Women's issues in social policy

For over a decade, a notable development in mainstream social policy in the United Kingdom has been the emergence of a feminist critique. *Women's Issues in Social Policy* is intended as a contribution to the social policy literature which can also be used in a women's studies context. It demonstrates the impossibility of understanding the welfare state without appreciating how it treats women, especially as dependants within the family, and the conflicts of interest between men and women as well as the unequal power relationships in the welfare context. It also highlights the fact that women's traditional role in welfare provision is as unpaid carers for children, the elderly and incapacitated people, and is particularly concerned with the everyday experiences and dissatisfactions of women which have largely been ignored within mainstream social policy research and literature.

Women's Issues in Social Policy incorporates recent research findings written from a feminist perspective and reveals the breadth and depth of recent work in previously unexplored areas such as time budgeting and transport, as well as developing analysis in traditional areas of interest such as health and personal care.

The editors have also looked into the wider European context and included is a chapter which examines whether the abortion issue will give birth to feminism in Poland.

Women's Issues in Social Policy will be of value to teachers and students of social policy and women's studies, as well as of interest to the general reader.

Mavis Maclean and Dulcie Groves have been members of the Social Administration Association (now the Social Policy Association) since its inception in 1967, and in 1987 convened a conference in Women and Social Policy in Oxford where this volume originated. Mavis Maclean is a fellow of Wolfson College, University of Oxford. Dulcie Groves is an Honorary Lecturer in Social Policy at the University of Lancaster.

Women's issues in social policy

Edited by Mavis Maclean and
Dulcie Groves

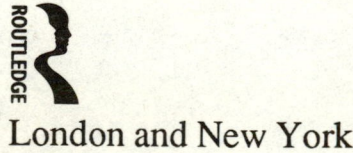

London and New York

First published in 1991
by Routledge
11 New Fetter Lane, London EC4P 4EE

Simultaneously published in the USA and Canada
by Routledge
a division of Routledge, Chapman and Hall Inc.
29 West 35th Street, New York, NY 10001

Reprinted 1992

Laserprinted by LaserScript Limited, Mitcham, Surrey
Printed and bound in Great Britain by
Biddles Ltd, Guildford and King's Lynn.

British Library Cataloguing in Publication Data
Women's issues in social policy.
  1. Great Britain. Women. Social conditions
  I. Maclean, Mavis   II. Groves, Dulcie
  305.420941

Library of Congress Cataloging in Publication Data
Women's issues in social policy/edited by Mavis Maclean and Dulcie Groves
  p.   cm.
  1. Great Britain – Social policy. 2. Feminist criticism – Great
  Britain. 3. Social problems. 4. Sex discrimination against women
  – Great Britain.   I. Maclean, Mavis.   II. Groves, Dulcie.
  HN390.W58   1990
  361.6'1'0941–dc20   90-8564
                                                              CIP

ISBN 0-415-04121-X
      0-415-04122-8 (pbk)

Contents

    critique of 'paid volunteering'   136
    John Baldock and Clare Ungerson

Part III   Research and progress

9   The long term effects for girls of parental divorce   161
    Mavis Maclean and Diana Kuh

10 Sex and motherhood as handicaps in the labour market   179
    Heather Joshi

11 Feminist research and social policy   194
    Janet Finch

12 Will the abortion issue give birth to feminism in Poland?   205
    Malgorzata Fuszara

    Name index   229

    Subject index   233

Tables and figures

Tables

Figures

Contributors

John Baldock is Lecturer in Social Policy at the University of Kent.

Sally Baldwin is Professor and Director of the Social Policy Research Unit, University of York.

Kristine Beuret is Lecturer in the School of Applied Social Sciences and Public Administration, Leicester Polytechnic.

Miriam David is Professor of Social Policy and Head of Social Sciences at South Bank Polytechnic.

Janet Finch is Professor of Social Relations and Head of the Department of Applied Social Science at the University of Lancaster.

Peggy Foster is Lecturer in Social Policy in the Faculty of Economic and Social Studies, University of Manchester.

Dulcie Groves is Honorary Lecturer in Social Policy in the Department of Applied Social Science at the University of Lancaster.

Caroline Glendinning is Hallsworth Research Fellow in the Department of Social Policy and Social Work at the University of Manchester.

Heather Joshi is Senior Research Fellow at the London School of Hygiene.

Diana Kuh is Research Officer at the Medical Research Council National Survey of Health and Development, University College, London.

Hilary Land is Professor of Social Policy at Royal Holloway and Bedford New College, University of London.

Malgorzata Fuszara works at the Dept of Sociology of Morals and Law, Institute of Social Prevention and Resocialisation, Warsaw University.

Mavis Maclean is a fellow of Wolfson College, Oxford, working for the Centre for Socio-Legal Studies.

Jane Millar is Lecturer in Social Policy at the University of Bath.

Julia Twigg is Research Fellow at the Social Policy Research Unit, University of York.

Clare Ungerson is Reader in Social Policy at the University of Kent.

Acknowledgements

In September 1984 the Joseph Rowntree Memorial Trust sponsored a wide-ranging social policy seminar at Leeds Castle, inviting forty distinguished public servants and policy analysts, of whom precisely two were women. The proceedings were later edited by Richard Berthoud (1985) as *Challenges to Social Policy*.

Such were the events which prompted the editors of this book to set up a two-day open conference in May 1987 entitled *Women's Challenges to Social Policy*. It was organised by Mavis Maclean at Wolfson College, Oxford, to which warm thanks are due for providing administrative support and a delightful venue for the meeting.

The conference was attended by most of the academics and researchers who had in the past two decades developed a feminist critique within the subject of social policy. The Wolfson College event has lingered long in the memories of those who attended it and the editors hope that this book will bring the flavour of the conference to a wider audience.

The editors wish to thank the Social Policy Association for its part in helping to promote the conference. We would also like to thank warmly Heather Gibson, our editor at Routledge, for the enthusiasm and support she has given towards the publication of this book. Finally, we are extremely grateful to our contributors for all their efforts in getting this collection together as an enjoyable co-operative enterprise in the best traditions of feminist scholarship.

Reference

Berthoud, R. (1985) *Challenges to Social Policy*, Aldershot: Gower.

Introduction

A notable development in the subject area of social policy in Britain in the 1970s and 1980s has been the emergence of a feminist critique within the mainstream subject area of social policy. This owes much to pioneer work published in the 1970s by Hilary Land (1971, 1976, 1977, 1978, 1979a, 1979b) and Elizabeth Wilson (1977). During the 1980s, further policy analyses and research findings have pointed out the extent to which the literature of social policy and teaching within that area, not to mention social services and welfare provision, have been characterized by blindness to gender divisions and issues, so that women and their concerns have remained largely invisible.

In recent years, a substantial literature on women and social policy has been published. The demand for such books and articles has been fuelled not only by the attempts of some mainstream social policy teachers to focus on issues of gender, but also by the enormous popularity of women's studies courses at all levels of further and higher education, leading to the establishment of specialist courses on women and social policy. This book is intended as a contribution to the mainstream social policy literature which can also be used in a women's studies context. In addition, while we have had the needs of students and their teachers firmly in mind while editing the book, we have also aimed to give the social policy and women's studies research community access to the findings of recent studies in the area of women and social policy.

With the growth of teaching on women and social policy topics, several key texts have been published which are now widely used. Many students have cause to be grateful to Dale and Foster (1986) and Pascall (1986) for wide-ranging textbooks, to Lewis (1983) for a collection of original papers and to Ungerson (1985) for a reader which drew together a number of previously published articles or book extracts in great demand by students. Certain themes are common to these books and will be echoed in this collection. They include the impossibility of understanding the welfare state without understanding how it treats women, especially as dependants within the family and as formal and informal carers; the conflicts of interest between men and women as well as unequal power relationships in the welfare context; and the invisibility of women in the earlier Fabian-influenced social policy literature of the 1950s and 1960s onwards. Mainstream social policy literature, including some well-known recent texts written from other perspectives, has continued to a surprising extent to marginalize women.

An example of this marginalization is found in *Challenges to Social Policy* (Berthoud 1985), which on other counts provides a stimulating and wide-ranging overview of topical issues in social policy. It was the absence of women contributors to the Berthoud collection and the limited discussion of social policy issues relevant to women which led the editors of this collection to think about questions which Berthoud *et al*. did *not* address. We were particularly interested in those aspects of social policy which touch upon the everyday experiences and dissatisfactions of women. It was those topics wherein women's issues have largely gone unremarked which were identified and addressed by feminist scholars at the 'Women's Issues in Social Policy Conference' in 1987. The papers given at this meeting represented work in progress: some have since been expanded into contributions to this volume.

The first part of the book highlights areas where women's interests have been largely ignored within mainstream social policy research and literature. Hilary Land discusses women's *time* as an invisible item in household and national accounting procedures. Caroline Glendinning and Jane Millar then address the absence of women from poverty studies and point out ways in which this might be resolved within the theory and practice of social policy. Dulcie Groves focuses on the Social Security Act 1986 in discussing the invisibility of women in relation to financial provision for old age. Kristine Beuret analyses differences in the ways in which women and men travel and the implications for public transport policy.

The second part is concerned with aspects of women's traditional role in welfare provision as unpaid carers for children and for elderly and incapacitated people and in relation to women's health. The topics addressed have to a greater or lesser extent been subject to feminist analysis and have by now gained some degree of recognition within the general literature of social policy. However, there is a constant need to rethink the implications of what has begun to be known. Miriam David addresses recent debates about child care in the context of the Children Act (1989), child protection and child sexual abuse and feminist critiques of child care and family policy. Sally Baldwin and Julia Twigg review the current state of the debate on community care and its exploitation of women's labour. Clare Ungerson and John Baldock discuss the use of low-paid quasi-volunteer carers. Peggy Foster scrutinizes 'well women' health care provisions.

The final part concentrates on current research, first giving an example of empirical work of the type to provide a base on which to build a more solid social policy agenda that takes full account of perspectives on women. Mavis Maclean and Diana Kuh examine the impact of parental divorce on women's work and family lives in adulthood, using longitudinal data. Heather Joshi uses the same data set to examine sex and motherhood as handicaps in the labour market. Janet Finch suggests an agenda for feminist research in the context of social policy. Finally, in celebration of renewed contacts with Central Europe, Malgorzata Fuszara describes the response of the emerging women's movement to proposals to change the law on abortion in Poland.

We hope that this book will be of use not only to students and teachers with a specific interest in social policy in a women's studies context, but especially as a mainstream social policy text which adds a missing dimension – the feminist perspective.

REFERENCES

Berthoud, R. (1985) *Challenges to Social Policy*, Aldershot: Gower.

Dale, J. and Foster, P. (1986) *Feminists and State Welfare*, London: Routledge & Kegan Paul.

Land, H. (1971) 'Women, work and social security', in *Social and Economic Administration* 5, 3: 183–92.

—— (1976) 'Women: supporters or supported?', in S. Allen and D.L. Barker (eds) *Sexual Divisions and Society*, London: Tavistock.

—— (1977) 'Social security and the division of unpaid work in the home and paid employment in the labour market', in DHSS *Social Security Research*, papers presented at a DHSS seminar on 7–9 April 1976, London: HMSO.

—— (1978) 'Who cares for the family?', *Journal of Social Policy* 7, 3: 257–84.

—— (1979a) 'The boundaries between the state and the family in C.C. Harris (ed.) 'The sociology of the family', *Sociological Review Monograph* 28, Keele, Staffs.

—— (1979b) 'The changing place of women in Europe' *Daedalus* 102, 2: 73–92.

Lewis, J. (ed.) (1983) *Women's Welfare: Women's Rights*, London: Croom Helm.

Pascall, G. (1986) *Social Policy: A Feminist Analysis*, London: Tavistock.

Ungerson, C. (ed.) (1985) *Women and Social Policy: A Reader*, Basingstoke: Macmillan.

Wilson, E. (1977) *Women and the Welfare State*, London: Tavistock.

Part I

Filling in the gaps

1 Time to care

Hilary Land

> Every day working men see their wives and mothers toiling for 12 to 16 hours at scrubbing, sweeping, cooking, tending young live things. Their attitude is but a fresh illustration of the truth that people accustomed to measure value in terms of money will persist, even against the evidence of their own eyes, in thinking meanly of any kind of service on which a low price is set and still more meanly of the kind of service which is given for nothing.
>
> (Rathbone 1924: 126)

Although it was written nearly seventy years ago and some of the tasks, or rather the methods of accomplishing them, have changed, this statement is still true. If it were not then this book would not have been necessary, for the issues raised here are those which we believe are still inadequately recognized (if recognized at all) by both male policy analysts and policy makers. Certainly they do not yet occupy mainstream social policy analysis, in spite of the activities of feminist scholars since the early 1970s, let alone the writing of generations of earlier feminists. However, as I shall argue, these issues must be taken seriously. First, because they raise important and challenging theoretical questions not only about the relationship between state provision, the market and families and the relative merits of each system as a mechanism for allocating and delivering resources and services, but also about the nature, purpose and impact of state intervention in the lives of individuals in society and thus about the meaning of what T.H. Marshall (1963) called social citizenship – for *women* as well as for men. Second, if these issues are not addressed, the practical consequences of social policy development will not be what were intended by the politicians and the policy makers. Within both the universalistic and the residual model of the welfare state this is true because the exploration of these issues gives insights into the ways in which markets and families operate and how the conceptualization of a dichotomy between public and private which is somehow 'natural' and unchanging, obscures this. Eleanor Rathbone understood this very well, for the quote above comes from her classic book *The Disinherited Family* in which she makes the case for family allowances and which contained, at its core, a trenchant attack on conventional economic theories for their exclusion of the family as a unit of distribution.

The current debates about community care illustrate this and show that the problem is not just one of altering the balance between paid and unpaid work, important though that is. Again, as Eleanor Rathbone recognized, measuring value only in money terms focuses on too narrow a range of issues. The Norwegian sociologist, Helge Hernes, has written recently that the welfare state has changed the traditional dividing lines between so-called public and private spheres, but she argues:

> Debates about the new balance are not only concerned with issues of paid and unpaid work and the social values they represent, but with the time spent on these activities and the civil, social and economic entitlements we attach to time spent in paid and unpaid work and activities. The extent of these entitlements is today still largely determined by status in the labour market. The perceived injustices created by this situation have become even more obvious since research has uncovered the large amount of unpaid work which is an integral part of the modern welfare mix. The issue for many is then that this new welfare mix must accept the consequences of the social changes it has itself created: one of which is the destruction of traditional views on the public and private use of time, which is now central in questions of care.
>
> (Hernes 1987: 120)

Helga Hernes was writing about Scandinavia, where public welfare provision (of child care, for example) is more extensive than in Britain, particularly in Sweden and Denmark, but where debates about community care have characteristics very similar to those of the British debates. As another Norwegian sociologist wrote recently, 'a belief in so-called "community care" is spreading rapidly because it is supposed to be cheaper and morally preferable to the public care-giving services' (Waerness 1987: 207). Her comments hold true for Britain, too. The post-war welfare state created hundreds of thousands of jobs for women. Between 1951 and 1981, the public sector workforce associated with health, welfare and education or what Martin Rein (1985: 38) has called the social welfare industry grew from 1.3 million to 3.4 million people. These jobs were held predominantly by women who by 1981 comprised 78 per cent of health workers, 72 per cent of local authority workers and nearly 90 per cent of those involved in local authority social services. Moreover, as Martin Rein's comparative studies show very clearly, a growing service sector is a feature of all modern economies, although the extent to which this falls into the public sector or the private sector varies between one country and another. However, whether or not they are defined as public or private employees, it is mainly women who are working in the social welfare industry, and, as Laura Balbo (1987) has argued, it is largely women who spend time enabling other members of their family to have access to and the use of these services, or as the Audit Commission (1986: 43) acknowledged, their unpaid care in the home is 'important to the economy and health of the Health and Social Services'.

Some caring and servicing work previously done in the home has become waged: time spent on these activities has been valued in money terms, albeit lowly. In Britain, however, in the 1980s, cuts in welfare spending have meant that the pay and working conditions of many of these workers has deteriorated, for already in 1981, half of the two million women employed in education and health services were employed part-time. Part-time employment in Britain has always had far fewer economic and social entitlements associated with it than in Scandinavia or indeed the rest of the European Community. Britain is alone in opposing the draft EC directive on part-time employment which would give part-time employees, on a pro rata basis, the same rights to state and occupational benefits as full-time employees. So there is considerable resistance against sustaining, let alone increasing, the value placed on women's time in the formal labour market, especially when it is associated with the social welfare sector.

Just as significant are changes occurring to the value placed on time spent on caring work when it takes place in the home. This is particularly important because the emphasis on 'community care' for elderly infirm, chronically sick and handicapped people has grown in the 1980s, although it is important to note that community care policies are neither entirely a product of the Thatcher administration nor confined to Britain. Throughout the 1960s and 1970s, there had been a shift in emphasis from community care meaning care *in* the community as opposed to large, isolated institutions, to mean, by the early 1980s, care *by* the community (see DHSS, 1981: 3). This, as feminists have long argued, means care by the family, which largely, although not exclusively, still means care by women.

Here too, the picture in the 1980s is of a reduction in the few economic and social entitlements arising from caring for a dependent child, sick, elderly or disabled person at home. During the 1970s, unpaid care in the home did begin to be recognized in the state benefit system. Those who left waged work to care full-time for a child or dependent adult had their rights to a basic state pension protected. The invalid care allowance was introduced and paid to those who gave up paid employment to care for a dependent adult, although it took over ten years before this was extended to include married or cohabiting women carers, and then only when challenged in the European courts in 1986. The method of calculating the earnings related component of the state pension introduced in the Social Security Pensions Act 1975 was based not on earnings averaged over a whole working life, but on the twenty best years. This meant that those whose earnings had been interrupted or reduced for a period of time because of their caring commitments at home did not face a reduced pension when they retired. All modest steps but, far from building on them, even these have been reversed in the 1980s.

First, there is no additional premium for carers within the new income support scheme included in the Social Security Act 1986. Carers were the only group previously eligible for the higher rate of supplementary benefit to receive no premium. The 1985 social security review on which the 1986 Act was based proposed to abolish the earnings-related component of the state pension altogether, but even the private pensions industry opposed that. Instead, the Social Security Act 1986 reduced its value and of particular importance to carers is that the calculation of the earnings-related com- ponent of the pension will in future be based on earnings averaged over the whole of their working life. In other words, part-time employment taken to allow time to care for someone at home will increase the risk of poverty in old age.

Changes in the regulations and administrative rules have made it harder to qualify for the non-contributory constant attendance allowance (CAA) paid to those who need attention during the day and/or night. In order to qualify for the invalid care allowance, the dependent adult must be in receipt of the CAA and either not receiving or willing to forgo the severe disability premium, introduced in the new income support system in April 1988. (Thus those caring for someone poor enough to qualify for income support cannot enhance the *household* income by claiming the ICA.) However, attention needed at night must now be frequent, requiring not just the *presence* of the carer but also their 'wakeful and watchful' presence. The rules affecting eligibility for contributory unemployment benefit have also been changed in ways which adversely affect carers. 'Availability for work' on which eligibility for the benefit depends, means being able to make alternative arrangements for the care of children or sick or elderly relatives *within twenty-four hours*. Unwillingness to travel longer distances from home, or take a job involving evening or weekend work may also debar a claimant from receipt of benefit. When the ICA was introduced, receipt of benefit not only safeguarded the carer's rights to the basic state pension, but also protected their right to unemployment benefit when they ceased caring. The new benefit rules in force since October 1988 have ended this protection which hits carers particularly harshly, because from the same date eligibility for unemployment benefit has depended on sufficient contributions *paid* in the previous *two* tax years, instead of one as was formerly the case.

In a moving account of caring for her sister for five years, Maureen Oswin described how she felt when she experienced the operation of this rule after her sister died. She said, 'After several years of caring one needs to feel wanted, to be part of the scene again, to feel valued. The new unemployment benefit rules made me feel very devalued' (*The Independent*, 28 June 1989). She was well aware, as Helga Hernes has said, that this care *could* have been provided by the State. 'I suppose in cold monetary terms I must have incurred some £80,000 in loss of earnings and must have saved the country at least £200,000 by looking after Nita at home on my own' (ibid.). All she was asking for was less than £50 a week until she found a job.

These are not just mean-minded, penny-pinching policies designed to save the public purse in a time when expenditure on social services and benefits is believed to be not only wasteful but, worse, an impediment to economic enterprise and success because it requires high levels of taxation. Neither is it, I suggest, just because to recognize the value of care in the home as measured in money terms, comparable to its cost in the public sector of the private market, would be *very* costly. (It has been estimated by the Family Policy Studies Centre (1989) that Britain's six million carers currently provide about £20 (UK) billion support annually.) That is a very important consideration, but the resistance is more fundamental because of the very nature and meaning of caring and what many call servicing work. Mrs Thatcher (1985: 150) herself understood this when she told the Women's Royal Voluntary Service at their Annual Conference in 1981: 'The voluntary principle is very important for reasons which are far beyond economics.' Earlier in the speech she had said that 'in the end real neighbourliness and understanding care comes more *naturally* from those who *choose* to give it' (author's emphasis). It is the issues of choice and the identification of natural caring with women, or at least with the definition of feminine, to which I now wish to turn.

Care is a multi-dimensional concept and very difficult to define. It has a number of different meanings associated with it. Maureen Oswin's article was entitled 'Neglected after a *job* of *love*' and Maureen Oswin herself was introduced as someone who 'gave up *work* for nearly five years to nurse her dying sister . . . [and] . . . describes how the state has devalued her *role*' (author's emphasis). As Hilary Graham has argued in her thought-provoking article exploring the meaning of care, 'care defines both the identity *and* the activity of women in western society' (Graham 1983: 30). But the activity is not just a set of tasks, it signifies a relationship. The relationship may be between equals, or more likely, it may not. 'Tending' describes these tasks – washing, dressing and cooking meals, etc. without, it seems to me, implying either anything about the nature of the relationship between the person for whom they are done and the person doing them, nor the existence of an emotional dimension to this relationship. (Did Eleanor Rathbone use the word 'tending' in the opening quote because, like many upper middle-class women of her time, she never had responsibility for the execution of domestic matters, did not have children and indeed left the management and organization of her household to her lifelong companion Elizabeth Macadam?) It is also a word empty of any moral obligation the carer feels towards the person, young or old, being cared for. It is significant, for example, that the female carers in Clare Ungerson's study were more likely to explain why they cared in terms of 'duty', whereas the men used the word 'love' (Ungerson 1987: 97).

Another aspect of the caring and servicing to which Laura Balbo and many others have drawn attention is that it involves more than the time needed to accomplish certain tasks. For example, one of the women interviewed in a study of women who had cared for their mothers conducted by Jane Lewis and Barbara Meredith, said 'Caring is not just washing and dressing them. It's time to talk to them, unpick their knitting that's gone wrong' (Lewis and Meredith 1988: 48). Moreover, in order to respond to these needs, the carer must be present or readily available (and not too preoccupied with their own activities, i.e. they must be paying attention even if not *doing* anything). To quote Laura Balbo again, 'Being there to wait, to listen, to respond, to attend to the needs and desires of others; to worry when difficulties are anticipated, to deal with one's own sense of guilt when problems are not successfully resolved: this is servicing' (Balbo 1987: 52).

Such preoccupation not only fragments time, but imposes a severe restriction on the carers' thoughts, let alone their activities. Vera Brittain, explaining how she hated domesticity, wrote 'only those who appreciate the different qualities of work produced by complete and by partial concentration can ever estimate the extent to which women's performance suffered from constant, small interruptions and petty time-wasting tasks' (quoted in Dyhouse 1989: 53). She did not feel she had the right, as Barbara Wootton's father, a Cambridge don, had, to make sure she could concentrate on her own work as he had done. Even when away on holiday with the children, in order to ensure no interruptions, he hung a red handkerchief out of the window of his room when he was studying, to warn the children not to make a noise.

The effect of *not* being so preoccupied was noted more recently by the wife of a contemporary Cambridge don, the mathematician Stephen Hawking, in an article giving 'the story behind the huge success of best-selling author, Professor Stephen Hawking' (*Guardian* 9 August, 1989). She had provided enormous support of every kind to her increasingly disabled husband, for the National Health Service had been able to offer only seven hours of nursing help each *week* plus two hours' help with bathing. She had given up all thoughts of her own career for years until more recently his success and the surrounding publicity had brought them the money needed to purchase substantial help. Looking at the positive side of his illness, she wrote: 'but then his condition enabled him to develop his mental capacity further than anybody else because it was totally unrealistic to expect any physical help from him in the home or with the children. And he put his time to best advantage. It wouldn't necessarily have happened if things had been different' (*idem.*). This is not to belittle either Stephen Hawking's illness, his determination or his achievements, or to suggest that he was happy with a situation not of his choosing.

Nevertheless, men, far more often than women, have the power and resources to be in a position to choose *not* to be involved in the time-consuming and preoccupying aspects of care, or indeed domestic work of any kind. This, Chiara Saraceno argues, is one of the sources of resistance against changing the division of responsibility for care and domestic work within the family. Not only do many women feel a loss of identity and gratification not easily found in the paid jobs available to them in the labour market, but, for men, more involvement in this aspect of family life 'translates most visibly and immediately into the loss of male privilege . . . (the privilege of being uninvolved, which is even more important than the privilege of being served) . . . (Saraceno 1987: 200). They have the time to enjoy more leisure, more sleep, become involved in political activities which may confer public status or power, and even if they have to spend more time in the labour market, at least that time entitles them to more money, not all of which is likely to be spent on the family. But it is too simple to see this entirely in terms of women's interests versus men's interests. Returning to Laura Balbo's analysis, she reminds us that 'women's work must be devalued in terms of the dominant interests in society; but it also becomes increasingly clear how other interests suffer within this process. Servicing allows women, and everyone else, to survive in spite of and in opposition to capitalism and patriarchy' (Balbo 1987: 57).

When women are freed from domestic preoccupations, even quite small ones, and they have interesting and fulfilling paid work, they acquire unexpected energy. For example, Barbara Wootton in her autobiography reflects on the coast-to-coast lecture tour she made in the US in the 1950s.

These tours are supposed to be terribly exhausting and strong men have been known to collapse under them. But I did not find it so, and I think that the reason is that the strain is much greater for men than for women. On such an assignment as this one becomes simply a speaking parcel. You do not have to look up a train, consult a map or make any decisions: you just go where you are told, when you are told, and you are not haunted as housewives so often are, by the fear that you have left undone some vital domestic duty – in my own case, typically, by the fear that I have forgotten to buy the bread.

(Wootton 1967: 159)

Barbara Wootton, a distinguished social science professor, was married but had no children. Nevertheless, even she had not escaped entirely from the demands of domesticity.

Another important feature of caring and the tasks associated with it is that even when they are not preoccupying they do fragment the carer's time. All the studies of women's paid employment show very clearly how paid work has to be fitted around responsibilities to take children to school, visit clinics, etc. Even ordinary mealtimes impose a schedule on the person responsible for them and if the person to be fed is either very young or incapacitated they are *very* time-consuming, allowing little 'free' time in between. For example, Maureen Oswin describes feeding her sister as her illness progressed. 'As Nita's swallowing reflex became weaker and weaker it sometimes took two hours to spoon-feed her a small meal. I used to do patchwork between her mouthfuls, so that she did not feel hurried. Within two years I had completed a gigantic multi-coloured quilt' (*The Independent*, 28 June 1989). This is a telling example, for Laura Balbo, in her thoughtful and perceptive article already cited, used patchwork quilting as a metaphor for women's work, arguing very convincingly that the analogy is as apt today as it was in former times.

Piece bags, sorting out, piecing patching and quilting, are all words which suggest parallels to concepts that have been used (by myself and by others) to describe women's work in contemporary society: the servicing, the pooling and packaging of resources, the self-help activities, emotional work and survival networks, how women keep at their endless tasks, how they put their vision into the planning and design of their own and others' lives whose responsibility they carry.

(Balbo 1987: 46)

However, the patchwork is not noticed because many of the pieces are ignored. When Peter Wilmott and Michael Young conducted their study of family life in the 1960s and purported to show a much more egalitarian relationship between husbands and wives, their time budget studies excluded mealtimes. In a footnote they admitted that 'such things not recorded as work might actually be so for housewives. A meal, for example, is not counted as work, though some mothers would think that feeding young children was. If finer distinctions had been made, it might have turned out that the husbands did not, by and large, do more work than their at-home wives' (Wilmott and Young 1965: 112). Indeed it might, and more comprehensive surveys have, of course, confirmed this. Instead, this study gave comfort to those who wanted to believe that women had far less to complain of than their mothers. A much more recent example of omitting an important piece of caring work is found in the General Household Survey of Informal Carers (Green 1988). This very useful survey, published in September 1988, gives us for the first time a national picture of the numbers of carers, who they are and for whom they care. Altogether, four out of five of the six million carers in Britain were caring for a relative, one in five were caring for more than one person and nearly one in four were spending at least twenty hours a week caring. However, this last figure is an underestimate of the time spent caring, for the survey excluded time spent 'on call' while sleeping. The Lewis and Meredith study cited above, as well as Maureen Oswin's story, illustrates all too clearly how wearing sleeping-in can be on the carer. Ironically, the publication of this study coincided with the junior hospital doctors' protests about the harmful effects that long hours of duty and broken sleep were having on their health and ability to provide proper care for their patients. When this happens inside the home, official surveys do not even bother to count it, although the ill-health of many of the carers was noticed.

This invisibility is not accidental, for, as Laura Balbo argues, 'it is best done if it is not even seen' (Balbo 1987: 52). This is likely to happen to the servicing of work of anyone in a subordinate and powerless position: it is not an experience just confined to women. Ronald Blythe, in his study of Akenfield, records the old gardener describing his work for 'the big house', and how it was deliberately kept hidden. For example, fresh flowers were arranged every day: 'We had to creep in early in the morning before breakfast and replace great banks of flowers in the main rooms. Lordship and Ladyship must never hear or see you do it, fresh flowers just had to be there, that was all there was to it (Blythe 1972: 109). Noticing, let alone counting, the cost of this work destroys the illusion that it is 'natural', and as far as care is concerned it is alleged that it destroys its very essence. But as Kari Waerness has pointed out, this serves the purpose of masking dependency. 'The fact that helplessness and dependency are part of life itself for all of us – in childhood, illness and old age – may in part be hidden and depressed as long as the caring function is left to an invisible, oppressed woman's culture' (Waerness 1987: 225). In a society which decries what John Moore, when Secretary of State to the DHSS, called 'the dependency culture' and where independence is the desired state – for men – it is better that care and carers remain out of sight and unacknowledged. At least in part this is so.

On the other hand, a society consisting of independent individuals is, of course, a contradiction in terms. As a leader in *The Times* noted when considering how to establish social order on a long-term basis, an emphasis should be put on 'a cliché that needs to be awakened, more neighbourliness, perhaps a new sense of altruism that may not be easy to marry with the enterprising go-getting temperament so vital to the economic life of the nation' (*The Times*, 14 March 1986).

Caring is not in conflict with the values of a so-called 'enterprise' society only when it takes place outside the formal sector. The growing emphasis on 'efficiency' and profits, as welfare services are either relocated in the private sector or have to adopt its criteria of success, is squeezing out the possibility of caring. Ursula Huws, criticizing this development, wrote recently:

> It seems to me that this is the wrong way to approach the problem of developing services to meet the real needs of users. In fact it could be argued that one of the great mistakes of the 1960s and 1970s was the wholesale adoption of private sector methods of management efficiency into public services in this country. . . . The men with the stop-watches were sent in, and tasks were analysed and subdivided so that they could be speeded up and monitored. Payment by results systems were brought in so that workers were encouraged to sacrifice all other things to productivity. Deskilling and stress brought surlier attitudes, workers were increasingly unable to step outside their rigid job descriptions to offer individual help – standards began to deteriorate. Refuse collectors no longer had the flexibility to carry an old lady's dustbin back into the house; one-man bus crews could not help a mother with her shopping and buggy; hospital cleaners were under too much pressure to stop and chat to a lonely patient.
>
> (Huws 1988)

Caring is being fractured in other ways too, within the formal sector, as some aspects of care have become professionalized and subject to a scientific as well as economic rationality. As a result, as Kari Waerness argues:

> because the head/heart quality is accepted in all sciences, it seems

probable that any kind of formal education based on scientific knowledge will to some degree promote a more instrumental attitude towards work, at the expense of the expressive.

(Waerness 1987: 223)

She cites nursing as an example where the development of formally acquired knowledge devalues the informally acquired and intuitive kind of knowledge and skills through practising bedside care. This enhances the value placed on some kinds of care but devalues others, leaving the mother, wife or daughter caring for a sick person at home feeling even less competent and more unsure, but of course, no less responsible.

As the number of professionals proliferates in the formal sector, systems of care become *less* flexible as well as more fragmented. Home helps have become 'home care assistants' who may no longer dust or wash up. The result is less personal and comprehensive care requiring more patching and piecing together by the carer at home – if there is one. But now even this is becoming professionalized as the recommendation of the Griffiths Report will require local authorities not to *provide*, but to *manage* 'packets of care'. 'Care managers' are thus the latest professionals to enter the field. What, asks a social worker writing in *New Statesman and Society*, is the difference between a social worker and a care manager? (16 September 1989). A more important question is where will that leave the carer in the family? Will these care managers concentrate their attention on those for whom there is no informal carer, as some of the groups representing disabled and elderly people fear? This will leave families struggling with inadequate services and support, as before. It will also avoid the awkward question of identifying the client on behalf of whom these packages are being managed – the carer or the person being cared for? Their needs and preferences may well conflict. Either way, this new development may enhance the value of certain skills in social workers and their assistants but will do little to recognize *and* value the informal care manager's skills and time. It will certainly not be experienced as having more 'choice', which purports to be one of the great virtues of increasing private sector influence.

The caring capacity of the so-called public sector is thus being reduced in more subtle and complex ways than straightforward cuts in services, and this adds to the growing criticism of, and lack of confidence in, public provision which, as noted earlier, is widespread. The more the public world is seen and experienced as 'uncaring', the more attractive, and indeed necessary, community care seems. As Richard Titmuss wrote, warning against confusing the rhetoric with the reality of community care, 'Does it not conjure up a sense of warmth and human kindness, essentially personal and comforting . . .?' (Titmuss 1979: 104). It is not however more attractive to the carers who are expected to take on even heavier burdens. Neither is it attractive to those being cared for by their families if they sense they are a growing burden. Much research shows that elderly and disabled people want 'intimacy – but at a distance' and this means not being *fully* dependent on their families. What is needed are services which allow families to balance these contradictory wishes and are neither based on the exploitation of women (whether they are in the formal labour market, in the family or in the community), nor destructive of the positive qualities of what Kari Waerness calls 'women's traditional caregiving work' (Waerness 1987: 220).

The issues surrounding care and the value placed on it wherever it takes place are complex and contradictory. Above all, caring needs to be valued more highly and this means recognizing that women's time is not just divided between paid work and leisure. Many economists assume a direct trade-off between time and money and build their models accordingly. But for carers the trade-off is not such a simple one. Moreover, as Rita Liljestrom has pointed out, leisure can be thought of as a *free time* with the emphasis either on *free* or on *time*. If the latter:

> the matter will boil down to an issue of negotiation concerned with the allocation of time, time measured in hours, time spent at work and time put at one's own disposal. But if the emphasis is placed on *free*, we get into the psychological import of time, irrespective of whether that time is remunerated or unremunerated. The word *free* includes those ingredients of interest, voluntariness, autonomy and meaningsfulness (*sic*) that people seek in their leisure but which they can also find in work (original emphasis).
>
> (Liljestrom 1978: 159)

She therefore concludes that 'the core problem with shorter working hours actually has to do with the supply of *freedoms* and not *time* in the mechanical sense of the clock' (ibid.: 160, original emphasis).

Current community care policies are doing little to alter the supply of freedoms in favour of carers and those for whom they care. Indeed, they are still based on what Hilary Rose and I have called women's 'compulsory altruism' (Land and Rose 1985). Too many women are not free to choose *not* to care without either damaging those whom they care about or their own self-esteem. Worse, those who do, face tasks and experiences little valued, supported or even acknowledged in material terms, and their reward is too often poverty which may extend years after the caring has ceased. This will continue unless we develop analyses and policies which take into account the complexity of the relationship between the family, the market and the State and challenge the assumption that caring is an attribute and activity which naturally belongs to women. This in turn means exposing, confronting and exploiting some major contradictions inherent within the welfare state in modern western societies.

REFERENCES

Audit Commission (1986) *Making A Reality of Community Care*, London: HMSO.
Balbo, L. (1987) 'Crazy quilts: rethinking the welfare state debate from a woman's point of view', in A. Showstack Sassoon (ed.) *Women and the State*, London: Hutchinson.
Blythe, R. (1972) *Akenfield*, Harmondsworth: Penguin Books.
Department of Health and Social Security (1981) *Growing Older*, London: HMSO.
Dyhouse, C. (1989) *Feminism and the Family in England 1880–1939*, Oxford: Blackwell.
Family Policy Studies Centre (1989) *Family Policy Bulletin* 6.
Graham, H. (1983) 'A labour of love', in J. Finch and D. Groves (eds) *A Labour of Love: Women, Work and Caring*, London: Routledge & Kegan Paul.
Green, H. (1988) *Informal Carers: A Study*, London: OPCS, HMSO.
Hernes, H. (1987) *Women, Power and the Welfare State*, Oslo: Norwegian University Press.
Huws, U. (1988) 'Consuming fashions', *New Statesman and Society* 19 August.
Land, H. and Rose, H. (1985) 'Compulsory altruism for some or an altruistic society for all', in P. Bean, J. Ferris and D.K. Whynes (eds) *In Defence of Welfare*, London: Tavistock.
Lewis, J. and Meredith, B. (1988) *Daughters who Care*, London: Routledge.
Liljestrom, R. *et al.* (1978) *Roles in Transition*. Report of an investigation made for the Advisory Council on Equality between Men and Women, Stockholm.
Marshall, T.H. (1963) *Sociology at the Crossroads*, London: Heinemann.
Rathbone, E. (1924) *The Disinherited Family*, London: Allen & Unwin.
Rein, M. (1985) 'Women, employment and social welfare', in R. Klein and M. O'Higgins (eds) *The Future of Welfare*, Oxford: Blackwell.
Saraceno, C. (1987) 'Division of family labour and gender identity', in A. Showstack Sassoon (ed.) *Women and the State*, London: Hutchinson.
Thatcher, M. (1985) 'Facing the new challenge', in C. Ungerson (ed.) *Women and Social Policy*, London: Macmillan.
Titmuss, R. (1979) 'Community care, fact or fiction', in R. Titmuss (ed.) *Commitment to Welfare*, London: Allen & Unwin.
Ungerson, C. (1987) *Policy is Personal*, London: Tavistock.
Waerness, K. (1987) 'The rationality of caring', in A. Showstack Sassoon (ed.) *Women and the State*, London: Hutchinson.
Wilmott, P. and Young, M. (1965) *The Symmetrical Family*, Harmondsworth: Penguin Books.
Wootton, B. (1967) *In a World I Never Made*, London: Allen & Unwin.

2 Poverty: the forgotten Englishwoman

Reconstructing research and policy on poverty

Caroline Glendinning and Jane Millar

INTRODUCTION

The invisibility of women's poverty – in Northern Ireland, Scotland and Wales, as well as in England – has a long and well-established history. In the study published in 1970 as *Poverty: The Forgotten Englishman*, the 176 participating Nottingham households were asked six questions about the employment of their 'breadwinner'; and just one question about the earnings of wives, children or other household members. Moreover, Coates and Silburn were not alone in largely ignoring the relationship between poverty and gender. In many of the studies of that time, gender differences in poverty were visible but generally not remarked upon.

One of the earliest studies which marked the 'rediscovery' of poverty in Britain in the mid-1960s was Cole and Utting's (1962) survey of 1,445 households of old people. They found that more than one-third of lone women were wholly dependent on state benefits, compared with a quarter of lone men and only 11 per cent of couples. 'In our view,' the authors concluded, 'the discovery of such a gulf between the income position of women and the rest of the over-retirement age group is of considerable importance' (Cole and Utting 1962: 57). Three years later, Townsend and Wedderburn confirmed Cole and Utting's findings, with single and widowed women emerging as the largest 'problem group' (*sic*). This was however apparently 'not due to sex *as such*, but to differences in employment experience, past and present, (Townsend and Wedderburn 1965: 110, authors' emphasis). The policy recommendations which stemmed from these conclusions were 'the need to protect or provide adequate rights for widows in private pension schemes' (ibid. 133). Perhaps most striking for the invisibility of women's poverty, however, was Abel Smith and Townsend's comparison of Family Expenditure Survey data from 1953 to 1960. The authors found that, in 1953-4, 29 per cent of men living alone had expenditure below 140 per cent of the (then) national assistance rates, as did nine per cent of couples; but as many as 42 per cent of women living alone had incomes below this poverty line. Yet the relationship between poverty and gender apparently merited little or no comment or explanation on the subsequent discussion and policy recommendations (Abel Smith and Townsend 1965).

The main intention of the poverty studies carried out around this time was to evaluate the impact of the post-war welfare state – especially the impact of retirement pensions, national assistance and family allowances in preventing poverty among families and the elderly. Where women's poverty was recognised, it was therefore largely interpreted as a residual problem, a consequence of minor technical deficiencies within the benefit system and, in particular, of the failure by individual women and men to take up the benefits and other opportunities now assumed to be available to all (Alcock and Shepherd 1987). This individualization of poverty further helped to divert attention away from the structural processes which create poverty and, in particular, the gender dimensions of those processes. This chapter represents an attempt to steer the study of poverty away from that diversion, by posing some fundamental questions about the methodologies which are commonly used in the course of those studies, and about the theories and assumptions which underpin those methods.

First, we will outline the two main approaches to defining and measuring poverty which have been used by Government and independent investigators in carrying out empirical research on poverty and inequality. We will illustrate how the issue of gender has been treated in this research. We will then undertake a detailed critique of the main standard approaches. We will argue that conventional approaches to the definition and measurement of poverty are consistently gender-blind, because the assumptions which underline them are erroneous. Conventional research thereby obscures both the empirical and structural dimensions of what is a highly gendered issue. Finally, we will indicate some of the major challenges for both research and the development of social policies on poverty.

DEFINITIONS OF POVERTY – ABSOLUTE OR RELATIVE?

Defining and measuring poverty, though in principle distinct and separate activities, are in practice closely related – interdependent, even. For example, the usefulness of any definition of poverty depends upon how easy it is to operationalize it, in order then to be able to estimate the numbers of people who are poor and the extent of their poverty. Conversely, operationally simple measures may, in effect, easily become widely used definitions of poverty.

The first of the two main approaches to the study of poverty has tended to take the definition of poverty as given and relatively unproblematic. For example, there has been a widespread convention of defining poverty in relation to current levels of minimum means tested benefits. However, such definitions of poverty do not on the whole question how those levels of means tested benefits have been set, their nutritional adequacy or their social or political acceptability. (Veit Wilson (1985) provides a very useful discussion of these issues.) Measuring poverty according to this approach essentially focuses on income, and compares the incomes or disposable resources of households with their notional supplementary benefit or income support entitlement. Thus, until 1988, the official Government statistics on poverty, published every two years, were derived from supplementary benefit administrative records and data from the Family Expenditure Survey. Poverty (or 'low income', to use the euphemistic official term) was measured by comparing normal weekly net income, after meeting housing costs, with the appropriate supplementary benefit scale rates for each 'tax unit'. (Tax units refer to the family unit liable for tax or the assessment unit eligible for means tested benefits. They therefore consist mainly of single people and couples with or without dependent children.)

A similar approach, again focusing on income and again involving relatively arbitrary judgements, compares the distribution of incomes among particular population groups (such as the elderly), or among the population as a whole, concentrating especially on the circumstances and characteristics of those in, say, the lowest decile or quintile of the distribution. Since 1988 this approach has been adopted by Government to replace the former means tested benefit measure of low income. Statistical analysis of households 'below average income' now show the numbers of individuals in households in the bottom 10, 20, 30, 40 and 50 per cent of the income distribution. They show each group's share of the total income and the changes in that share, in real terms, in recent years. This approach has been criticized for masking the impact of changes in social security and wages policies, and for obscuring information on poverty (LPU and CPAG 1988).

These two approaches are similar in that they both focus on the income entering the household and employ ready-made, standardized definitions whose scientific basis is not questioned.

Some of the advantages of these income based approaches are that they can provide standardized measures of the numbers of people in poverty, enabling easy comparisons to be made between different survey groups, between different points in time and at different stages in the life-cycle. They can also provide an easy means of investigating income based wealth and inequality as well as poverty (although this advantage is perhaps not made use of as often as it might be). Nevertheless, the use of income to define and measure poverty is long-established and widespread, not only by Government but also by independent academic researchers (Rowntree 1902; Abel Smith and Townsend 1965; Layard *et al.* 1978; Fiegehen *et al.* 1977).

The second broad approach to the study of poverty starts from the premise that the definition of a poverty 'line' is itself highly problematic. It therefore focuses on the development of appropriate nutritional, social or political bases for the construction of such definitions. In essence, this approach involves the construction of a definition of poverty which bears some relationship to socially approved norms, standards or values. These might include the range, quality and quantity of food and other items consumed by an 'average' or modal household; particular consumer durables and social activities which are commonly enjoyed or considered desirable; or the levels of benefit or public expenditure judged appropriate by the general public. The debate about what elements should be contained in socially relative, consumption-based definitions of poverty, and how those definitions should be devised, is a heated one (Townsend 1987; Piachaud 1987; Bradshaw *et al* 1987; Veit Wilson 1987; Walker 1987). However, regardless of their methods of construction, socially relative definitions of poverty essentially all involve elements of consumption. Poverty is defined in relation to actual consumption patterns, or majority views of what normative consumption patterns should be.

Perhaps the most unequivocal advocate of a definition of poverty which is related to the social values, culture and norms of a particular society at a particular time is Townsend. In *Poverty in the United Kingdom* (1979: 915) he argued that such a definition should be based on:

> the absence or inadequacy of those diets, amenities, standards, services and activities which are common or customary in society. People are deprived of the conditions of life which ordinarily define membership of society. If they lack or are denied resources to obtain access to these conditions of life and so fulfil membership of society, they are in poverty. . . . The 'subsistence' approach ignores major spheres of life in which deprivation can arise.

Comparing actual patterns of consumption with socially defined norms was also the basis of Mack and Lansley's (1985) study of poverty. However, instead of deciding for themselves, as Townsend did, exactly which 'diets, amenities, standards, services and activities are common or customary in society', Mack and Lansley asked a representative quota sample of 1,174 people to decide for them.

Socially relative definitions of poverty have enormous potential in that they can encompass non-monetary and even non-material dimensions of poverty. They draw attention to the fact that poverty is the outcome of a set of social and economic processes, rather than a personal attribute of those individuals who find themselves without adequate resources. Relative definitions stress powerlessness and exclusion from 'normal' or customary social activities as key causes – and consequences – of poverty. They also draw attention to the ways in which the lack of access to adequate financial resources is actually experienced and is also associated with other aspects of inequality and powerlessness.

What do these various methods of defining and measuring poverty tell us about the poverty experienced by women?

RENDERING WOMEN INVISIBLE

Some studies, quite simply, ignore women altogether; the possible link between poverty and gender is just not made. The data which are presented give no analysis whatsoever of the sex of those living in poverty (or of their household heads). The most consistent offender in this 'presentational invisibility' is probably the Government itself. The former DHSS statistics on 'low-income families' provided information on the numbers of 'tax units' (and individuals living in those tax units) with net incomes below 100, 120 and 140 per cent of supplementary benefit rates, as well as figures for those actually in receipt of supplementary benefit. No information on the composition of those 'tax units' was given. Looking at the last published set of figures for 1985 (DHSS 1988), we are therefore left wondering exactly how many of the 3,150,000 single pensioners living on or below 140 per cent of supplementary benefit are women and how many are men; and likewise for the 570,000 lone parents. In fact over 80 per cent of single pensioners living or below the poverty line are women, as are over 90 per cent of lone parents. These two groups of women have much the highest risk of poverty of any family type. The 'low income families' statistics cannot tell us this. Nor can the new 'households below average income' data, which again do not provide breakdowns by sex.

However, most researchers do provide some analysis of their results by sex, although not always in any great detail. Those who do consistently find that women living alone or as 'heads of households' have a greater risk of poverty than men in similar circumstances and that such 'female-headed' households are greatly over-represented among the poor. How do they then interpret these results? First, often by treating them in a very perfunctory fashion. As we have already shown, Abel Smith and Townsend (1965) made no mention of the sex differences which were clearly visible in their results – gender was simply not an issue. For Mack and Lansley, using a completely different approach to defining and measuring poverty twenty years later, this was still the case. Only one mention of the relationship between poverty and gender was made:

> The fact that one-parent families are headed by mothers means that there are many women who face a high risk of poverty: though, in general, women are not significantly more at risk of poverty than men.
>
> (Mack and Lansley 1985: 189)

If the authors had been more aware of the gender dimensions of poverty, they would have regarded this finding as highly significant. Considered together with the circumstances of female pensioners, they might have been discouraged from asserting such a sweeping, unsubstantiated (and incorrect) conclusion.

Even among those researchers who do acknowledge the high incidence of poverty among women, little attempt is made to explain its causes. Fiegehen *et al.*'s explanation is so perfunctory that it virtually constitutes some kind of apparent biological reductionism. In their discussion of the causes of poverty, they attempt to distinguish between 'demographic' and 'economic' causes of poverty. Their examples of people whose poverty arises from demographic causes include 'those whose employment is hindered by retirement and/or old age; being a single parent; being female (not retired); and other reasons (unoccupied)' (Fiegehen *et al.* 1977: 66; Table 5.8). Women's poverty is simplistically attributed to sex – to women being women – rather than to gender – to the economic and social processes which are constructed upon this basic biological distinction. This latter explanation only appears as an afterthought: 'the poverty of single parents and single women in employment [could be] attributed to economic causes (the adverse employment opportunities of women compared with men)' (ibid. 67).

Another approach is to assume that, although being a woman may increase the risk of poverty, in many instances being a women actually decreases that risk. Thus, single women are poor because they do not have access to men's resources, but married women are, apparently, not poor because they do. For example Layard *et al.* (1978: 24) explain that low pay and household poverty are not correlated: 'the reason is of course that most of those on low hourly wages are married women, and married women are not usually poor'. Fiegehen *et al.* (1977: 43) propose a similar explanation: 'some people do not enjoy income in their own right and, since these are mainly dependent children or married women not in employment, information about individuals' incomes tells us little about the extent of poverty.'

The widespread failure to recognize the relationship between gender and poverty stems from the near-universal use of aggregate living units as the basis on which information is collected and analysed. Aggregate units –

whether defined as 'families', 'assessment units', 'tax units' or 'households' – are the focus of both theoretical discussions and empirical studies of poverty. This widespread use of aggregate units rests upon a number of key assumptions which are generally taken for granted, but which, from a feminist perspective, are highly problematic. These assumptions are, first, that the distribution of resources within families or households is broadly equal; second, that the levels of consumption and living standards of all those who live in the same household are also broadly equal; and, third, that living standards are mainly determined by income and other material resources (housing conditions, consumer assets and so forth), rather than by the ways in which these resources are generated or managed.

In addition, the use of aggregate units for research into poverty has implicit ideological overtones. It allows us to ignore the issue of women's direct access to resources, because there is an implied assumption that this is of less significance in determining women's living standards than the access which they have to resources through their relationships with others (usually men). Thus, even when evidence is clearly found that women do receive low incomes or experience other kinds of deprivation, it is somehow assumed not to matter. Indeed, the whole issue of women's lack of resources is discounted as entirely unimportant and unproblematic, *because* women are deemed to share in the resources of, and derive their financial position from, the men with whom they live:

> Many people, and overwhelmingly married women and children, are not in poverty by virtue of any *personal* characteristics so much as indirectly by virtue of the labour market, wage or social security characteristics of the principal income recipient of the family unit.
>
> (Townsend 1979: 899)

In the next section of this chapter we will discuss these various assumptions in more detail. In particular, we will examine them in the light of both historical and recent feminist research on the patterns of resource control and management within households.

WOMEN'S POVERTY WITHIN THE FAMILY

The study of poverty on an aggregate rather than an individual basis obscures the particular circumstances of women in several ways. First of all, it means that women are included among the numbers of people in poverty *only* if the income of the family or the household in which they live is below the 'poverty line' currently in use. They are not counted among the poor if household resources are above that line, regardless of the actual amount of income to which they themselves have access. It is assumed that there is a degree of equality in the distribution of resources within households, which pays no regard whatsoever to the dynamics of power and command over resources which are known to take place within households and, especially, in households which women share with male partners and/or children. In reality, the patriarchal structuring of conjugal relationships means that, within the household, men are likely to exercise greater control over whatever resources come into the household. They are also likely to benefit from those resources to a greater extent than other household members, through bigger or more expensive patterns of consumption. For example, it is common, even in households where income is very limited, for men to retain some money for their own personal use, whether that is spent on alcohol, tobacco, or more expensive hobbies (Townsend 1979; McKee and Bell 1985; Graham 1987). The limited evidence available so far (Land 1983; Pahl 1988; Kellerhals and Lazega 1988) on the uses to which women put any earnings or other sources of income of their own suggests that rarely is any retained for personal spending money in a comparable way. Instead it is much more likely to be used in such a way that other household members share in its benefits – on children's clothes, family holidays, redecorating or new furniture, for example.

Townsend (1979: 271) does allude to some of these issues when he states that 'individual members of the household vary in the extent to which they pool and retain incomes for common or individual use'. However, this is treated as an essentially technical problem to be dealt with in the course of exploring the relationship between income and deprivation, rather than as a significant social fact with important economic and policy implications. He was concerned that the amount of money which was actually available to spend on the items of food, social activities and household amenities which constituted his deprivation index might have been less than the total household income because some of the latter was retained for personal, non-collective, consumption. The implications of the fact that different members of the household might have had unequal access to household resources or may have been able to enjoy higher levels of consumption than others were not explicitly considered.

Second, and paradoxically, although women are likely to exercise less command or control over household income than men, they are likely to bear a greater responsibility for the day-to-day management of whatever resources are available. Women are far more likely than men to be responsible for the week-by-week household budgeting. Moreover, as household income decreases, the likelihood that this responsibility will fall exclusively on female household members and the onerousness of the burden which it imposes both increase. Meredith Edwards' (1981) Australian research and Jan Pahl's (1990) research in Britain both demonstrate that the 'whole wage' system of allocating household resources, in which one partner (usually the wife) is responsible for managing all the household's financial affairs, is typical in lower income households.

This highlights a further conceptual flaw in aggregate, or household based, studies of poverty. They implicitly assume that within poor households all the members experience equally the deprivation caused by poverty. But there is ample evidence, both historical and contemporary, to show that the burden of poverty – of doing without and making ends meet – falls mainly on women. Even in poor female-headed households, where there are no men present to divert scarce resources, women make savings and sacrifices in their own comfort for the benefit of children (Graham 1987). Moreover, such self-sacrifice on the part of women is viewed as an entirely legitimate aspect of their altruistic and care-giving 'nature'. Land and Rose (1985) draw attention to the lack of comment with which case studies of poor families have described the small treats and indulgences which are only afforded to men from very meagre household resources because of the self-denial of women: 'the mother . . . accepts these as real human needs for her children and her husband but does so by denying her own. Her satisfaction is seen to lie in her altruistic practices.' Land and Rose conclude that 'self-denial is still seen as women's special share of poverty'.

Moreover, it is not just day-to-day and week-by-week consumption from which men and women derive unequal benefits. Major consumer durables which are conventionally assumed to enhance the standard of living of an entire household in fact confer different kinds of benefits (and costs) on different household members. So-called 'family' cars, for example, are predominantly owned by and used by men (Dale 1986); women's access to the freedom which car usage confers is largely at the discretion of male car owners. Furthermore, expenditure on 'his' car may be a serious drain on limited household resources, contributing yet further to the living standards of men at the expense of the needs of women and children. In contrast, women's unrestricted access to the 'family' washing machine or dishwasher, although it may confer freedom of a kind, is certainly not of an equivalent status to that of car ownership.

In summary, the use of household based definitions and measures of poverty rests upon an assumption that both the distribution of income and the consumption of resources *within* households are unproblematic and equal. Household based measures thus ignore the differences in men and women's access to, and control over, household income; they ignore the differences in men and women's consumption of the various goods and services which that income buys; and they ignore women's intensified experience of poverty through their role in managing scarce household resources on behalf of others.

TIME – AN UNVALUED RESOURCE

As well as overlooking the differences between women and men in their access to, and consumption of, resources, most studies of poverty also tend to overlook the important resource of time. Although time is generally uncosted, it does have both potential and actual value and is an immensely important factor in both the generation of financial resources and their actual use. Both the amount of time expended in generating and using financial resources, and the value placed upon that time differ substantially between women and men; and both factors contribute to the economic and material inequalities between men and women.

For example, men are on the whole better paid than women. (A decade after the Equal Pay Act, women's average earnings are still less than two-thirds those of their male counterparts.) Men, until the 1990 budget established independent taxation for women if they were married, were also more favourably taxed than women. These differences mean that men, on average, will have to work fewer hours to obtain a given level of income. Conversely, an 'average' woman would have to work 50 per cent *more* hours to achieve the same level of income as her male counterpart (Millar and Glendinning 1989). Furthermore, if the time taken to maximize the benefits of that income through efficient consumption ('shopping around' for bargains; mending rather than buying new; making home produced cakes, clothes or beer rather than buying ready-made) were taken into account, it would almost certainly point up yet more substantial differences between women and men. Women spend far more time on these activities and other unpaid domestic tasks, yet again this time and effort is both ignored and given no value in research on poverty. An analysis which included unpaid as well as paid work, and which assumed that all income represented payment for work done, would vastly increase the income differentials between women and men (Scott 1984: x).

DEPENDENCY – THE SOLUTION OR THE CAUSE OF WOMEN'S POVERTY?

Conventional poverty research therefore tells us little specifically about the poverty experienced by women and, in particular, about the poverty experienced by the vast majority of women who are married or living with a male partner. Moreover, there is evidence to suggest that these gender inequalities are not unique to men and women who are married or living together in marriage-type relationships. Historical evidence on the family circumstances of women who remained unmarried or were widowed (Gittins 1986) and contemporary research on unmarried women who are providing a substantial amount of care for an elderly relative (Glendinning 1988) indicate that similar patterns of inequality may exist between adult unmarried sisters and brothers who remain living in their parental home. In turn, all these dimensions of inequality in the relative power of men and women within marriage and the family reflect, and are reflected in, inequalities between women and men in the public domain outside the home. Women on the whole bring home lower wages, through their shorter working hours and lower rates of pay, than men; women also generally receive lower levels of benefits from State and occupational welfare systems. These wider economic inequalities are mirrored in the respective economic positions of individual heterosexual couples, as Christine Delphy describes:

> all the efforts a man may make to treat his wife as well as possible, and I am prepared to be optimistic about this, will neither hide nor abolish nor even mitigate the fact that he owes his material situation to the discrimination which women – the group to which his wife belongs – suffer in the employment market. We cannot separate the situation which men – and hence this particular man – occupy, from the situation which women – and hence this particular woman – occupy in the market.
>   The interpersonal relationship of a man and a women is not an island. . . . Even if a husband and wife or two lovers do not work together, their respective situations in the labour market, as members of differently treated groups in this market, are part of their overall situation – and therefore of their relationship, even though the latter appears to have nothing to do with labour or the market. The involuntary benefits the man in a couple derives from his group membership on the 'occupational' scene, are not absent from the loving, relational, conjugal scene. . . . They are part of the objective resources which he brings to it, whether he wants to or not, simply in bringing his person. The non-benefits of the woman in the couple are also part of what she does, or does not, bring into the relationship.
>
> (Delphy 1984: 115)

If not being poor means not just having adequate material resources but also opportunities for independence and self-determination, then the structuring of family and gender roles will make it much more difficult for women not to be poor than men. Yet, paradoxically, even socially relative definitions of poverty which give emphasis to important non-material phenomena such as powerlessness and social exclusion, or which focus on non-monetary aspects of deprivation and inequality, have not been extended to any examination of the relative positions of women and men. For even if it is the case that domestic relationships with men do protect women against poverty – that men share 'their' incomes with women sufficiently to ensure that women are not poor – it is still a strange reasoning which argues that women are not in some way impoverished by dependency itself and by the relative powerlessness which accompanies this dependency.

For underlying attitudes towards women in both official and independent studies of poverty lies the pervasive assumption that, within marriage or other male–female relationships, women are financially dependent upon men. However, this assumption is, statistically, largely inaccurate. According to estimates derived from the 1981 Census, the vast majority of adult women are first, either single, widowed or divorced, and second, employed or retired. At any one time, less than one-fifth of all adult women are wholly dependent on the earnings of a man with whom they live. Moreover, for most women, this period of complete financial dependency is relatively short, lasting only a few years while their children are very small. Yet because of this, financial dependency is assumed to be the norm for all women, all the time. This also somehow makes it legitimate for researchers to ignore the lower resources commanded by most women. The inequalities which are actually experienced by women because they receive lower wages or lower welfare benefits than men (or no wages or benefits at all) have usually been regarded as entirely unproblematic and rarely questioned.

This enormous discrepancy between the reality and the myth of women's financial dependency on men suggests that it also has an important normative dimension. The presumed financial dependency of women within marriage is believed actually to *protect* women against poverty. Hence, Layard *et al.*'s assertion, quoted earlier, that the lower pay received by married women is not an accurate indicator of poverty because 'married women are not usually poor'.

The assumptions that women are dependent on, and derive their standard of living from, the men with whom they live, and that this dependency protects them from the experience of poverty together render women invisible in both Government and independent studies of poverty. Because of their assumed economic dependency on a man, women's access to resources in their own right is deemed unimportant, and the issue of how those resources are allocated *within* the family is considered to be equally unproblematic.

However, the assumed financial dependency of women not only renders invisible their widespread poverty; it has also, time and time again, obscured the structural causes of that poverty. Poverty researchers have therefore also largely failed to address and explain just why it is that being female brings with it a high risk of financial inequality and poverty. This invisibility in research is mirrored in the absence of serious policy discussions about measures to alleviate that poverty.

The structural causes of women's poverty are rooted in a sexual division of labour which assigns to women a primary role (which is nevertheless largely hidden and unpaid) in the private domestic sphere, and a secondary position in the labour market. Moreover, this sexual division of labour is translated into and reflected in the private, occupational and the public systems of welfare provision, so that the inequalities which women experience in paid work are mirrored in their unequal access to, and levels of, income replacement benefits. And, of course, the inequalities of both the labour market and welfare systems are underpinned and legitimated by the ideology of dependency.

INTO THE OPEN: WOMEN'S POVERTY AND THE CHALLENGE TO SOCIAL POLICY

The challenges to social policy which follow from this analysis are twofold. They lie in social policy as an academic discipline – the concepts, theories and methodologies which are used for understanding and exploring our social world; and in the practice of social policy – the serious develop- ment of measures embracing both the public worlds of employment and welfare and the private domain of household labour and care, to combat the structural causes of women's poverty.

Women's poverty *is* gradually becoming more visible – in particular through the growing numbers of women living without men, as lone parents and in old age; and through women's increasingly clear segregation into low wage sectors of the labour market. This growing visibility has given rise to the notion of the 'feminization' of poverty, with its implication that poverty is somehow a relatively new experience for women (Scott 1984). This is however not the case; again, historical data provide a remarkably consistent picture of women's experience of poverty over the last hundred years (Lewis and Piachaud 1988). It is important that we do not allow the new visibility of women's poverty to confuse our understanding of its longer-term structural causes.

In order to increase that visibility yet further, we must tackle the issue of how poverty can be conceptualized and measured on an individual rather than an aggregate basis. As a very minimum first step, it is essential that Government departments responsible for collecting and presenting data about income and living standards begin to provide, at the very least, basic information which is disaggregated by sex. (Indeed, it may be possible to do this already in a preliminary fashion through analysis of existing Family Expenditure Survey and General Household Survey data, both of which contain some individual as well as household based data.) Following on from this, we need to begin collecting much more information about how different types of income and other resources come into households – who contributes what and how, and under what conditions they obtain that income. We need to make a clear distinction between 'direct' income (received by an individual through earnings or benefits) and 'indirect' income (obtained on the basis of dependency on another person). We need to pay much more attention to how, on what and by whom income is spent and how this spending is related to the different sources of income. This requires much more detailed information about the patterns of financial responsibility and consumption within households and how these are determined. (An important start on this has already been made by the contributors to Brannen and Wilson (1987).)

Conventional poverty research tends to assume that material resources are the main – if not the sole – determinants of living standards. However, it seems likely that, at any given income level, outcome living standards will vary according to the different inputs and usages of time by individual household members. It is therefore important to examine the different uses of time by women and men, how these are differentially rewarded, and how these uses variously contribute to their own and others' living standards. Related to this, more work is also needed on different ways of costing time (as, for example, the work of Nissel and Bonnerjea 1982; Joshi 1987). Large-scale survey research as well as small-scale in-depth research is essential – much of the research so far on the distribution of resources within households has focused on fairly small samples. Many problems exist in conducting this sort of research using survey techniques, but if these approaches are to be used in the study of poverty it is important that the methodology for survey work be developed.

These methodological considerations are important not only from the point of view of conducting more accurate and sensitive research. They also suggest some of the directions in which appropriate policy measures need to be developed. For example, discussion of the principles on which resources are distributed between former partners following the breakdown of marriage needs to be based on much more detailed and precise information about the respective contributions of women and men to both the material and the non-material resources of the family during marriage. (Funder (1988) provides an example of how such research could be pursued.)

More broadly – and most importantly – in both research and social policy analysis, we need to challenge the existing sexual division of labour and the assumptions which arise from it. In particular, we must tackle the assumptions about women's financial dependency and what Cass (1985: 16) terms the 'dangerous myth' that dependency protects women from poverty. The implementation of that challenge must take place on two fronts: in the public worlds of paid work and welfare; and in the private domain where unpaid domestic work and caring are performed. In the public domain, we must develop policies which are no longer based on the assumption that men are the main (or sole) breadwinners. If men and women were instead regarded as breadwinners of equal status, a number of positive policy measures immediately spring to mind. These include improving the training and labour market qualifications available to women; improving equal job opportunities and combating the increasingly pervasive vertical and horizontal segregation of jobs; and pursuing policies for equal pay, job sharing and parental leave far more aggressively than at present. By tackling labour market inequalities, women are also likely in both the short and longer terms to derive greater benefits from those systems of state and occupational welfare which are tied closely to labour market participation and earnings, although both of these also need considerable modification in order to meet women's particular needs and reduce their experience of poverty. It is important to recognize that action on these issues needs to come not only from Government, both in enacting and enforcing regulatory legislation and as a major employer itself, but also from the organized labour movement.

However, only if women are also relieved of their present high levels of responsibility for domestic and caring work within the home can they have any chance of participating 'equally' in the labour market. What is therefore needed is a simultaneous challenge to the conventional sexual division of labour within the home. This involves a challenge, too, to the firmly-held notions of men on both the political right and left about the 'protection of the family' – meaning, implicitly, that activities, relationships and responsibilities in the private domestic domain should be beyond the reach of the regulatory arm of State intervention. Because we do not seem to be overwhelmed by increasing numbers of men choosing on an individual basis to take on a bigger share of unpaid domestic work and the care of dependants, it is important to consider the development of statutory policies which would lift some of the burdens of responsibility for domestic work from women's shoulders. Such policies should ideally have both fiscal and service dimensions. For example, levels of social security benefits need to be raised, and particularly levels of income maintenance for those women (and men) whose responsibility for the care of children or other dependants limits their labour market opportunities and earnings potential. Fiscal policies of this kind would help to make visible the currently invisible value of at least some of the work done in the home. More importantly, such policies, combined with positive employment policies, would help to increase the sources of income to which women have independent access.

The development of services is also an important plank in any set of policies aimed at alleviating women's poverty. In particular, services which help to share more broadly the responsibilities of caring for children and others would do much to combat the current private context of care, by promoting the notion that caring is a legitimate collective concern. One way of doing this might be to reassert the notion of a 'social wage', encompassing the provision of a comprehensive network of supportive health, education and welfare services. This has at least as much to offer women as, say, straightforward campaigns for equal pay.

Research and policy are interdependent. The principles and assumptions which underlie policy goals also frame the concepts and questions we employ in our research, the data we collect, and the analysis and presentation of that data. Conversely, our research informs (or fails to inform) specific policy issues. This two-fold challenge – to research and policy – must be integrated and simultaneous.

REFERENCES

Abel Smith, B. and Townsend, P. (1965) *The Poor and the Poorest*, London: Bell.

Alcock, P. and Shepherd, J. (1987) 'Take up campaigns: fighting poverty through the post', *Critical Social Policy* 19, Summer: 52–67.

Bradshaw, J., Mitchell, D. and Morgan, J. (1987) 'Evaluating adequacy: the potential of budget standards', *Journal of Social Policy* 16, 2: 165–182.

Brannen, J. and Wilson, G. (eds) (1987) *Give and Take in Families: Studies in Resource Distribution*, London: Allen & Unwin.

Cass, B. (1985) *Poverty in the 1980s: Causes, Effects and Policy Options*, Paper presented to ANZAAS Congress, Monash University, August.

Coates, K. and Silburn, R. (1970) *Poverty: The Forgotten Englishman*, Harmondsworth: Penguin.

Cole, D. and Utting, J. (1962) *The Economic Circumstances of Old People*, Welwyn: Codicote Press.

Dale, A. (1986) 'Differences in car usage for married men and married women: a further note in response to Taylor-Gooby', *Sociology* 20, 1:91.

Delphy, C. (1984) *Close to Home: A Materialist Analysis of Woman's Oppression*, London: Hutchinson.

Department of Health and Social Security (1988) *Low Income Families 1985*, London: DHSS.

Edwards, M. (1981) *Financial Arrangements within Families*, Canberra, Australia: National Women's Advisory Council.

Fiegehen, G., Lansley, P.S. and Smith, A.D. (1977) *Poverty and Progress in Britain 1953-1973*, Cambridge: Cambridge University Press.

Funder, K. (1988) 'Women, work and post-divorce economic self-sufficiency', in

M.T. Meulders-Klein and J. Eekelaar (eds) *Family, State and Individual Economic Security*, Brussels: Story-Scientia.

Gittins, D. (1986) 'Marital status, work and kinship 1850-1930', in J. Lewis (ed.) *Labour and Love: Women's Experience of Home and Family 1850–1940*, Oxford: Basil Blackwell.

Glendinning, C. (1988) 'Dependency and interdependency: the incomes of informal carers and the impact of social security', in S. Baldwin, G. Parker and R. Walker (eds) *Social Security and Community Care*, Aldershot: Avebury Gower.

Graham, H. (1987) 'Women's poverty and caring', in C. Glendinning and J. Millar (eds) *Women and Poverty in Britain*, Brighton: Wheatsheaf Books.

Joshi, H. (1987) 'The cost of caring', in C. Glendinning and J. Millar (eds) *Women and Poverty in Britain*, Brighton: Wheatsheaf Books.

Kellerhals, J. and Lazega, E. (1988) *Individual Property Rights and Conceptions of Privacy in the Family*, Oxford, Wolfson College: Centre for Socio-Legal Studies.

Land, H. (1983) 'Poverty and gender: the distribution of resources within families', in M. Brown (ed.) *The Structure of Disadvantage*, London: Heinemann.

Land, H. and Rose, H. (1985) 'Compulsory altruism for some or an altruistic society for all?' in P. Bean, J. Ferris and D.K. Whynes (eds) *In Defence of Welfare*, London: Tavistock.

Layard, R., Piachaud, D. and Stewart, M. (1978) *The Causes of Poverty*, Royal Commission on the Distribution of Income and Wealth, Background Paper No. 5, London: HMSO.

Lewis, J. and Piachaud, D. (1988) 'Women and poverty in the twentieth century', in C. Glendinning and J. Millar (eds) *Women and Poverty in Britain*, Brighton: Wheatsheaf Books.

Low Pay Unit and Child Poverty Action Group (1988) *An Abundance of Poverty: Joint Briefing Paper*, London: LPU and CPAG.

Mack, J. and Lansley, S. (1985) *Poor Britain*, London: Allen & Unwin.

McKee, L. and Bell, C. (1985) 'His unemployment, her problem: the domestic and marital consequences of male unemployment', in S. Allen, K. Purcell, A. Waton and S. Wood (eds) *The Experience of Unemployment*, London: Macmillan.

Millar, J. and Glendinning, C. (1989) 'Gender and poverty', *Journal of Social Policy* 18, 3: 363–82.

Nissel, M. and Bonnerjea, L. (1982) *Family Care of the Handicapped Elderly: Who Pays?* London: Policy Studies Institute.

Pahl, J. (1988) 'Earning, sharing, spending', in R. Walker and G. Parker (eds) *Money Matters: Income, Wealth and Financial Welfare*, London: Sage.

Pahl, J. (1990) *Money and Marriage*, London: Macmillan.

Piachaud, D (1987) 'Problems in the definition and measurement of poverty', *Journal of Social Policy* 16, 2: 147–164.

Rowntree, B.S. (1902) *Poverty: A Study of Town Life* (2nd edn), London: Macmillan.

Scott, H. (1984) *Working your Way to the Bottom: The Feminisation of Poverty*, London: Pandora Press.

Townsend, P. (1979) *Poverty in the United Kingdom*, Harmondsworth: Penguin Books.

—— (1987) 'Deprivation', *Journal of Social Policy* 16, 2:125–146.

Townsend, P. and Wedderburn, D. (1965) *The Aged in the Welfare State*, London: Bell.

Veit Wilson, J. (1985) *Supplementary Benefit: What is to be Done?* School of Applied Social Science: Newcastle upon Tyne Polytechnic.
—— (1987) 'Consensual approaches to poverty lines and social security', *Journal of Social Policy* 16, 2: 183–212.
Walker, R. (1987) 'Consensual approaches to the definition of poverty: towards an alternative methodology', *Journal of Social Policy* 16, 2: 213–226.

3 Women and financial provision for old age

Dulcie Groves

Major changes in retirement and survivors' pension provision introduced from April 1988 via the Social Security Act 1986 were preceded by a Green Paper (DHSS 1985a) which made it clear that Conservative policies on financial provision for old age posit a residual role for state retirement pensions. By contrast, a heavy emphasis is placed on individual responsibility for generating income and capital for old age and on the exercise of choices in selecting the best means towards this end. This chapter comments on some implications of these policies for women.

Policies on financial provision for old age are liable to have a differential impact on women, as compared with men, given the major responsibility which women typically take for the unpaid work of the home (see Brook, Jowell and Witherspoon 1989), their characteristically interrupted records of paid employment and lower lifetime earnings (see Joshi 1989; Martin and Roberts 1984). The Green Paper was heavily criticized (DHSS 1986; Land 1985; Land and Ward 1986) for its failure to address the position of women with regard to social security in general. This chapter argues that with regard to income maintenance policies on retirement and survivors' benefits, the current government emphasis on individual responsibility for making financial provision for old age (over and above the very modest National Insurance basic state contributory retirement pension) makes it particularly important to consider the implications for women.

Low waged and intermittently employed workers, among whom women are overrepresented, have been largely excluded from occupational pension provision (Groves 1987). In addition, women have until recently been treated by state and occupational pension providers largely as actual or potential economic dependants within marriage (Groves 1983). It is still the case that many women continue to spend substantial periods of their adult lives in a state of partial or total economic dependency within marriage or a marriage-like relationship (see Joshi 1989; Land 1986). The principles underpinning current government policies on financial provision for old age and, especially, the respective roles and responsibilities envisaged for the state, the employer, the private insurance market and the private individual in making such provision, call into question some very important aspects of female financial dependence and independence within and without marriage.

This chapter aims to explain and comment upon current pensions and retirement benefit legislation in relation to the particular position of women, noting the extent to which pension providers are subject to sex discrimination legislation. It then more briefly addresses the Conservative emphasis on individual responsibility for making financial provision for old age in the context of a system of pension provision which, historically, has been geared much more in the case of women towards replacement of a family wage lost on the death of a husband, via a widow's benefit (potential access to which is lost on divorce), than on enabling women themselves to generate an adequate income for old age.

CURRENT RETIREMENT PENSION PROVISIONS

The Social Security Act 1986 modified the provisions of the Social Security Pensions Act (SSPA) 1975, passed after lengthy parliamentary and wider national debate on pensions. This debate hinged on the appropriate balance of responsibility between State and employer with regard to the provision of pensions at a level sufficient to lift recipients above the point at which means tested social assistance could be claimed. The outcome retained basic National Insurance pension provision and required employees to contribute to a new state earnings-related pension scheme (SERPS) or to an approved employer's pension scheme which would pay a guaranteed minimum pension (GMP) and widows' benefits at least as good as SERPS entitlements (Groves 1986; Hannah 1986; Helowicz 1988; Shragge 1984).

SERPS was designed to meet the needs of lower paid and intermittent employees, basing eventual entitlements on the 'best twenty years' of earnings, averaged out and revalued to reflect general increases in the value of earnings (SSPA 1975, 21: 12). The scheme provided for an earnings-related widow's pension payable in addition to a basic state widow's pension and also introduced an innovatory widower's pension payable to men whose insured wives died when both were over pensionable age. SERPS was intended for employees without access to occupational pension provision and was to be phased in over a period of twenty years to 1998. Its potential importance is clear from a 1983 survey which showed that only half of all employees were in an occupational scheme, of whom about one-third were women. In addition to the eleven million scheme members, a further two million, mainly men, had some pension rights from previous employment (Government Actuary 1986: 5).

By the mid-1980s it was the assumed future high cost of SERPS which provoked the government into proposing to abandon it completely (DHSS 1985a I: ch. 7) though some commentators disagreed that the finance of the scheme would inevitably be problematic (Cullen and O'Kelly 1985; Independent Pensions Research Group 1986; Walker 1986), arguing that there are wider grounds for the retention of SERPS such as the interests of those 'vulnerable' groups, including women, for whom the scheme was largely designed (DHSS 1985b: ch. 2). Financial provision for old age was a major area scrutinized in the 1984 Social Security Reviews undertaken by the second Thatcher administration. Though as the actuary Kaye notes (1987: 17) while evidence was taken on pension provision from specialists and the general public, subsequent proposals 'appeared to pay rather little attention to the majority evidence presented, but picked up ideas that had been vigorously argued by a minority'.

In the event, SERPS was retained in a much less advantageous version. The White Paper (DHSS 1985b) proclaimed a continuing role for the state in providing flat rate retirement and widows' pensions. Above this, individuals (seemingly conceptualized as male) were to have greatly increased responsibility for generating income (and capital) above a modest second-tier minimum prescribed by the state. All but the lowest earners would have to belong to a second-tier pension scheme, but the guaranteed benefits would be much lower for people retiring or being widowed beyond the end of the century. Membership of an employer's scheme would be optional. For their second-tier pension scheme, employees would be able to choose between employer's provision (if available), SERPS or an innovatory 'personal pension' (DHSS 1985b: Ch. 2).

The 'pensions choices' now available (see Wilson and Davies 1988) are extremely complex, as will be indicated in the next section. Younger people especially have a potential plethora of decisions to make as to the most appropriate way, given their particular personal circumstances, to make adequate financial provision for their old age (which they may not reach) and for any dependants. Other forms of more immediate expenditure compete for available resources and no crystal ball is available to reveal an individual's life course or employment career. 'Pensions choices' are immensely complicated for women in particular, given their greater propensity to spend a substantial period of their lives outside paid employment and/or in low paid jobs. The next section addresses the position of women in relation to pensions legislation and provision subsequent to the passing of the Social Security Act 1986.

WOMEN AND THE SOCIAL SECURITY ACT 1986

Detailed proposals within the Green Paper (DHSS 1985a) stated that basic National Insurance (NI) pensions were to remain 'as the foundation from which those retiring in the future can build their own additional pension'. The principle governing this provision was that the current generation of 'working people . . . provide this level of income to their predecessors in retirement' (DHSS 1985a II, 1.41: 5). And given that making provision for retirement is, in theory if not in practice, the task of a 'working lifetime', the Social Security Act (SSA) 1986 ruled that those reaching pensionable age before the end of the century would not be affected by modifications to SERPS (SSA 1986, 18–19: 22–4).

The Social Security Pensions Act 1975 required that all employed women, married or single, should in future be charged full NI contributions. From 1948, employed wives had been allowed to pay a reduced contribution and forgo benefits on the grounds that they had husbands to support them on whose contribution records an eventual dependent wife's retirement pension would be payable when the husband reached 65. This pension, worth 60 per cent of a single person's pension, was a disincentive to a married woman's opting to pay full contributions for a single person's retirement pension at 60, for once the dependent wife's pension became available, the married woman contributor had, effectively, bought herself only 40 per cent of a retirement pension. An even stronger deterrent lay in the 'half-test' which required a wife to pay full contributions for at least half of her married life or lose the entire value of her contributions made while single or married. This ruling was particularly punitive for women who married or had their children late in life and then withdrew from the labour market for a substantial period (see Groves 1983: 43–9).

From 1977, all women initially joining the labour force or returning after a gap of more than two years have been charged full contributions regardless of marital status, the half-test has been revoked and only those wives already paying the reduced contribution have been allowed this facility. From 1978 all but the lowest paid employees (an overwhelmingly female and part-time category) have been required to make earnings-related contributions for NI benefits. Basic retirement credits have been made available to women (or men) claiming child benefit, provided that they are either non-employed or earning less than the weekly wage point which triggered liability for NI contributions. Similar credits have been granted to 'carers' whose adult dependants are so severely incapacitated as to qualify for an attendance allowance. Married women can claim such credits (without an invalid care allowance) provided that they have revoked any continuing right to pay reduced contributions (Matthewman and Sloss 1988, 3.16: 24,

7.4: 116). On divorce, women are, where necessary, credited with their husband's NI contribution records up to the time of the divorce: widows are granted the same facility. Only women who were under pensionable age in 1979 and who were divorced or widowed after that date can get such credits (Matthewman and Sloss 1988, 17.11: 353).

As a result of these changes, although it is still a minority of married women currently reaching pensionable age who can claim a full state retirement pension of their own at 60, the number of wives with a minimum of ten years' paid or credited contributions and a consequent personal entitlement does appear to be increasing (DHSS 1988, Table 13.30: 86, 13.40 92; Walker and Hutton 1988: 59). From 1985, women affected by the half-test have been retrospectively permitted to use all their previous contributions (Masson 1985: 321) and can combine individual and dependent wife's retirement pension entitlements, but only up to the level of a dependent wife's pension (Matthewman and Sloss 1988, 17.16: 354–5). However, some non-married women will continue to have particular problems in establishing a complete record of entitlement to a basic state retirement pension unless they can pay Class Three voluntary NI contributions. This category includes women who exceed the permitted number of twenty years allowed for claiming home responsibility credits or who undertake 'caring' without in fact qualifying for an invalid care allowance or who find themselves, for whatever reason, unable to establish a right to NI credits when unemployed or in a situation of 'non-employment' such as early retirement (see Matthewman and Sloss 1988; 11.19–29: 230–4; 16.33 343). A woman who has been in receipt of a state basic widow's pension during the period immediately prior to reaching the age of 60 qualifies for a Category B widow's retirement pension of the same amount. A reduced widow's retirement pension can be topped up to the amount of a full single NI retirement pension by any allowable contribution or credits due (Matthewman and Sloss 1988; 17.14, 17.16: 354–5). Given regulations which link entitlement to a state widow's pension to age and the presence of dependent children, widows are at risk of ending up with a reduced retirement pension if they are not able to compensate adequately in this event from their own or their husband's contribution records.

Conservative party policies, however, now conceptualize the state retirement pension merely as a 'foundation' on which more adequate financial provision for old age can be based. It is constructing the remainder of the edifice which is potentially even more problematic for women, not least because of the downgrading of SERPS benefits. The possibilities are membership of an occupational pension scheme, SERPS, purchase of a personal pension (or pensions) or permitted combinations of these alternatives.

The state requires that all employees liable for NI contributions pay towards a specified entitlement to a second-tier pension, but from 1988 has offered more choice as to how this might be done. If a woman's employment contract offers her membership of a 'contracted-out' occupational pension scheme she may take that option (but is no longer obliged to do so) in which case she will be entitled to benefits at least as good as the revised SERPS. Alternatively, she may reject both her employer's scheme and SERPS in favour of an 'appropriate personal pension', in which case a level of contribution is laid down but the benefits are not guaranteed.

One of the few ways in which the government radically altered its original intentions on pensions reform was by retaining SERPS, albeit with seriously diminished benefits. Was the limited access of women to existing occupational retirement pension provision a major factor in persuading the government to leave a version of SERPS in place? How anxious were the potential providers of personal pension schemes to sell their products to women, given their tendency to occupy low paid, part-time jobs and to interrupt their employment careers? The terms of the Social Security Act 1975 have enabled employers to exclude women in gender-segregated job categories as well as part-timers from access to membership of occupational pension schemes. Employers have demonstrably never been keen to include part-time, low paid or temporary employees in their schemes (see Groves 1986). Hence it is not surprising to read that organizations such as the Confederation of British Industry and the National Association of Pension Funds argued for the modification of SERPS into a 'cheaper' version (DHSS 1985b, 1.28–1.34: 3–5). Nor were the insurance industry and associated financial institutions seemingly interested in being required to provide small personal pensions to a category of potential purchasers (such as women) who might be thought to carry an above-average risk of ceasing to pay premiums through leaving the labour force and who did not appear to be potentially profitable customers (see Ward 1988: 49–50).

SERPS in its original version, with its 'twenty best years' formula, was an enormous potential gain for those people (mainly women) who took time out of the labour market owing to domestic responsibilities. It also helped men and women who had suffered spells of unemployment, chronic ill-health or disability and favoured those whose highest real earnings came earlier in their careers, a typically female profile (see Martin and Roberts 1984). Early retirers, a category which potentially includes female 'carers', also benefited from the 'twenty best years' rule. In 1986 only 52 per cent of women in the 55–9 age cohort were economically active as compared with 74 per cent of those aged 40–50 (OPCS 1989, Tables 8.8: 93 and 9.17: 130). The original 1978 SERPS formula allowed for a £ for £ replacement of earnings in retirement up to a base rate (£41 for 1988–9) by the state retirement pension plus a second-tier SERPS pension equivalent to 25 per cent of averaged-out and revalued earnings between that base level and a ceiling (£305).

Thus, by 1998, it appears that a woman fully participating in SERPS with a record of twenty years in employment and with revalued earnings equivalent to the female full-time manual worker's New Earnings Survey 1988 weekly average of £124 (Employment Gazette 1988: 601–5) could expect to retire at 60 with the equivalent of a basic State retirement pension of £41.15, assuming maximum entitlement, plus a SERPS pension equal to 25 per cent of revalued earnings between the lower earnings limit of £41 and £124. Taking this revalued band of earnings as £83, the woman would on current values be in line for a SERPS pension of £20.75, making a total pension of £61.90 which replaces at gross level around 50 per cent of her earnings. By contrast, a prototype woman non-manual worker earning the 1988 New Earnings Survey average of £176 would receive a SERPS pension of £33.75 making a total of £75.70, replacing 43 per cent of her earnings. The biggest SERPS pension potentially available under the original arrangements, based on £305 revalued weekly earnings, would be £66, making a total of £107.15 replacing 35 per cent of the earnings. As can be seen, the scheme was designed to favour the low paid, among whom women are greatly over-represented, including the many who work part-time though earning sufficient to trigger liability for NI contributions.

Under the revised formula operative from 1999 (with the basic state retirement pension guaranteed under contributing conditions of entitlement), SERPS will be based not on an employee's 'best twenty years' but on lifetime average earnings (Wilson and Davies 1988: 46) and on 20 per cent (not 25 per cent) of the relevant earnings band. The 'best twenty years' rule will never now come into operation as those people retiring before the end of the century will only have paid a maximum of twenty years' contributions. The 'working lifetime' will seemingly in future be a stringent 44 years for women and 49 for men (SSA 1986, 18–19: 22–6) which is a less generous interpretation of a 'working lifetime' than that used (nine-tenths) for calculating entitlement to a full basic state retirement pension at 39 years for women and 44 for men (Matthewman and Sloss 1988, 17.9: 352). No allowance is to be made for periods spent in full-time education or outside the labour market unless the person concerned was formerly granted a home responsibilities credit for which disregards are permitted to a maximum of twenty years (SSA 1986, 18(3)(2b): 22–3). A credited year is discounted when averaging out and revaluing earnings.

From the point of view of women, the revised SERPS is a far less generous arrangement, reminiscent of the meagre 'State Reserve' pension scheme proposed by an earlier Conservative government (DHSS 1971), though never enacted. Unless some future government moves the goal-posts yet again before 1999, no woman will ever receive a SERPS pension based on that notion of 'twenty best years' which went some way towards compensating women for diminished economic activity as a consequence of major domestic responsibilities. Not only will the maximum SERPS pension which a woman might expect be lower because it will be based on only 20 per cent of the requisite earnings band: she will need to work for a far greater number of years in order to achieve that maximum, unless she has an entitlement to home responsibility credits.

Furthermore, a most fearsome poverty trap for old age is now laid for women who do part-time work for lengthy periods, usually on account of motherhood or other domestic responsibilities (see Beechey and Perkins 1987). A home responsibilities credit can only be claimed by someone who is, during the relevant contribution year, entitled to child benefit and/or the invalid care allowance and earning, if at all, too little for inclusion in the NI scheme. Part-time employment remunerated at or above the NI lower earnings limit disqualifies a woman from receiving home responsibilities credits and means that, if she is in the SERPS scheme, low part-time earnings will be counted in when the final calculation of her pension entitlement is made. Thus, women in SERPS will run the risk of greatly depressing their eventual SERPS pension entitlement if they work part-time at a rate of pay above the lower earnings limit because such pay will be counted into the total revalued earnings on which the eventual SERPS retirement pension will be based. Previous higher earnings will lose their value. The discarded 'best twenty years' arrangement was calculated to avoid this, even if a woman did spend a period of years in lower paid and/or part-time work.

It would appear that a woman with dependent children or who cares for someone potentially entitled to an attendance allowance (which is a trigger for claiming the invalid care allowance) will achieve a better end result under the revised SERPS scheme by not engaging in paid work at all. At the least she should earn so little that she can be credited with NI contributions on the grounds of her home responsibilities. Credited contribution years will not count towards the total of years by which her lifetime earnings will be divided in order to produce the applicable level of SERPS pension. However, for best results in the SERPS scheme, a woman now needs to work full-time rather than part-time and to maximize her earnings opportunities up to the weekly ceiling (a point which few women are likely to achieve) throughout her working life.

The revised arrangements allow for a phasing out of the 1978 formula for women who are between 50 and 60 in 1999. The 25 per cent rule will be applied to earnings in the tax years 1978–9 to 1987-8 with a gradual tapering to the tax year 2008–9 at which point all earnings will be subject to the 20 per cent rule (See SSA 1986, 18: 22–4). For those women under 50 when the cutbacks in SERPS are fully in place, the scheme will offer severely diminished entitlements. The depressing effect of part-time work is particularly worthy of note.

Hence, for women, as for men, there is much to be said for membership of a good 'contracted-out' occupational pension scheme which is based on 'defined benefit' principles, that is, a final salary arrangement so that the contributor knows what will be due to her on retirement. A useful feature of the 1986 legislation, especially for women, is the universal introduction of arrangements whereby members of employers' pension schemes can make good 'missing years' or simply add to the value of their future pension by paying additional voluntary contributions up to the permitted limit. Contributions to an employer's pension scheme, unlike those made to SERPS, are tax relieved at the employee's highest rate.

An 'approved' contracted-out occupational pension scheme enables both employer and employee to pay lower NI contributions since the employee's GMP will come via the employer's scheme, not SERPS. The typical occupational pension scheme at the time of the most recent Government Actuary's Survey (data collected 1983, survey published 1986) was a final salary scheme into which a defined percentage of earnings was paid, resulting in a retirement pension calculated as a fraction of final salary (commonly one-sixtieth) multiplied by completed years of service. Members typically had the opportunity to commute part of their pension into a lump sum on retirement, though in the public sector, employees such as teachers had a multiplier of one-eightieth, but were automatically entitled on retirement to a lump sum worth three times that factor (Government Actuary 1986: 41–50). Membership of a good occupational scheme is, typically, a fringe benefit offered to full-time, better paid and well organized employees, the majority of whom are male (see Groves 1986; Hannah 1986). Contracted-out schemes have, since 1978, included a guaranteed widow's pension where such would be available via SERPS: many offer more generous survivors' benefits. From 1988, schemes have been required to incorporate a modest widower's pension, an entitlement not incorporated in SERPS other than on the limited basis already mentioned.

In 1983, around half of all full-time workers were in occupational pension schemes, including 37 per cent of all women in full-time work (Government Actuary 1986: 3). Full-time public servants, male and female, have hitherto been near-universally covered by employer's retirement pension provision, with facilities to transfer their accrued benefits from one part of the public sector to another. Had the prototype woman non-manual worker on £176 weekly, last observed drawing a 'best twenty years'

SERPS pension, retired after twenty years' service as a full-time worker in the public sector, she could have expected an occupational retirement pension equivalent to £44 per week. This, with a full State pension of £41.15 would give her a 48 per cent replacement of her previous salary as compared with 43 per cent under SERPS. However, the employer's pension scheme would also offer a lump sum of three times her annual pension, that is, £6,864 and, had she achieved more than twenty years of service, her eventual lump sum and pension would considerably exceed the maximum available under the original version of SERPS and will be even more advantageous in the future.

The Social Security Act 1986 reduced the GMP payable to members of occupational pension schemes in proportion to the reduction of potential entitlement to SERPS. However, as illustrated, membership of a 'final salary' employer's pension scheme is liable, potentially, to be more profit-able to the employee with long service, producing eventual benefits well above the guaranteed minimum. But a further important modification of the 1975 pensions legislation now allows employers to gain approval from the Occupational Pensions Board for 'contracting-out' a new form of occupa-tional pensions scheme. This is a 'defined contribution' scheme (a COMPS), analogous to the personal pension plans which will be discussed below (see Ward 1988: 38–40).

Hitherto, around 10 per cent of the members of occupational pension schemes have been 'contracted-in' so that employees continued to belong to SERPS but got additional benefits such as lump sums or survivors' pensions. Most such schemes are very small (Government Actuary 1986, Table 5.1: 5). Some 18 per cent of 'contracted-in' scheme members were in defined contribution or money purchase schemes, this category being reported as increasing (Table 7.5: 44). The future benefits derived from money purchase schemes depend entirely on the investment performance of those contributions. Investments are made via the pension scheme's trus-tees or by the company's own pensions personnel and professional advisers, or by the insurance companies to whom this task is directly entrusted (see Ward 1988: 254–66). Where COMPS are concerned, an assumption will be made by the Government that the end result will enable the scheme member to purchase an annuity equal to the GMP, though there is no guarantee of that outcome and the individual could end up with a pension even lower than that which might have been obtained from SERPS. It may well be that if employers continue to be permitted to exclude certain occupational groups from their final salary schemes (such as part-timers) they may offer COMPS as an alternative, which will not necessarily be advantageous to women (see Ward 1988: 38–9).

The major innovation in the retirement pensions field arising from the

Social Security Act 1986 is a new form of second-tier provision – the personal pension. There are in fact two types of personal pension. The first is an approved personal pension (APP) with what are defined as 'protected rights' which can be chosen as an alternative to SERPS, or an occupational pension scheme. This represents a basic and modest level of second-tier pension provision which must incorporate a widow(er)'s pension. Secondly, one or more personal pension plans can be taken out in addition to an APP or SERPS.

An appropriate personal pension is an alternative to SERPS or a contracted-out occupational scheme and satisfies the official requirement that all employees liable for NI contributions must be covered for a minimal level of second-tier pension provision. Where an APP is the preferred option, the employer and employee NI contributions are partially diverted (with tax relief) to the APP selected by the employee from a range of schemes now offered by approved pension providers, that is, life insurance companies, unit trusts, friendly societies, banks and building societies. Employees already in SERPS who opted for an APP by 5 April 1989 are entitled to a Government bonus, payable to their plan, equal to 2 per cent of earnings between the lower earnings limit and their own earnings, up to the maximum level (the NI 'ceiling') and for a maximum of six years, the exact amount depending on individual circumstances.

The whole of the APP proceeds (less charges and commission of whatever amount) must eventually be used for the purchase of an annuity, that is, a 'personal pension' available at 60 (women) or 65 (men), which must be 'unisex' with respect to the actuarial calculations upon which it is based. When taken, it must increase by whichever is the smaller of 3 per cent, or the rise in annual prices. It must provide a survivor's pension of 50 per cent of its value for a widow(er). However, there is in fact no guarantee that the final pension will be as good as that which would have been obtained by paying a similar amount of contributions to SERPS.

Employees may also take out personal pension plans over and above the required APP or remain in SERPS and take out one or more additional personal pension plans available on retirement at any age between 50 and 75. Under the terms of the Social Security Act 1986, it is an individual employee decision which has to be taken – in the first place whether to participate in SERPS, an APP or an employer's pension scheme (if available), *one* of these being compulsory. In the second place, a decision can be taken to make contributions over and above the required minimum to one or more personal pension schemes, again selected as an alternative to an occupational pension scheme if such is available. There is no requirement that a personal pension plan must incorporate survivors' benefits (unlike the APP) and one-quarter of the eventual capital proceeds may be taken as a lump sum, the rest being used to purchase an annuity. Again, unlike the APP, a personal pension is quite legally based on sex-specific actuarial calculations which means that women's annuities are somewhat lower than men's because, statistically speaking, women live longer than men. (For sources and detail on APPs and PPs see Wilson and Davies 1988.) The 1989 budget made it possible for people to contribute a greater proportion of their annual earnings to pension schemes, from 17.5 per cent (under 36) to 35 per cent (over 60) (*Guardian* 6 May 1989).

Personal pensions and the 'bonus' were widely advertised in the early months of 1989, one general message within the detailed information available being that it was younger men (under 50) and women (under 45) who should consider leaving SERPS for an APP. In a bank on the Lancaster University campus in February 1989, there was a poster featuring a youngish man, soberly dressed, while the accompanying leaflet featured a unisex hand, emerging from the sleeve of a track suit, clutching at least £90 in £10 notes. Given women's typical rates of pay, the handful of £10 notes is likely to be rather more representative of the bonus accruing to the typical woman who leaves SERPS than the maximum £1,600 quoted in an assurance company advertisement.

The Technical Annexe to the White Paper on Social Security (DHSS 1985c) gives estimates as to the likely relative performance of an APP as compared with the revised SERPS. While the APP looks more favourable for men, it has to be reiterated that for contributors of either sex, the ultimate performance of any form of money purchase pension is only as good as the investments made with the contributions. For lower paid women with career breaks, for instance, it is highly questionable as to whether the eventual fund and annuity will provide a better return than would have been obtained from the 'old' SERPS with its 'twenty best years' rule. It seems unlikely that women are in fact the major targets of pension marketers since, for best results, a money pension scheme must be maintained over a 'working lifetime'. One of its selling points is its 'portability' between jobs, though some occupational pension schemes, notably those within the public sector, are also portable.

A major issue for women contemplating the purchase of an appropriate personal pension (APP) is that only people in paid employment can pay the annual premiums. While a woman can contract to pay by means of variable annual premiums, as a proportion of her annual earnings, she will necessarily miss out on any years when she is out of the labour market due to motherhood or 'caring' duties and she will have a lower permissible maximum from which to contribute if she works part-time, like many women with time-consuming domestic duties. She may have some scope for recouping her losses at a later stage by increasing her premiums to the permitted maximum, but, especially if inflation has remained moderate, it is the earlier contributions which particularly enhance the value of a money purchase arrangement, provided always that the premiums are profitably invested. For, as Ward (1988: 44) notes, the Stock Exchange crash of 1987 wiped 25 per cent off its prices within three weeks, so that anyone forced to retire then might well have had a severely eroded sum with which to buy an annuity to last the rest of their life.

PENSIONS AND SEX DISCRIMINATION LEGISLATION

Before going on to discuss some wider issues, it may be helpful to comment on the limited extent to which sex discrimination legislation applies to pensions, death and retirement benefits, which were specifically exempted from the remit of the Sex Discrimination Act 1975 on promise of further legislation (Groves 1986). The Social Security Pensions Act 1975 made some moves, already noted, towards the elimination of discrimination against women in State pensions provision, and SERPS can fairly be said to have originally contained an element of positive discrimination, given the 'best twenty years' rule, which favoured women. As regards occupational pensions, an 'equal access' clause required scheme membership to be 'open to men and women on terms which are the same as to age and length of service and as to whether membership is voluntary or obligatory' (SSPA 1975: iv: 46–9). From 1978, if men and women were in a job category where an occupational pension was available, it had to be available to both sexes, though women could be required to retire earlier than men. However, women's under-representation in those better paid full-time job categories typically covered by occupational pension schemes and their over-representation in jobs which carry no such fringe benefits remains a wholly legal form of indirect sex discrimination. Meanwhile, the two major areas of permitted inequality in the state system remain the differential age of eligibility for state pensions (60 for women and 65 for men), together with provision of survivors' benefits for certain categories of widow in circumstances where widowers cannot benefit.

Some changes in UK law have come about, not as a result of official enthusiasm for promoting the equal treatment of men and women as a matter of principle, but as a result of legal judgments and directives from the European Community. A 1981 judgment prevented Lloyds Bank from continuing to operate a form of 'delayed entry' for women bank clerks (Ellis and Morrell 1982). The 1986 judgment in the *Marshall* case has made it illegal for employers to operate a differential 'normal retirement age' for men and women, typically requiring women to retire at 60, while men are permitted to remain at work until 65 (Ward 1988: 32). Immense legal confusion has followed this judgment in that the Sex Discrimination Act 1986 requiring employers to set equal 'normal retirement ages' has not yet been reconciled with other aspects of occupational provision, many schemes being organized to pay benefits to women at 60 and men at 65 (Ward 1988: 122–3).

Legislation going through Parliament in 1989, following publication of a consultative document by the Department of Social Security in the previous year, will further implement equal treatment by acting on an EEC Directive on Occupational Social Security Schemes (86/378/EEC). This makes it obligatory for occupational pension schemes to charge equal contributions from men and women members, which final salary schemes in the UK have done almost without exception. The Directive gives money purchase schemes thirteen years in which to comply. Schemes are also required to provide equal lump sum benefits (which most do), equal accrual rates and to calculate transfer values, preserved pension rights and any return of contributions on a 'unisex' basis (EOC 1986, 6: 5). However, benefit levels for men and women members in money purchase schemes can be varied according to actuarial data and 'contributions paid by employers can vary according to the sex of the employee where this is intended to make more equal the benefits provided to men and women by contribution-defined schemes' (EOC 1986, 4.1: 3).

UK legislators also have to take note of recent European Court judgments. For instance, the *Bilka* case indicates that the exclusion of part-timers from occupational pension schemes is a form of indirect discrimination, as is the exclusion of employees by 'occupational group' (EOC 1988a: 2–3). A further draft directive (COM (87) final 494) has been placed before member states which aims to complete the implementation of the principle of equal treatment of men and women in statutory and occupational pension schemes. It proposes the eventual equalization of pensionable ages and aims to replace benefits granted as 'derived' rights to wives or husbands, contingent on a legal relationship to an insured person, with a system of individual rights. In its commentary on the proposed directive, the Equal Opportunities Commission, a body which has consistently argued the case for equal treatment of men and women in pension provision, points out that further legislation is needed so as to prevent 'money purchase' and other insurance based death, retirement and pension benefits, including the payment of additional voluntary contributions, being based on crude assumptions as to women's statistically longer life span (EOC 1988b, 56–9: 17–19).

The EOC has further noted (1988a, 1.4: 1) that in relation to the Directive 86/378, the Government's approach has been 'one of strict adherence to the minimal requirements of the Directive, rather than of thorough-going review of how this principle can most effectively be expressed in practice'. During 1989 the House of Lords Select Committee on the European Communities has completed a wide-ranging report in response to the draft EC Directive COM (87) 494 final. The arguments for and against actuarial exemptions from the principles of equal treatment are clearly set out (H of L 1989, Appendix 5, 32–3). The broad issue under consideration is whether occupational money purchase schemes should be forced to be 'unisex' under Community law while the life insurance industry continues to be permitted to apply sex specific mortality tables. From the social policy perspective, issues of sex equality are at stake. From the point of view of commercial (personal) pension plan providers, the issues are also related to the potential profits to be derived from a particular course of action.

SELF-RELIANCE AND RETIREMENT BENEFITS

Envisaging social security in general as 'a partnership between the individual and the State' (DHSS 1985a I, 1.5:1), the Green Paper stated that 'The organization of social security . . . should respect the ability of the individual to make his (*sic*) own choices and take responsibility for his (*sic*) own life' (1.6:1). 'State provision has an important role in supporting and sustaining the individual: but it should not discourage self-reliance or stand in the way of individual provision and responsibility.'

The extent to which these organizing principles are meant to apply directly to women, especially if married, is uncertain, though a hint as to the Government's intention may be gleaned from its quoting of the Beveridge report, published four decades earlier. 'The State . . . should leave room and encouragement for voluntary action by each individual to provide more than that minimum for himself and his family' (Beveridge 1942, 9: 6–7). The Green Paper argues that 'The ability of most people to make their own provision has substantially improved' (DHSS 1985a I, 1.8: 2). Hence the Government's original plans to retain the basic State retirement pension, but to leave all additional provision to the employer or the private insurance market.

The Government's emphasis on individual responsibility for generating income and capital for old age was highlighted in the Green Paper by reference to positive public responses to policies on expanding opportunities for home ownership and for 'wider ownership of shares in former public sector companies' (DHSS 1985a I, 7.22: 26). The proposed pension arrangements were in line with other policies which set out to encourage people to gain equity in flats and houses and to generate capital via the market. The tone of the argument appears to highlight the notion of investment for capital gain, rather than mere saving for old age or making financial provision for dependants by taking out life insurance. The proposed pension arrangements would give 'greater freedom and choice to individuals'. The 'two nations in pensions – those with their own pension provision and those dependent on the state' would be replaced by 'a nation in which everyone is saving through their job for a better retirement' (7.22: 26). This begs the question of the prospects for those persons of 'working age', including women, who, for whatever reason, are excluded from the paid labour force or from opportunities to engage in entrepreneurial activities for profit.

Both the National Insurance pension arrangements (with their origins in the Beveridge Report which presumed that married women would normally be fully occupied by unpaid domestic labour) and occupational pension schemes (incorporating similar assumptions) have a history of making provision for married women as widows rather than as 'breadwinners' in their own right. The existence of widows' pensions as a replacement for a family wage or a husband's deferred earnings is one factor which has helped to structure the financial dependence of wives in marriage (Groves 1983). It is doubtless one of the reasons why the text of the Green Paper is ambiguous when it comes to exactly *who* is meant to be demonstrating financial self-sufficiency with regard to provision for old age. There are by now many contradictions incorporated within provision for survivors, not least because widows' pensions originated in assumptions of total financial dependency of wives in marriage, whereas at the present time most married women are economically active during at least part of their marriages. Younger women display a greater propensity to engage in paid work, but the earnings of the typical wife are far less than those of her husband. Furthermore, on motherhood she characteristically forgoes a very large amount of potential earnings as one of the opportunity costs borne by women who have children (see Joshi 1987; 1989).

A notable feature of the Social Security Act 1986 is its actual reduction of the benefits available to widows through raising the age of entitlement to a full basic 'childless' widow's pension to 55 and cutting by half a wife's entitlement to inherit her husband's SERPS pension under the new provisions. Widow's benefits within 'final salary' occupational pension schemes have tended to become more generous in recent years. However, the new legislation allows for a man to opt out of his occupational scheme in favour of a personal pension plan, seemingly without any requirement that his wife be informed. An APP must incorporate minimal widows' and widowers' benefits, but there is no obligation for a spouse to provide over and above that minimum.

The history of pension provision reflects the traditional domestic division of labour in marriage with men generating deferred earnings from their family wage for old age. The prototype 'good husband' has been expected to provide for his widow with pension entitlements and life insurance policies. It has not been the place of a wife to provide for her own old age. There is evidence in recent studies of the division of financial resources in the household (Brannen 1987; Brannen and Moss 1988; Brannen and Wilson 1987; Mansfield and Collard 1988; Wilson 1987) that a wife's earnings, across socio-economic classes, tend to be constructed as applicable to short-term family expenditure and, in more affluent households, for extras. It is the husband's earnings which are constructed as more permanent than those of the wife and therefore applicable to long-term expenditure like life insurance and provision for old age. Mothers with earnings tend to use them for meeting the expenses of child care. Such attitudes help to explain why government documents are apt to characterize the individual exercising pension choices as a man. Indeed, with legislation which allows employees to opt out of their occupational pension scheme, it is now possible for a wife earning a good salary, with access to an excellent employer's pension scheme, to opt to pay only the approved minimum via an APP, leaving her husband to make the 'real' provision for old age or death in service or provision for survivors. In the light of Britain's high divorce rate, this must be a questionable strategy.

On divorce, a former wife can make good any deficiencies in her basic NI record by making use of any available contributions from her ex-husband's record. Post divorce she is on her own. She loses all potential entitlement to the benefits she might have received had she been widowed while still married to her husband and, despite a consultative document from the Vice-Chancellor's department in 1985, no action has ever been taken on the question of compensation for loss of potential widows' or widowers' benefits on divorce. Indeed, it does seem that the advent of the Matrimonial and Family Proceedings Act 1984, with its emphasis on the goal of economic self-sufficiency on divorce, has disinclined the government to act on this matter. It is by no means clear what the best course of action might be on this issue. Meanwhile, many divorced women who have subordinated their earning potential to the performance of unpaid domestic work are distinctly at risk of poverty in old age (see Masson 1986; Freedman *et al.* 1988: Ch. 6).

The Conservative administration of 1983–7 clothed its discussion of financial provision for old age in the rhetoric of individualism and, in cutting state pension entitlement for younger middle-aged widows with regard to the basic pension and, potentially, for all widows in terms of SERPS, gestured in the direction of married women's increased economic activity. However, as the Social Security Advisory Committee concluded, not least with regard to pension proposals within the Green Paper, the review failed 'to take full account of the changing position of women in society or of the continuing importance of the service they provide as carers' (DHSS 1986, 7.12: 84). The changing position of women in society has included an increasing propensity to experience divorce, at which point all entitlement to potential widows' pensions and benefits are lost without necessarily being compensated for when the financial settlement is made after divorce. At the present time, older divorcing women, as well as younger wives whose responsibilities for child care preclude full-time employment are particularly likely to have little or no entitlement to occupational pension benefits (Groves 1987). The Thatcher Governments' 'individualistic' policies for financial provision in old age need careful scrutiny in relation to the realities of women's lives.

WOMEN AS FINANCIAL PROVIDERS FOR OLD AGE

For a woman to achieve merely the 'foundation' for an adequate income in old age, on present government policies, she must ensure, if she can, that she reaches pensionable age with a full state retirement pension entitlement, for which she will need to have contributed or been credited for a total of 39 years. As previously indicated, even this may be difficult for some women. While it is possible to pay voluntary contributions (£3.95 weekly in 1988–9) with limited opportunities for back-dating, for this strategy a woman needs to know how to obtain information about her NI record and about the voluntary payments procedure, and needs the wherewithal to produce the cash for contributions. Basic retirement pensions have, however, lost their value steadily since the Conservative party took office in 1979. They were formerly uprated in relation to whichever was the more favourable of prices or earnings, but for the past decade have been linked to increases in prices only. The many elderly women subsisting on basic retirement pensions have not shared in Britain's rising living standards in proportion to the rise in the real value of wages and salaries.

Individuals seeking to generate income and capital for old age over and above the basic state provision need command over financial resources. Women are less likely than men to have such command, especially during their husband's lifetime or while in a marriage-like relationship. Most women are financially at their most vulnerable when rearing children or caring for a severely incapacitated close relative. It is paid work which is most likely, barring substantial inheritance, to provide opportunities for the generation of income and capital for old age, mainly through contribution to a second-tier pension scheme and acquiring equity in an owner-occupied home, bolstered, for those who can afford it, by savings, life assurance and other investments. Yet, a substantial minority of the population, male and female, have such low incomes that few, if any, such opportunities can be grasped, which places some question over the notion of universal economic self-sufficiency for old age. Many younger people, especially in the south of England, now have to devote a substantial part of their incomes to the repayment of large mortgages on their homes or to the payment of high rents. Some of these people may be tempted to minimize their retirement benefit provision. Furthermore, younger people may well also be faced in the future with repaying debts incurred for post-school education.

'Women on the whole, have not achieved an equal economic footing with men in British society and they will not achieve it universally over-night. Meanwhile it would be a mistake for legislation on divorce, taxes or pensions to assume they had' (Joshi 1989: 174). Much evidence has become available in recent years on women's typically low earnings, their interrupted careers and the 'opportunity costs' of motherhood and caring duties. As Joshi (170–2) has shown, motherhood typically has very depressing effects on women's earning power. For women, the inequalities of the workplace and of the home are reproduced in old age. Widows' pensions are meant to compensate to some degree for this, which helps to explain why divorce without re-marriage is a poor prognosis for economic well-being in old age, especially for those ex-wives who left the labour market for a substantial period or habitually worked for low pay or who lived on state benefits during or subsequent to marriage (See Ermisch 1989: 43-6).

Marriage and marriage-like relationships, especially where there are children, typically incorporate unequal economic relationships between men and women. It appears uncertain whether official policies are, or are not, seriously inviting women as well as men to become economically self-sufficient for old age, making 'pension choices' to that end. Certainly, the literature on the financial consequences of divorce would appear to indicate that women, married or single, would do well to aim for some measure of economic self-sufficiency prior to, as well as during, old age. However, given the provisions of the Social Security Act 1986, women aiming to make serious provision for retirement will need to become more economically active, earn more and spend more of their adult lives in full-time paid work than do most women at present. Given the almost total lack of publicly provided child care provision, greater economic activity on the part of women would appear to indicate a need for greater sharing of unpaid domestic work (especially child care) by men or, perhaps more realistically, that women will need to earn sufficiently well to purchase (if their principles allow) the domestic labour of others in order to perform a greater degree of paid work themselves. Younger women with children are currently being targeted as potential skilled employees, given the coming drop in the number of school leavers. Perhaps similar lines of argument will be followed in relation to those older women who, traditionally, have borne major responsibility for the care of elderly relatives.

The second-tier pension provisions offered from 1988 require the exercise of choices and also the acquisition of knowledge about the ramifications of available options. A certain amount of 'consciousness-raising' on the subject of pensions has taken place as a result of the aggressive marketing of personal pensions. The Occupational Pensions Board (1989: 55) has emphasized that the extension of options means that people need information about employers' pensions of all types. The same sentiment can be echoed with regard to personal pensions, with the added complication that independent advice is becoming harder to find. Many well-known financial providers are now tied to the products of one particular life assurance company, because there is profit in it. Yet as Hamish Macrae (*Guardian*, 3 March 1989) argues, making the right decision about such a long-term investment as a personal pension 'is enormously important: it is one of the areas of finance where people most need expert advice'.

Who is advising women? Getting financial advice is a problem, but women are hampered by traditional attitudes which construct them as being incompetent to make financial decisions or to take financial responsibility beyond dealing with 'housekeeping'. The history of occupational pension provision well illustrates this point (see Groves 1983). Another amusing illustration was the sight of a wife being interviewed in 1988 on film at a 'money fair' about her choice of personal pension provision. The interviewer (male) not only set the wife up to defer to the opinions of the husband who was standing by her side, but constantly directed questions about the wife's financial circumstances to her husband. Evidence from previously cited studies of the division of household resources indicates that for a wife (even when earning a good salary) to take an assertive stance on providing for her own financial future, especially if she is a mother, is liable to pose a considerable challenge to the typical marital relationship. It is men, still, who are constructed as the 'real' financial providers. The vaunted disaggregation in 1990 of a personal tax system which has played no little part in helping to construct women as financial incompetents, will retain a 'married person's allowance' to be paid, automatically, to the husband, if he is entitled to that level of tax relief.

In order to make adequate financial provision for old age, women will need to be well informed and assertive with respect to their pension options including ways in which they can make good missing contributions when returning to paid employment after an absence. Part-timers need equal rights with full-timers to join occupational pension schemes. It is to be hoped that the women's movement increasingly reflects the interests of older and retired women and that as more women qualify and practise in the area of financial services, so women's interests will be better served. Only when women can demonstrably exercise independent command over financial resources will the argument stand that widows' benefits are a total anachronism. For many years to come, they will continue to provide some compensation in old age (and earlier) for that unpaid domestic labour which places many married women at an economic disadvantage. Unmarried women, of course, receive no such compensation.

Finally, a question may be posed as to what extent an individualistic and workplace-related approach to financial provision for old age, let alone any arrangements which depend on the continuation of married status, are really in women's best interests, given the economic uncertainty of many women's lives. It can be argued that what women need for decent financial security in old age is access to a really adequate basic state pension available via collective provision as a citizen's right. The combination of basic state retirement and SERPS pension introduced in 1978 was a step in this direction, though the conditions of entitlement were perhaps too closely related to occupational and marital history to offer the promise of real financial security for all women in old age. It can also be argued that the financial situation of older women is immeasurably improved by access to a wide range of community and public services, including transport, at a cost which relates realistically to the incomes of female pensioners and does not involve an individual test of means. Citizens' rights are good news for older women and offer some recompense for all the low-paid and unpaid work which the typical woman does over her lifetime. For, as Joshi (1989: 174) has observed, 'British women are still taking better care of their families than their pension rights. It should not be beyond the wit of woman (and man) to devise more adequate forms of compensation.'

REFERENCES

Beechey, N. and Perkins, T. (1987) *Women, Part-time Work and the Labour Market*, Cambridge: Polity Press.

Beveridge, Sir W. (1942) *Social Insurance and Allied Services*, Cmd. 6404, London: HMSO.

Brannen, J. (1987) *Taking Maternity Leave: The Employment Decisions of Women with Young Children*, London: University of London, Institute of Education.

Brannen, J. and Moss, P. (1988) *New Mothers at Work: Employment and Child Care*, London: Unwin.

Brannen, J. and Wilson, G. (1987) *Give and Take in Families: Studies of Resource Distribution*, London: Allen & Unwin.

Brook, L., Jowell, R. and Witherspoon, S. (1989) 'Recent trends in social attitudes', *Social Trends 19* London, HMSO.

Commission of the European Communities (1987) *Proposal for a Council Directive completing the implementation of the principle of equal treatment for men and women in statutory and occupational social security schemes*, COM (87) 494 final, Brussels: Commission of the European Communities.

Council of the European Communities (1986) *Council Directive on the implementation of the principle of equal treatment for men and women in occupational pension schemes*, 86/378/EEC, Brussels: Council of the European Communities.

Cullen, J. and O'Kelly, R. (1985) 'The cost of pensions and the myth of funding', in R. Silburn (ed.) *The Future of Social Security*, London: Fabian Society.

Department of Health and Social Security (1971) *Strategy for Pensions: The Future Development of State and Occupational Pensions*, Cmnd. 4755, London: HMSO.

—— (1985a) Green Paper: *Reform of Social Security*, London, HMSO.
I *Reform of Social Security*, Cmnd. 9517.
II *Reform of Social Security: Programme for Change*, Cmnd. 9518.
III *Reform of Social Security: Background Papers*, Cmnd. 9519.

—— (1985b) White Paper: *Reform of Social Security: Programme for Action*, Cmnd. 9691, London: HMSO.

—— (1985c) White Paper: *Reform of Social Security, Technical Annexe*, London: HMSO.

——(1986) *Fourth report of the Social Security Advisory Committee 1985*, London: HMSO.

—— (1988) *Social Security Statistics 1988*, London: HMSO.

Ellis, E. and Morrell, R. (1982) 'Sex discrimination in pension schemes: has community law changed the rules?' *Industrial Law Journal* II, 1: 16–28.

Employment Gazette (1988) 'Pay in Great Britain: results of the 1988 New Earnings Survey' 96, 11: 601–5.

Ermisch, J. (1989) 'Divorce: economic antecedents and aftermath', in H. Joshi (ed.) *The Changing Population of Britain*, Oxford: Blackwell.

Equal Opportunities Commission (1986) *Commentary: European Directive on Equal Treatment for Men and Women in Occupational Social Security Schemes*, Manchester EOC: Opportunities Commission.

—— (1988a) *Response of the Equal Opportunities Commission: DSS Consultation Document on the implementation of the EC Directive 86/378*, Manchester EOC.

—— (1988b) *Response of the Equal Opportunities Commission to the DSS on the EC Draft Social Security Directive*, Manchester EOC.

Freedman, J., Hammond, E., Masson, J. and Morris, N. (1988) *Property and Marriage: an Integrated Approach: Property, Tax, Pensions and Benefits in the Family*, Institute for Fiscal Studies, IFS Report, Series 29.

Government Actuary (1986) *Occupational Pension Schemes 1983*: Seventh Survey by the Government Actuary, London: HMSO.

Groves, D. (1983) 'Members and survivors: women and retirement pensions legislation', in J. Lewis (ed.) *Women's Welfare, Women's Rights*, London: Croom Helm.

—— (1986) 'Women and Occupational Pensions 1870–1983: An Exploratory Study', unpublished PhD thesis, University of London.

—— (1987) 'Occupational pension provision and women's poverty in old age', in C. Glendinning and J. Millar (eds) *Women and Poverty in Britain*, Brighton: Wheatsheaf.

Hannah, L. (1986) *Inventing Retirement*, Cambridge: Cambridge University Press.

Helowicz, G. (1988) 'A look at the past' in B. Benjamin, S. Haberman, G. Helowicz, G. Kaye and D. Wilkie, *Pensions: the Problem of Today and Tomorrow*, London: Allen & Unwin.

House of Lords (1989) *Equal Treatment for Men and Women in Pensions and Other Benefits (With Evidence)*, 10th Report of the Select Committee on the European Communities, H of L 51, 1988–89, London: HMSO.

Independent Pensions Research Group (1986) *Stealing Our Future: the Government's Plans for our Pensions*, London: IPRG.

Joshi, H. (1987) 'The cash opportunity costs of childbearing: an approach to estimation using British data', *Centre for Economics Policy Research*, Discussion Paper 208, London: Centre for Economic Policy Research.

—— (1989) 'The changing form of women's economic dependency', in H. Joshi (ed.) *The Changing Population of Britain*, Oxford: Blackwell.

Kaye, G. (1987) 'Current regulation', in B. Benjamin, S. Haberman, G. Kaye and D. Wilkie, *Pensions: the Problem of Today and Tomorrow*, London: Allen & Unwin.

Land, H. (1985) 'Fair means or Fowler', *Trouble and Strife* 7, Winter.

—— (1986) *Women and Economic Dependency*, Manchester: EOC.

Land, H. and Ward, S. (1986) *Women Won't Benefit: the Impact of the Social Security Bill on Women's Rights*, London: National Council for Civil Liberties.

Mansfield, P. and Collard, J. (1988) *The Beginning of the Rest of Your Life*, London: Macmillan.

Masson, J. (1985) 'Women's pensions', *Journal of Social Welfare Law* 319–40.

—— (1986) 'Pensions, dependence and divorce', *Journal of Social Welfare Law* 343–61.

Martin, J. and Roberts, C. (1984) *Women and Employment: A Lifetime Perspective*, London: HMSO.

Matthewman, J. and Sloss, E. (1988) *Tolley's Social Security and State Benefits 1988-89*, Croydon: Tolley.

Occupational Pensions Board (1989) *Protecting Pensions: Safeguarding Benefits in a Changing Environment*, A Report by the OPB in accordance with section 66 of the Social Security Act 1973, DSS, CM 533, London: HMSO.

Office of Population Censuses and Surveys (1989) *General Household Survey 1986*, Series GHS, no. 16, London: HMSO.

Shragge, E. (1984) *Pensions Policy in Britain: A Socialist Analysis*, London: Routledge & Kegan Paul.

Walker, A. (1986) 'Pensions and the production of poverty in old age', in C. Phillipson and A. Walker (eds) *Ageing and Social Policy: A Critical Assessment*, Aldershot: Gower.

Walker, R. and Hutton, S. (1988) 'The costs of ageing and retirement', in R. Walker and G. Parker (eds) *Money Matters: Income, Wealth and Financial Welfare*, London: Sage.

Ward, S. (1988) *The Essential Guide to Pensions: A Workers' Handbook*, London: Pluto Press.

Wilson, G. (1987) *Money in the Family: The Distribution of Resources and Responsibilities in the Family*, Aldershot: Gower.

Wilson, J.V. and Davies, B. (1988) *Your New Pensions Choice: An Independent Guide to Help You Understand the New and Important Pensions Legislation* (3rd ed.) Croydon: Tolley.

4 Women and transport

Kristine Beuret

INTRODUCTION

Since the 1970s there has been growing awareness of wide differences in the ways in which men and women travel.[1] Yet the integration of this knowledge into other areas of social policy has been slow to develop. Most discussion has concentrated on general disadvantage rather than the particular issue of gender and transport. Even textbooks about women and social policy have tended to neglect this area and it has been left to the disciplines of politics and social geography to introduce relevant material, although here, too, only in recent years.[2] Therefore, it seems timely to set out some of the basic facts about women's transport opportunities, since such material may be relatively unfamiliar to students of social policy.

Table 1 Travel methods according to age/sex of person

| | Per cent of all journeys by | | | | | Journeys |
	Walk/ Cycle	Car driver	Car passenger	Public transport	Other	(000s)
Child under 10	57	0	35	8	1	65
Teenagers, 11–20	53	6	18	20	3	83
Men aged 21–64	25	57	7	9	2	144
Women aged 21–59	42	21	23	14	1	122
Men 65 and over	52	25	6	16	1	100
Women 60 and over	50	6	19	25	1	100

Source: 1978–9 National Travel Survey from Potter (1982: 63)

HOW DO WOMEN TRAVEL?

Evidence from the National Travel Survey (Department of Transport 1978–9) shows marked differences between the methods of travel of men and women. It can be seen from Table 1 that the most common method of travel for women is walking (42 per cent of journeys) and for men it is car driving (57 per cent of journeys). This is partly explained by the structure of car owning households, whereby these are less likely to be headed by women.

Table 2 UK household type and car ownership

	Car/van %
One adult, non-retired	43.9
One adult, one child	24.2
One adult, two or more children	34.8
One man, one woman, non-retired	80.1
One man, one woman, one child	80.9
One man, one woman, two children	84.6

Source: Family Expenditure Survey (1986: 56)

Given that households comprising one adult and one or more children are predominantly female (89 per cent), Table 2 clearly shows the low rates of car ownership in such families, compared to others with both a man and woman. This is hardly surprising when recent figures published by the Automobile Association suggest that the overall cost of running a small car for a modest mileage totals £46 a week.

The GLC Women and Transport Surveys (Greater London Council 1984; 1987) also found that Afro-Caribbean women and women with disabilities were much less likely to travel by car than other women (see Table 3).

Table 3 Percentage of women using car at least once a week

	Car driver	Car passenger
Afro-Caribbean	10	45
Asian	22	64
With disability, under 60	14	61
With disability, over 60	4	40
All women (including white)	27	57

Sources: GLC (1984) *Women on the move* vol. 5, Table 1, p. 2
GLC (1987) *Women with Disabilities* vol. 9, Table 3, p. 5

Yet, even in car owning households containing both men and women, there is a greater likelihood that women will be car passengers, rather than car drivers. This is partly accounted for by figures for licence holding.

As shown in Table 4, in 1986 41 per cent of women held licences, compared to 74 per cent of men, although over time the gap has been narrowing. Yet, holding a licence, even if there is a car owned by a household member, does not ensure ready access to it. Very often the car is used by the main wage earner for the journey to work and is thus not available to the woman for her own work or other purposes. This is especially likely in households using company cars (one in ten of total UK cars). Of those provided with a company car in 1986, 85 per cent were men and 15 per cent women (Transport and Environmental Studies 1984). Furthermore, even if the household buys its own car, there is a marked tendency for the car to be seen as 'his' and this is demonstrated by the preponderance of male drivers and women passengers. A recent survey of couples arriving in cars to visit the Thames Barrier found that even when both had a driving licence, 97 per cent of drivers were male (London Tourist Board 1987).

Table 4 Private motoring: full driving licence holders

Within age and sex group						Percentage
	Male		*Female*		*All persons*	
	1975/6	1985/6	1975/6	1985/6	1975/6	1985/6
Full car licence						
17–19	31	31	17	25	24	28
20–29	75	72	42	53	58	62
30–39	85	86	48	62	66	74
40–49	82	87	38	56	60	71
50–59	75	81	26	41	51	60
60–69	59	72	15	24	36	46
70 or over	33	51	5	11	15	33
All ages	69	74	29	41	48	57

Source: Department of Transport (1975–6, 1985–6)

If many women do not travel by car, how else do they get about?

The short answer is by walking. But this is a form of transport widely ignored in many travel surveys and much available data are unsatisfactory. This is because there is a tendency for the Department of Transport to discount short walk trips of less than a mile. Yet these make up 37 per cent of total walk trips. Exclusion has the effect of reducing the total proportion of walk journeys by three-quarters and increasing the total proportion of car journeys by one-third, as shown in Table 5.

Table 5 Variation in modal split according to method of recording (per cent)

Mode	Train/ Underground	Bus	Car	Bicycle	Walk	Motorcycle
Excluding walk trips of less than a mile	2.6	21.9	60.0	3.8	10.2	1.4
Including walk trips of less than a mile	1.6	13.2	40.6	2.8	40.8	0.9

Source: An analysis of travel patterns using the 1972/73
         National Travel Survey by J.P. Rigby, TRRL, Crowthorne

Yet, most Department of Transport published statistics still omit short walk journeys or tag these on as a separate chapter (Department of Transport 1988). The result of this practice is that many published figures underestimate the amount of walking, and, given that women are nearly twice as likely as men to walk, by implication they underestimate women's travel. Yet walking is particularly important for women of *all* ages (Hillman and Whalley 1979). The GLC survey (1984) found that walk trips fell only slightly with age.

The survey also showed that Afro-Caribbean women were more likely to walk than other women. This is related to the low rate of licence holding

Table 6 Percentage of women using walking as a travel mode at least once a week
         by age group, ethnic group and disability

	Walking
16–19	93.4%
20–59	88.6%
60–74	85.1%
75+	77.0%
Afro-Caribbean	92.0%
Asian	86.0%
Women with a disability under 60	84.0%
Women with a disability over 60	69.0%
All women	87.2%

Sources: GLC (1984) vol. 4, p. 3; vol. 5, p. 2; and GLC (1987) vol. 9, p. 4

(15 per cent) in this group compared with the average for all women (41 per cent). Perhaps even more surprising, the survey found that 'walking is still on average the most common way of getting around in London by women who have a disability'.

Yet it is also still the norm that local authority transport policy plans ignore walking as a method of transport. Even when it is mentioned and provisions for pedestrians are included, such provisions are more for the convenience of motorists or perceived primarily as road safety techniques. Examples are the building of underpasses, vehicle triggered traffic lights and barriers which force detours by pedestrians. Another example of this is the recent publicity given to the decline in road deaths, hailed as a triumph for seatbelt legislation. Less well publicized, however, are the ways in which pedestrian deaths have increased, probably as a result of faster driving speeds resulting from the confidence gained from wearing a seatbelt. For example, in the two years after the introduction of compulsory seatbelts, the number of pedestrians killed in two-party collisions involving cars or light vans went up by an average of 130 per year (Durbin and Harvey 1985). As Mayer Hillman has suggested, a better option for pedestrian safety would be to have a 6 in. nail sticking out of the middle of steering wheels (Plowden and Hillman 1984)! More feasible is the fitting of speed governors which limit the maximum speed and have had to be installed on all new express coaches from 1989.[3] In addition, the lack of awareness of walking as a method of transport has resulted in low priority for pavement repairs and enforcement of pavement parking, lack of street lighting, litter clearance, and police foot patrols. A study of highway maintenance for Kent County Council showed that women were far more likely to prioritize spending money on these issues compared to men (Montgomery *et al.* 1988).

A similar neglect of pedestrian issues can equally be seen in relation to provision for cycling. Given that women have lower incomes, cycling could be an attractively low cost method of transport; yet twice as many men as women cycle (Finch and Morgan 1985). Reasons for this vary; among young women they are partly embarrassment and the experience of sexual harassment, later in life the reasons lie with the difficulty of transporting shopping and children by this method.

Another important method of travel for women is by public transport, and especially by bus. In many areas, women account for 75 per cent of bus passengers. The Greater London Council survey on Women and Transport (GLC 1984) showed that the bus was the most important mode of motorized transport for women, with more than half the women in London travelling by bus at least once a week.

The same survey found that women under 60 years of age with a disability were *more* likely than those without a disability to travel by the bus and even for disabled women over 60 it was the second most common method after walking. Travel by bus is also high for women under 20 and for women of pensionable age. Finally, the survey found that Afro-Caribbean women were far more likely to travel by bus than most other women, apart from those under 20, as reflected in the lower rate of licence holding for this group.

Table 7 Percentage of women using buses at least once a week by age group, ethnic group and disability

16–19	85%
20–59	44%
60–74	75%
75+	
Afro-Caribbean	79%
Asian	42%
Women with a disability under 60	52%
Women with a disability over 60	50%
All women	53%

Source: GLC (1987) vol. 4, p. 3; vol. 5, p. 2; and GLC (1987) vol. 9, p. 4

Bus travel itself involves difficulties for women passengers. It is difficult to get on and off with shopping, children or disability, especially since the phasing out of conductors who used to help. High steps up and lack of luggage space are other problems. A survey of women shoppers in Slough found that some women who were disabled or pushing young children in prams, chose (reluctantly) to walk long distances rather than struggle to use the bus (Steer, Davies & Gleave Consultants 1987).

Women are also concerned about the danger of using public transport, especially at night. Waiting at bus stops (especially if the bus is late or cancelled) and walking home are especially frightening to women, and many take taxis in spite of the cost, to allay these fears. Women use taxis twice as often as men (West Yorkshire Centre for Research on Women 1987) and the GLC survey found that almost 25 per cent of women use taxis or minicabs at least once a month (GLC 1984). But they are too expensive for some women, and even those who do are often exposed to unpleasant sexual harassment by taxi drivers. In London, over 30 per cent of women who used minicabs say they would not feel safe travelling in them late at night on their own. Another survey in Leicester found that many women used private taxi firms rather than the official ranks so that they could specify a woman driver, and that there was a considerable unmet demand for more women taxi drivers.

On the other hand, rail travel seems to be relatively less important to women. But this is not to minimize the crucial role it may play for some, even if they use trains infrequently. Women are only 10 per cent of first class train passengers, just under half of standard class and the only area in which they outnumber men is in leisure travel where they form 60 per cent of passengers (Department of Transport 1988). Here, too, it can be argued that transport policy discriminates against women's travel. Buses receive less subsidy than rail (Le Grand 1982) and this situation has been exacerbated since the deregulation and privatization of bus services has reduced rural and offpeak bus services predominantly used by women. In many areas, the costs of public transport have increased in recent years. A recent survey in Liverpool showed how families in poor areas now save up for bus trips to the city centre (Dodson and Katsoulacos 1988).

All this adds up to a picture of considerable disadvantage for women in comparison to men in the area of transport. Yet the real interest in relation to women and social policy lies in relating this disadvantage to other aspects of women's lives, and asking whether this disadvantage is a serious hindrance to women's opportunities. The next section of this chapter therefore looks at several areas of women's lives, namely, employment, education and leisure, health and shopping, to assess the effect of transport on access.

EMPLOYMENT

The average journey distance travelled by women to and from work in 1985–6 was 5 miles compared to 8 miles for men (*Social Trends* 1989: 151). The commentary to this table, which, like so many, excludes short walk trips, explains tautologically that 'working women tend to take jobs closer to home'. Behind this statement lies the reality of women's lives whereby household responsibilities typically have to be fitted in with low wages and the transport opportunities available (Pickup 1988). In the GLC survey (GLC 1984), 20 per cent of women said that convenience of work to home was a major factor in job choice. Yet very little is known about the advantage, if any, of, for example, car ownership in obtaining employment. We can only surmise at the commonsense level, that there are considerable advantages.

In many big cities, transport provision, and particularly public transport provision, tends to follow radial routes, reflecting the historical importance of the city centre. However, in more recent years, much employment has grown up in suburban areas or on 'greenfield' sites; in the 1960s this was encouraged by Government policy, e.g. the Location of Offices Bureau. The realization of this trend formed part of the argument for building the M25 orbital road around London. It is generally much easier to travel by car from one suburb to another. By public transport, it is often necessary to go into the city centre and out again, and this can be expensive, time-consuming and sometimes impractical, especially for shift workers and part-timers (predominantly women). In rural areas, women may be prevented from gaining *any* employment due to lack of transport.

Other surveys show how car ownership widens the area in which it is feasible to work. Research by Blumenfeld *et al.* (1975) shows that the distribution of the homes of car users is much more dispersed than that of the homes of bus and tube users in the London area. Transport problems have been overcome in some places by the use of private buses to carry people to inaccessible work places. Elsewhere, community minibuses have been used to transport people to work, for example on the Isle of Dogs in the East End of London, an area relatively poorly served by public transport, before the opening of the Docklands Light Railway in 1987. An experiment in Los Angeles reported by Falcocchio and Cantilli (1974) introduced special bus services from an area of high unemployment to another where there were job vacancies. The results of this experiment were inconclusive since it was found that the unemployed had so many other problems it was difficult to isolate the influence of transport. On the other hand, the PEP survey (Hillman *et al.* 1976) showed that car ownership extended the range of work opportunities, enabling jobs to be fitted in with domestic duties, especially by young mothers.

Finally, it is worth noting that although work journey lengths were slightly shorter for bus users compared to car users, journey times are much less for car users. The average mean speed for journeys to work by car drivers is 20 mph, compared to 8 mph by bus (Department of Transport 1988). Even in a busy city such as London, average journey times (between the same pairs of points) are often less by car than by bus, in spite of the development of some bus priority routes. This trend is emphasized by the growing tendency for women to use a car to get to work. While bus travel by women to work has declined from 38 per cent to 19 per cent between 1972 and 1984, car travel has increased from 39 per cent to 59 per cent (*Social Trends 15* 1985; *19*, 1989). Even in the congested London area, the car is the most commonly used method of travel to work (24 per cent). Of those who did not use cars, 32 per cent said that public transport services were unreliable or infrequent, and concluded that 'good, cheap and reliable public transport is of key importance if women's choice of jobs is not to be restricted and that this is particularly important in relation to buses' (GLC 1984 2: 7).

For longer journeys to work, rail travel has clear advantages, although many rail commuters are dependent on a car to get to the station. In the UK as a whole, men make more rail journeys than other people and over two-thirds of this is for work (Department of Transport 1988). The growing cost of rail travel is reflected by evidence that 'The earned income of women commuting between 1.6 and 3.2km of home was 27 per cent higher than those commuting under 1.6km' (Pickup 1988).

UNWAGED WORK

It should also be acknowledged that as well as family responsibilities, women are more likely than men to undertake voluntary work. The GLC Survey found that voluntary work was an important reason for travel for about 10 per cent of the women in their sample. It has long been acknowledged that women play a major role in social visits and informal community care. A survey in Tyneside (Association of Carers 1983) in 1983 found that one in four women were actively involved in caring and that many more had cared for elderly relatives in the past. Many journeys made during the course of caring are to accompany a child or neighbour, the GLC Survey found that over 40 per cent of women regularly take someone to hospital or the doctor's (GLC 1984).

To conclude, as Laurie Pickup writes in his analysis of the British National Travel Survey data for 1975–6, 'it was the lack of car use that influenced the wider job locations where women did not seek jobs, for example requiring journeys across suburbs, jobs on the urban fringe and jobs requiring inter-urban travel, i.e. jobs much less accessible to the public transport user.'

He also suggests that, 'within women's limited labour market, they can substantially improve incomes if able to commute beyond the local job market' (Pickup 1988).

EDUCATION

Surveys conducted by PEP and PSI (Hillman *et al.* 1973) show that car ownership permits a wider choice of schools and extra-curricular activities. When children are bussed to school they may not be able to stay on late for extra activities unless they can be collected (usually by the mother) in a car. Some of the advantages of car ownership are borne out by a survey conducted by Norfolk County Council in 1977 (Norfolk County Council 1977). The results given in Table 8 show how use of the local swimming pool was affected by car ownership.

Table 8 Percentage of people using different forms of travel; also changes with
distance, e.g. to Thetford swimming pool

Distance from pool	Car	Motorcycle	Bicycle	Bus	Train	Foot
Under one mile	44	1	7	0	0	48
1–2 miles	62	3	5	2	0	30
2–5 miles	numbers small and unreliable					
5–10 miles	95	0	0	2	1	0
10+ miles	91	0	1	6	0	0

Source: Norfolk County Council (1977) *mimeo* (p. iv)

It is significant that even those who lived less than a mile from the pool
made a good deal of use of the car for the visit, and this is the same in inner
city areas. One of the most common uses of a community bus service in the
London inner city area of Tower Hamlets, for example, was to take children
swimming (Beuret 1978).

Another area of education much affected by car ownership is attendance
at evening classes. Whereas there may be a reasonable public transport
service at peak hours, many educational establishments can become inaccessible by public transport in the evenings. The use of a car can also be
helpful for the carriage of equipment such as easels, DIY tools, musical
instruments or sports gear. Another advantage of the car is the feeling of
safety it can give to people, especially women, who fear muggings, etc., in
walking the streets at night. This is especially true in the winter, the main
season for evening classes, when it can be very comforting to drive from
door to door in a warm and cosy car.

In other areas of leisure, car access can be a great advantage. The trend
in recent years has been away from non-participatory sport towards a
greater interest in participatory sport. Sailing, golf, fishing, rockclimbing,
rambling, camping, model racing, hang-gliding, etc., have all increased in
popularity, and these activities require the ability to get to out-of-the-way
places, which are unlikely to be accessible by public transport, and also to
carry relatively bulky amounts of equipment. Many opportunities would
thus be impossible without car access, and as might be expected, men are
more likely to pursue such activities than women who are faced with both
time and transport constraints (Hillman and Whalley 1977).

SHOPPING

Recent years have seen a steady decline in the number of small neighbourhood shops and the growth of large supermarkets. In addition, the development of superstores and hypermarkets on out-of-town sites has catered almost exclusively for car owners. These retail outlets are often cheaper than smaller shops because they can take advantage of economies of scale (Piachaud 1974). In addition, they are able to offer a larger choice and also convenience and a saving of time to the shopper. The average weekly shopping for a family of four weighs 100lb and for a non-car owning individual to carry this weight would clearly involve several trips. The growth of home freezer ownership has also resulted in new patterns of bulk buying and storage. Driving out into the country to 'pick your own' food is an increasingly popular activity available only to car owning families.

HEALTH

Many recent studies have documented the way in which NHS health services are used more by the better off. For example, the Black Report (Black 1974) shows that women from Social Class V received the lowest degree of intensive care. Much health education is targeted at persuading pregnant women to attend antenatal classes. Yet time and effort spent travelling when pregnant and accompanied by other children, may actually be so stressful as to be counterproductive. Other women may lose pay by needing time off work to attend clinics. The same is true of visiting children in hospital. One study in Wales (Earthrowl and Stacey 1977) found that parents without cars were less likely to visit children in hospital, and that the explanation was income and transport difficulties. Another survey carried out in Cumbria (Development Commission 1984) described the difficulties experienced by those living in rural areas in gaining access to essential hospital services. The average journey to a full district general hospital involved a round trip of 90–95 miles, and the poorest who were reliant on public transport took longest, some spending more than six hours with numbers of bus and train changes.

Similarly, hospital closure policies are centred on the cost of staff and make no attempt to value patients' time. Other evidence suggests that when health care *is* provided at the neighbourhood level, problems of lower take-up can be overcome. For example, a mobile health clinic in Southwark was used by groups representative of *all* the community (Waddington 1977). Similarly, mobile family planning and cervical smear facilities have experienced high rates of take-up when parked outside factories, or in neighbourhood centres. There is growing evidence that lack of transport particularly affects the use of preventive health facilities.

CONCLUSION

Thus, despite many gaps in our knowledge, all the evidence which is gradually becoming available suggests that transport disadvantage makes a major contribution to limiting women's opportunities in employment, family and leisure activities.

It can also be said that, although a minority of women (especially those with access to their own car) do not experience such disadvantages, the majority of women do not drive, and, even in car owning households, are constrained by gender roles which reduce their mobility. There is a growing body of research which shows that for most women of all classes, ages, disabilities, and ethnic groups; walking and public transport are crucial in enabling access to jobs, education, health, leisure, shopping and other community activities. This conclusion gives rise to suggestions for policy reform. In recent years, various views have been developed about what could be done and these can be divided into four broad ranges of options, although they are not mutually exclusive.

First, there are policies which advocate the *improvement* of public transport. Ideas range from increasing subsidies in order to reduce fares or increase services, redesigning vehicles, stations and bus stops, improving the co-ordination and service level of community and social transport, providing more buses and trains, providing better information, more staff and safer environments. A good example of the last are the recent improvements introduced by London Underground such as video cameras, convoying and information points in corridors. On a more general level, improving safety on the streets is also crucial – there is no point in making buses safer if the walk to and from the bus stop is still dangerous.

Second, there are those who advocate measures to help more women *gain access to cars*. Suggestions here include grants or encouragement for women to take driving lessons and tests and to assert their claims for access to the household car, to attend car maintenance classes, the setting up of shared car or car pooling schemes and the further development of special-ized cars for those with disabilities.

A third range of options have emanated from the transport industry itself, often as a result of *market research*. This view emphasizes the commercial opportunities available to public transport operators in pro-viding good transport at reasonable prices to women. This can be especially attractive to operators in off-peak periods when many women want to travel anyway. There are a growing number of marketing initiatives which have been designed with women's needs in mind. A good example is the growing number of 'hail and ride' minibus services which penetrate housing estates and provide a virtual door-to-door service. Many of these initiatives have been developed by the growing number of women (although still very few) attracted to careers in transport. But this is not philanthropy, rather a growing realization that women's transport needs are increasing and that as people who travel at all times of the day, women represent opportunities for operators to generate marginal income. Similarly, recent provision of better facilities for people with disabilities results from commercial decisions, taken in the light of evidence that one in eight potential passengers has some form of disability (Frye 1989). British Rail now has a wide range of services for disabled travellers, and, in the bus industry, the kneeling bus, which allows easier entry, is cheaper and becoming more common.

Finally, there are *more radical approaches* which focus on the propensity of women of all types to walk, to operate in the locality and to juggle demands of home, work and community. Solutions here advocate transport policies which emphasize accessibility rather than mobility (Hagerstrand, 1970), i.e. reducing the need to travel so much in the first place. Such policies relate to land use planning and point to decentralization and the prioritization of walking and cycling over motorized transport. They also emphasize the unacceptability of the 5,000+ annual road deaths. These ideas link with other political philosophies of the 'deep green' variety and to writers with concern about the future of the Third World (Illich 1974).

Indeed, differences between these four strategies also raise familiar feminist debates which are addressed throughout this book, i.e. whether to concentrate on improving transport conditions for women in a society which is basically organized around the lives of men, or whether to advocate more fundamental changes in the broader society in which transport is only a part.

NOTES

1 Although this awareness has come from many directions, the pioneering work of Mayer Hillman, Anne Whalley, Irwin Henderson and others at PEP and later the Policy Studies Institute, deserves special mention. Their *Personal Mobility and Transport Policy*, June 1973, PEP Broadsheet 542, was the first comprehensive study to relate the evidence of women's low personal mobility to policy implications.
2 See also Wistrich (1983).
3 For a detailed discussion of how the 5,000 plus annual traffic deaths could be reduced, see Plowden and Hillman (1984).

REFERENCES

Association of Carers (1983) *Who Cares?*, London.

Beuret, K. (1978) *Community Transport in Tower Hamlets*, London: Dame Colet House.

Black, D. (1974) *Inequalities in Health*, London: DHSS.

Blumenfeld, N., Shrager, F. and Weiss, G.H. (1975) 'Spatial distribution of homes to journeys to work by different modes of transport', *Transportation Research* 9 Issue 1: 19–23.

Department of Transport (1975–6) *National Travel Survey*, London: HMSO.

—— (1978–9) *National Travel Survey*, London: HMSO.

—— (1985–6) *National Travel Survey*, London: HMSO.

—— (1987) *National Travel Survey*, from Transport Statistics Great Britain 1976–1985, London: HMSO.

—— (1988) *National Travel Survey 1985–6*, part I, 'An analysis of personal travel', London: HMSO.

Development Commission and the South Cumbria Development Health Council (1984) *Survey on Travel to Hospital*.

Dodson, J.S. and Katsoulacos, Y. (1988) 'Quality competition in bus services: some welfare implications of bus deregulation', *Journal of Transport Economics and Policy*, September 1988.

Durbin, J. and Harvey, A.C. (1985) 'The effects of seat belt legislation on road casualties in Great Britain', in *Compulsory Seat Belt Wearing*, Report by Department of Transport, London: HMSO.

Earthrowl, B. and Stacey, M. (1977) 'Social class and children in hospital', *Social Science and Medicine*, vol. 1, no. 2, pp. 83–8.

Falcocchio, J.C. and Cantilli, E.O. (1974) *Transportation and the Disadvantaged*, Lexington, Mass.: Lexington Books.

Family Expenditure Survey (1986) Table 3 quoted in EOC, *A Research Profile*, London: HMSO.

Finch, H. and Morgan, J.M. (1985) *Attitudes to Cycling*, Research Report RR14, Crowthorne: Transport and Road Research Laboratory.

Frye, E.A. (1989) 'The situation in Europe', Keynote address to the Fifth International Conference on Mobility and Transport for Elderly and Disabled Persons, Stockholm.

Greater London Council (1984) Women's Committee, *Women on the Move*, GLC Survey on Women and Transport, vol. 5, 'Afro-Caribbean and Asian Women', London: GLC.

—— (1987) *Women with Disabilities*, London Strategic Planning Unit, vol. 9, London: LPSU.

Hagerstrand, T. (1970) 'What about people in regional science?', Paper delivered to the Regional Science Association, reproduced in E. de Boer (1985) *Transport Sociology*, Oxford: Pergamon.

Hillman, M. and Whalley, A. (1977) *Fair Play for All*, PEP Broadsheet 571, London: Political and Economic Planning.

—— (1979) *Walking is Transport*, London: Policy Studies Institute.

Hillman, M., Henderson, I. and Whalley, A. (1973) *Personal Mobility and Transport Policy*, PEP Broadsheet 542, London: Political and Economic Planning.

—— (1976) *Transport Realities and Planning Policy*, PEP Broadsheet 567, London: Political and Economic Planning.

Illich, I. (1974) *Energy and Equity*, London: Marion Boyars.

Le Grand, J. (1982) *The Strategy of Equality*, London: Allen & Unwin.

London Tourist Board (1987) 'Tourism in London in the 1990s', Unpublished Report, London: Touche Ross.

Montgomery, T. *et al.* (1988) 'Public perceptions of highway maintenance', in *Proceedings of Planning, Transport, Research and Computing Conference, Bath, 1988*, London: Planning and Transport Research and Computation.

Norfolk County Council (1977) *Sporting Facilities in Norfolk.*

Piachaud, D. (1974) *Do the Poor Pay More?*, London: Child Poverty Action Group.

Pickup, L. (1988) 'Hard to get around: a study of women's travel mobility', in J. Little, L. Peake and P. Richardson (eds) *Women in Cities: Gender and the Urban Environment*, London: Macmillan.

Plowden, S. and Hillman, M. (1984) *Danger on the Road: The Needless Scourge*, no. 627, London: Policy Studies Institute.

Potter, S. (1982) 'The transport policy crisis', Unit 27 of Open University Course D202, *Urban Change and Conflict*, Milton Keynes: Open University.

Social Trends 15 (1985) London: HMSO.

Social Trends 19 (1989) London: HMSO.

Steer, Davies, and Gleave (1987) 'Consumer attitudes to bus travel', Consultants' report to London Country NW (Unpublished).

Sutton, J. (1988) *Transport Co-ordination and Social Policy*, London: Gower.

Transport and Environment Studies (1984) *The Company Car Factor*, Report produced for London Amenity and Transport Association, September.

Waddington, S. (1977) 'The relation between social class and the use of health services in Britain', *Journal of Advanced Nursing*, vol. 2, pp. 609-61.

West Yorkshire Centre for Research on Women (1987) *Women and Transport in West Yorkshire, Phase 1: A Preliminary Report*, University of Bradford.

Wistrich, E. (1983) *The Politics of Transport*, London: Longman.

Part II

Our traditional concerns

5 Well Women Clinics

A serious challenge to mainstream health care?

Peggy Foster

Previous chapters have featured women as providers of care – looking after disabled relatives, volunteering and providing child care. While the State and men undoubtedly benefit greatly from women's unpaid caring within welfare services, it is far less clear that women benefit unequivocally from the caring services which the State and men provide for them. For example, feminist health activists have become so dissatisfied with women's experiences of male dominated mainstream health care that they have campaigned throughout Britain for the establishment of separate health clinics run by women for women. This chapter will attempt to evaluate alternative feminist strategies in relation to the expansion of these Well Women Clinics. First, however, for the benefit of those readers who may be unfamiliar with the feminist critique of mainstream health care services, I will very briefly outline its key points.

First, feminists have claimed that doctors exercise patriarchal control over their female patients. For example, feminist research has revealed GPs giving so-called medical advice and treatment to women which clearly reinforces both the ideology and practice of women's subordinate caring role within the home (see Barrett and Roberts 1978). A second type of social control over women exercised by the medical profession is their control over women's access to contraceptive advice, abortions and infertility treatment. Feminists have claimed that some doctors exercise this control in a way which distinguishes – often along class or race lines – between potentially 'good' mothers who should be encouraged to breed and 'unsuitable' mothers who should be discouraged from breeding for the good of society as a whole (see Aitken Swan 1977).

Second, feminists have complained that women suffering from a variety of female health problems including PMT, menopausal problems, vaginal discharges and pelvic pains are all too often dismissed by their doctors as neurotic or uninteresting. Many women thus fail to secure adequate investigation and treatment of debilitating and distressing health problems (see Leeson and Gray 1978).

Third, feminists have exposed the many negative side-effects suffered by women who have received certain types of modern medical treatment. In particular, feminists have emphasized both the physical and emotional dangers of the over-use of inductions, Caesarean sections, mastectomies, hysterectomies, and psychotropic drugs, particularly minor tranquillizers (see Ruzek 1978).

Fourth, conventional medicine tends to treat women patients – and, indeed, male patients – as a collection of physical or psychosomatic symptoms. Feminists object to this on the grounds that many of women's so-called health problems arise from social problems such as male violence, poverty and poor housing. Women therefore need a health care service which will look at their lives as a whole rather than defining their problems within a very narrow medical model (see Smith 1987).

Finally, feminists complain that too many doctors still expect their female patients to play a very passive role in their own health treatment. Women giving birth, for example, are often expected to lie back and allow the birthing process to be taken over by the medical profession. Women who try to ask their doctors intelligent questions about their treatment are too often labelled as awkward, and a nuisance (see Bieggs, 1979).

Having outlined some of the key complaints feminists have made against conventional health care, there are still some preliminary points which must be explored before we can begin to evaluate Well Women Clinics as a feminist strategy for improving women's health care.

A serious preliminary problem involved in any evaluation of the current provision of Well Women Clinics in Britain is that the title has been applied to a very disparate range of health care services, some of which have no explicitly feminist aims or objectives. In 1987 a survey by Jo Richardson found that out of 196 replies from 220 District Health Authorities and Health Boards, 107 reported having set up Well Women Clinics in their areas. However, 78 per cent of these clinics were clearly being run along traditional professionally orientated medical lines (Richardson 1987). Some authorities, for example, have simply renamed family planning/ cervical cytology clinics as Well Women Clinics without altering the style or philosophy of the service provided. Well Women Clinics which have been established and run without any explicitly feminist involvement tend to emphasize screening, particularly cervical smear testing. This service is usually provided by an all female staff, including a female doctor, and some advice on women's general health problems may be given. Nevertheless, the dominant approach is still very doctor centred and primarily concerned with women's physical health and health problems as defined by the medical profession. I would strongly suggest that clinics run along these lines, which have no specifically feminist aims and objectives, should not be counted by feminists as genuine Well Women Clinics. Most feminists welcome any attempts by the NHS to improve its screening programmes for cervical and breast cancer, but medical screening can still be carried out in a way which continues to oppress women as patients. There is some evidence that women attending Well Women Clinics run along traditional medical lines continue to be treated very much as passive objects of screening and may even in some cases be subjected to just the type of insensitive treatment against which feminist health care activists have long been campaigning. For example, one feminist GP I interviewed had worked briefly in a so-called Well Woman Clinic where women were expected to get undressed and line up in a corridor to wait for a five minute consultation with a doctor which was almost entirely taken up by the taking of a smear test.

Leaving aside so-called Well Women Clinics which have no feminist input, we still face a confusion of feminist run clinics and centres which vary considerably in terms of the services they provide and the philosophy on which they are based. Pat Thornley has identified two models of Well Women Clinics which claim to be based on feminist principles and objectives (Thornley 1987). She calls these two models the holistic model and the self-help model. Clinics based on the holistic model tend to operate within the NHS and place at least some emphasis on medical screening and professional advice. A doctor is normally available although she is not the sole source of advice and information. Whilst providing some medical services, these clinics do take a holistic approach to women's health needs and problems, including their psychological and emotional needs. According to Pat Thornley, this model also 'incorporates self-help in its approach and seeks to demystify medicine and treat women as equal participants in their health care' (1987: 101).

The second type of feminist clinic or centre is far less medically orientated. Some radical feminists claim that since *all* doctors, male or female, oppress women as patients, the only possible way for women to achieve liberation in health matters is for them to eschew all professionally provided medical help and to learn to help themselves and each other. Thus, in Britain, some feminists have attempted to set up and run non-medical, non-professional women's health centres. These centres provide health education, advice and support based totally on a self-help approach. They are usually run by lay volunteers and explicitly exclude the services of a doctor.

As well as distinguishing ideal types of Well Women Clinics, we must also look briefly at where such clinics are placed in terms of the structure and organization of Britain's mainstream health care services. The most radical, non-medical self-help centres operate outside the NHS, usually on very small budgets, although some have attracted Urban Aid, local authority grants and other types of 'soft' funding. In the long run, such centres might pose a serious challenge to health care professionals by enabling women to take more control over their own health and medical treatment. In the short term, however, self-help centres do not pose much of a threat to patriarchal medicine. Most women – for whatever reason – still wish to consult a doctor when they believe they have a medical problem. Since radical self-help women's centres explicitly exclude the provision of professional medical care, they leave the great majority of women entirely dependent on mainstream health care services. Partly for this reason, it is not appropriate to evaluate this type of clinic here.

The most well-known Well Women Clinics have been set up by feminists within the community services branch of the NHS. For example, in 1981 a group of feminist health care providers joined forces with lay volunteers to found the Wythenshawe Well Women's Clinic in South Manchester. The clinic was set up without any specific funding using an empty session within a mother and baby clinic. Once the concept of Well Women's Clinics had been put into practice within community medicine, a number of feminist GPs began to set up similar clinics within their own practices. Before evaluating the advantages and disadvantages of these similar, but organizationally very distinct, feminist strategies for improving women's health care, it is essential to establish the key principles against which feminist health care in practice should be judged.

The British women's health movement is a heterogeneous, unstructured organization with no clearly agreed publicly stated goals other than the long term objective of increasing women's autonomy and improving their total sum of health and well-being. However, despite the diversity of feminist theories and practices, it is just possible to identify some key guiding principles which underpin a feminist model of health care delivery. First, feminist health care providers, whether professionally trained or lay volunteers, should work together in non-hierarchical, co-operative teams. Second, they should be concerned not just with a woman's physical health, but also with her social, psychological and emotional well-being. In other words, feminist health care should be holistic and should allow women themselves to determine their own health care priorities. Third, feminist health workers should share their medical knowledge with their patients and always encourage women to play as active a role as possible in the health care process. Fourth, feminist health care should be equally accessible to all women regardless of class, race or sexual orientation. To these four key principles which can be found in various forms in the literature on feminist health care, I would like to add a fifth less overtly stated goal – that the women who use feminist run health care services should find them acceptable and beneficial. There seems little point in feminists putting a great deal of energy into providing an alternative form of health care if it cannot achieve greater consumer satisfaction than traditional services.

Having set out very briefly the principles or objectives of feminist health care, it is now possible to attempt to evaluate Well Women Clinics by assessing the extent to which those who have set them up have been able to put these principles into practice.

My research into Well Women Clinics in the North West of England[1] suggests that at least some community medicine-based feminist clinics have managed to create non-hierarchical working relationships, despite the many obstacles placed in their way. One clinic co-ordinator told me that although consensus management posed some problems, clinic policy was still made democratically, with everyone, volunteers as well as health care professionals, having equal rights and an equal say. A founder of one of the South Manchester clinics has written: 'all decisions about the clinic are taken at monthly policy meetings at which all workers are expected to attend. . . . No individual worker has the authority to make a decision without the meeting's approval' (Armstrong 1987: 135).

One factor which appears to facilitate the development of non-hierarchical decision-making in community clinics is that doctors are employed on a sessional basis. This gives them less organizational power than doctors usually have – whether they want it or not – within the NHS. Some evidence from feminists who have attempted a similar feat within general practice suggests that it may be much more difficult in such settings to avoid other workers, volunteers and patients all seeing the doctor as team leader. Eisner and Wright (1986) have written about the contradictions of attempting to run a feminist general practice on egalitarian lines. Whilst decisions were taken in a democratic way, the doctors were still in reality the employers of the rest of the staff and the experiment ended – with a bitter dispute – after four years. Another problem identified by feminists who set up a Well Women Clinic within general practice was that volunteers tended to 'underestimate their own abilities compared to those of the feminist doctors' (Cooke and Ronalds 1987: 143). They concluded: 'obeisance to the medical hierarchy is still powerful for patients, doctors and volunteers.' This hierarchy may well be weakened if doctors perform their role away from their natural power bases. On balance therefore, although some feminist GPs have struggled valiantly to overcome their imposed position of power and authority over 'their' 'less qualified' staff, I would suggest that egalitarian team work is more likely to flourish or, at least, survive in some modified form in settings such as community clinics where doctors can – in the nicest possible way – be somewhat marginalized.

The second principle against which to test Well Women Clinics is that feminist health care providers should take a holistic approach to women and their problems. Community based Well Women Clinics do offer attenders conventional screening and a consultation with a doctor, but those running such clinics emphasize that they aim to provide much more than just a purely medical service. One health visitor explained to me: 'We take an holistic, whole woman approach. We are interested in how she feels, the pressures on her life, not just her body.' A volunteer at another clinic explained: 'Here we discourage people from coming for just a smear. We see our key role as much wider than prevention. As volunteers we aim to see someone as a whole.'

Not only did volunteers in these clinics emphasize non-medical holistic objectives, but the doctors who worked in them were unable to treat patients in the conventional way. Some doctors, including feminist ones, may regard the fact that doctors working in community based clinics cannot prescribe as a major limitation of this type of medical provision. To others, however, the fact that they cannot reach for their prescription pad in response to a patient's problems may be seen as an incentive to develop alternative, more holistic, forms of practice. One clinic doctor told me: 'The women who come along know I can't prescribe anything ... which in a way helps them to accept a whole variety of other different sorts of approaches. It also encourages me to think of alternative treatments, especially self-help, rather than tablets.'

In contrast, a feminist GP who had set up a Well Women Clinic within her own practice admitted that in such a setting it was very difficult to get away from a predominantly medical model. 'Everyone wanted to see the doctor. As the idea was to demedicalize a lot of things that was somewhat counter-productive. It meant that I was doing no different than I would have been doing in surgery except that there was slightly more time.'

Another feminist GP running a clinic with her own health centre explained to me that as a GP her priority had: 'probably got to be to get women to have smears – a lot of young women in our practice are very much at risk and need to be chased up. We have a very high proportion of abnormal smears so we have to concentrate on that but we try to make the atmosphere such that if one does come along it is not just a quick smear – in and out in five minutes.' This, albeit extremely limited, comparison of approaches tentatively suggests that community based clinics may be more successful at getting away from the medical model than general practice based clinics. This certainly does not mean that feminist GPs who set up Well Women Clinics within their own practices give their patients a poor service. Indeed, in some ways, they may well provide a more adequate medical service than that provided in separate clinics. One feminist GP claimed, for example, that community based Well Women Clinics provided inadequate care because it was not integrated care. 'PMT, for example, cannot be dealt with in isolation. At our clinics we had access to patients' records so we could explain to them what had been happening.'

A third key objective of feminist health activists is to enable patients to gain as much knowledge as possible about their own health, and health care; to encourage women to take control over their own health care and to facilitate a variety of self-help activities. Both staff and volunteers working within community based clinics strongly emphasized this objective. Volunteers at one clinic explained, 'A lot of GPs think we don't provide any sort of unique service. They think women could get everything we provide through other services. This is not true at all since we try to be on an equal basis with the women who come to us.' A health worker at another community clinic told me: 'We do not say to a woman 'You have got so and so'. We ask her 'What do you think might be the matter?' We discuss symptoms together and let the woman come to her own conclusions about what is wrong. . . . At the end we reflect back her problem and ask what would you like to do? Is there anything you can do? Anything you want to do? . . . We need to educate women to be assertive and to seek the things they want.'

Feminist GPs have also emphasized their strong commitment to giving patients more knowledge and autonomy. For example, Cooke and Ronalds (1987) have written about their desire to share power and expertise with women within a health centre, although they also emphasized the difficulties of achieving that aim within a general practice setting. Both types of clinic have attempted to set up and sustain self-help groups for women with a particular type of problem such as PMT or smoking. Workers in both types of clinic explained to me that it was quite difficult to sustain self-help groups for any length of time. One feminist GP admitted: 'We didn't have enough extra energy to get self-help groups going.' Another explained that if she, as a GP, got too personally involved in running a self-help group, it would not be self-help. On the other hand, the organizer of a community based clinic admitted that they, too, currently had very few self-help groups because they were very short of volunteers to facilitate them.

It seems clear that feminist health care providers in all settings (see Savage 1986) have in common a strong commitment to sharing their expertise and knowledge and encouraging autonomy in their female patients. However, the more radical self-help model of feminist health care does not fit easily into any setting which includes the services of a doctor. In both community based and general practice based clinics, women can usually talk over their problems with a volunteer or a nurse without consulting a doctor. In practice, however, nearly all attenders want to see 'the doctor'. As one feminist GP put it: 'Fourteen people were involved in providing the service but everyone wanted to see the doctor.' Equally, the organizer of a separate Well Women Clinic emphasized: 'In my own mind, I knew that to be credible we needed a doctor. . . . The general public are happier if you are backed by the professionals.' On the other hand, the co-ordinator of a more radical non-NHS clinic which had tried to operate without the services of a doctor admitted: 'Getting women to contact us has been one of our problems. It is hard to explain what we actually provide. People think if it's "health" it has to have a doctor and be within the health service.'

Possibly community based clinics which include the services of a doctor but which are not 'doctor led' may have the edge over general practice based clinics in enabling volunteers and other health workers to emphasize a self-help non-medical approach to women's problems. However, neither type of clinic is particularly radical in this respect. On the other hand, they both appear to give women what they want – i.e. access to sympathetic, medically qualified advice and support and thus, in the short term at least, may attract far more women than more radical non-medicalized women's health centres.

Nearly all feminist health care activists strongly emphasize that any alternative forms of health care which feminists manage to set up must be available to all women regardless of class, race or sexual orientation. One of the key publicly stated goals of community based Well Women Clinics has been 'to reach women who may otherwise stay away from their doctor because of class, cultural or religious differences.' In practice, however, although evidence is very limited, community based clinics have not demonstrated a great deal of success in putting this key goal into practice. Unfortunately there are no national statistics on the class or ethnic origin of those who have attended either a community based or a general practice based Well Women Clinic. An unpublished evaluation of Wythenshawe Well Women Clinic undertaken in 1982 found that the distribution of attenders by social class, as calculated by the partners' occupations, appeared to be broadly representative of the area from which the clinic population was drawn (i.e. a predominantly working-class area), 22 per cent of attenders in the sample were from social classes IV and V while a further 40.3 per cent were from social class III (Spencer *et al.* 1982). A doctor working in a clinic based in a more middle-class area admitted to me, however: 'It is predominantly white middle class reasonably well educated women who come to this clinic and work as volunteers in it.'

The evaluation report on Wythenshawe Well Women Clinic claimed that: 'Attenders were representative of the "high risk" group of women who normally have little contact with preventive health services' (Spencer *et al.* 1982: 23). However, the figures showed that only 5 per cent of attenders had never had a cervical smear test, while over 80 per cent had had a smear test within the last five years. My own examination of attenders' post consultation questionnaires given out at two South Manchester clinics[2] suggested that for a significant proportion of attenders (the information was insufficiently standard to allow any statistical analysis), the key reason for attending the clinic was dissatisfaction with the advice or treatment they had previously received from their GP. For example, one attender, suffering from PMT, complained that her doctor had treated her 'as a nuisance over the years'. Another who had period problems stated that her GP had prescribed hormones but that 'he appeared unsympathetic'. Several attenders no longer wanted to take the pills prescribed by their GP. For example, one woman stated as the reason for her visit: 'I did not want my GP to give me more anti-depressants.' This very small amount of non-quantitative evidence suggests that community based Well Women Clinics may be providing a very valuable alternative service for patients who are dissatisfied with more conventional forms of treatment or with un-sympathetic treatment and advice. However, if such clinics wish to broaden access to include women who rarely, if ever, use conventional services, they may well have to put more resources into outreach programmes – resources which they simply do not have. Several of those working in such clinics expressed their frustration to me that they could not mount any effective outreach programmes. By contrast, one clinic had succeeded in obtaining urban aid money to fund an Asian development worker, and she was successfully reaching out to Asian women who had not previously used the clinic. 'She goes out there and asks them what they want, where they want it and at what time – it may be a Sunday afternoon – you can't just say we are having health education for Asian women at the centre on Tuesday afternoon please come along – they won't come. Asian women need outreach. You go out there and talk to them and they say when and where they want to meet.' This one example of successful outreach indicates what feminist run clinics might achieve in terms of access if only they were better resourced.

In principle, feminist general practitioners are much better placed to implement a successful access drive than those running community based clinics. GPs can use their practice files to contact specific cohorts of women, or women who rarely consult their GP. They can thus reach out to 'non- attenders' and specific 'at risk' groups. Katy Gardner (1983) has written abut her practice's attempt to attract more working-class women and older women to a Well Women Clinic. She admitted that on analysing the social class composition of the practice, the women who had attended the clinic had been representative of the practice as a whole rather than predominantly from classes IV and V. On the other hand, there had been an 'encouraging response' to an attempt to attract women over 35 by sending them a letter and following up non-respondents with a phone call or even a visit from the practice nurse. Cooke and Ronalds (1987) have described how at first few women turned up to their general practice based Well Women Clinic. Posters put up in the health centre to advertise the clinic inevitably only reached women already attending the health centre. Those running the clinic then sent out leaflets in English and three Asian languages to the 40–50 age group of women patients. They later also mailed all 35–40-year-old women. Unfortunately their account does not give any information on the impact of this outreach, although they do state that the majority of women attending the clinic were between 20 and 35.

It is clearly not easy to attract women who rarely use the NHS to any type of Well Women Clinic. Any type of outreach is likely to be expensive in terms of time, energy and money. Nor do we as yet have any firm quantitative evidence that outreach programmes are effective. Nevertheless, we can tentatively conclude that general practitioners, particularly those with computerised age/sex registers have at least the potential for targeted outreach initiatives, designed to put into practice the feminist priority of enabling working-class women and ethnic minority women to have access to good health care.

There is little point in feminist health workers putting so much effort into running Well Women Clinics if the services which they provide do not meet women's self-perceived health care needs. Outcome studies in relation to any type of health care are still rare and feminist run Well Women Clinics have even fewer resources than other types of health services to mount large scale studies of their effectiveness. Very preliminary small scale evidence, however, does suggest high levels of consumer satisfaction among attenders of feminist run clinics. For example, the replies of 175 attenders to a post consultation questionnaire given out at the two South Manchester clinics were 'overwhelmingly' positive. Under a section reserved for further comments, 45 per cent of respondents had spontaneously expressed their appreciation of the sympathy and understanding they had received. One woman wrote, for example: 'It was a great comfort to find someone here to show interest and understanding in my problems.' Another had particularly liked: 'The welcome, warmth and understanding and being able to talk over my problems which I would not do with own GP.' Forty per cent spontaneously commented favourably on the help and advice they had been given. For example: 'I found the clinic was most helpful to me. The advice given helped a lot and was in fact very simple.' and 'As I write this I have never felt so "well" for years. Everything the doctor suggested has worked. . . . Such simple remedies but what a dramatic effect. I wouldn't have thought it possible.' Thirty-six per cent of respondents emphasized how much they had appreciated having been given so much time, for example: 'Personally I found it reassuring to discuss a problem with someone who has time to listen, as GPs seem to write you a prescription as soon as you walk into the surgery, without getting to the root of the problem.' and 'I was able to discuss my problem without having to hurry for the next patient as in a doctor's surgery.'

Unfortunately there is no similar evidence of consumers' views of general practice based clinics. We cannot therefore make any evaluative comparisons between the two types of clinics in terms of attenders' satisfaction levels. We can hypothesize, however, that the amount of time given to each patient in both types of clinic may be a key factor influencing patients' views of the service. GPs who do not provide such a service may claim that they simply do not have the time to provide lengthy consultations for women with relatively 'minor' problems. Even feminist GPs have recognized that Well Women Clinics tend to provide a quality service for a relatively few women. The implications of this for feminist health care activists are two-fold. First, genuine feminist health care cannot be provided on a shoestring. Second, feminists need to campaign for major developments in the roles played by nurses and volunteers within primary and preventive health services. Doctors are currently the most expensive members of Well Women Clinic teams. If women could gradually be weaned away from a dependence on doctors towards a new confidence in the advice and services of other health care providers, Well Women Clinics might eventually be able to offer them a 'luxury' service without costing the NHS a great deal more than conventional health care services.

DISCUSSION

Feminist run Well Women Clinics based within community medicine appear to have at least one key advantage over similar clinics set up within general practice: they appear – albeit on very limited evidence – to be potentially the more radical type of clinic. Thus they enable feminists to create pockets of a genuinely feminist model of health care practice which – whilst not fully accepted or appreciated by NHS managers and other health care providers – are at least tolerated within the NHS. Several factors may contribute to their radical potential. First, because doctors are only employed on a sessional basis, they are unlikely to dominate the rest of the clinic team. Second, since clinic doctors cannot prescribe, they are encouraged to adopt alternative more holistic responses to patients' requests for help. Third, those attending separate community based clinics may be more prepared to accept the advice and support of lay volunteers and other health workers than those attending a clinic run by their own GP.

As well as the above advantages, two other strengths of community based Well Women Clinics have been identified. First, they appear, again on extremely limited evidence, to be very popular with most women who use them. Second, they seem to offer a much appreciated escape route for those women who have become thoroughly dissatisfied with the advice and/or treatment which they have received from their own doctor.

Unfortunately, separate Well Women Clinics are by no means an ideal feminist strategy for reforming British health care services. The strategy has at least two significant disadvantages. First, access to such clinics is severely limited due primarily to their chronic underfunding. NHS managers may tolerate the existence of feminist clinics within their areas, but they show absolutely no sign of actively supporting their growth with adequate staffing and funding. Feminist health workers and volunteers thus find themselves putting a great deal of unpaid time and effort into a service which has too few resources to begin to meet some of their key objectives. For example, most clinics have no resources for outreach activities designed to attract working-class women and women from ethnic minorities. Second, there are no signs that the existence of a few, very small scale feminist clinics has exerted any pressure on the majority of mainstream health care providers to reform their own services for women. Indeed, one Well Women Clinic co-ordinator admitted to me: 'There is a danger in that it takes a lot of energy to organize these places and the impetus to do something that's much more widespread and would reach many more women gets lost. It's a very hard battle to improve health services on a wide scale.' In sum, whilst community based feminist run clinics may provide an excellent alternative model of health care, they actually reach very few women indeed and do not appear to have stimulated any great interest from mainstream health care managers and doctors.

Those feminists who have put so much work into setting up and sustaining separate Well Women Clinics deserve much praise and support from all less active feminists. I must suggest, however, that, in the long run, the only way to improve health care for a significant number of women, particularly less privileged women, is to ensure that feminist health care gains more than just a tentative foothold within general practice itself. Feminist health care within general practice is likely to be more watered down and more medically orientated than a separatist service, but this may be a price worth paying for achieving much more widespread change. Undoubtedly, the obstacles to be overcome before such a widespread change could occur are formidable. First, most GPs, even feminist or pro-feminist ones, have been strongly socialized into traditional forms of practice. Moreover, whether they like it or not, GPs enjoy a privileged, powerful position within their own practices. It will not therefore be easy for them to share that power with both other health workers and their patients. As one feminist health activist pointed out to me: 'For GPs and a lot of other doctors, the notion that the service should be what the users want instead of what they think patients should have . . . is very uncomfortable, as is the idea that you should have lot of people who are not professionally trained messing about in a clinic. . . . It just does not fit with their experience of medicine.'

Second, there are still far too few women GPs, let alone committed feminist GPs. One feminist GP who was not very impressed by the strategy of separate Well Women Clinics explained why thus: 'Having more women's clinics won't ensure an adequate standard of primary health care. If women go to work in clinics like that and aren't fed into mainstream general practice – then it will stay forever the same. So you don't set up the clinics. You have to push the GPs to take on more women doctors and educate the male doctors.' In 1987, only 20 per cent of principals in general practice were women and Isobel Allen's recent study of doctors and their careers (Allen 1988) revealed a number of serious obstacles to any significant improvement in this figure; for example, the lack of any rights to maternity leave for self-employed principals.

Third, setting up a Well Women Clinic and running it on a regular basis takes a great deal of organization, time and energy. Coping with high lists and sick or emotionally unhappy people can be very draining. After normal surgery hours, many GPs, particularly those in overstretched inner-city practices may not have enough energy left to run a successful Well Women Clinic on a long term basis. One GP admitted, for example, 'The Clinic was successful for those who came but it needed a big input at the end of a working day. We ended up offering a quality service but for a small number of patients. . . . In the end we burnt out.' A sympathetic NHS manager whom I interviewed in 1987 made a similar point: 'Even if GPs in inner cities have the ideology and the right approach, they have too high lists to have the capacity to take on extra things.'

Despite these very real obstacles, there are some hopeful signs that general practice is ready for at least limited change. In recent years, the Royal College of General Practitioners, CHCs and central Government have all stressed the need to improve the quality of general practice and, in particular, to make it more responsive to the consumer and more orientated towards preventive medicine. At present, there is no indication that extra resources will be forthcoming to facilitate such changes, nor is the present Government likely to endorse any radical reform programme based on feminist health care objectives. Nevertheless, winds of change are beginning to blow through the NHS, and feminists should ensure that their voices are heard above the growing general clamour for new improved primary and preventive health care services.

A realistic package of demands designed to strengthen feminist approaches to health care within the NHS might include the following proposals.

First, career prospects and working conditions for women doctors must be significantly improved, if necessary by direct action by central Government. Women are unlikely to make any further headway in male dominated medical specialities until a medical career can be more easily combined with motherhood. Health authorities should provide far more part-time training posts and job sharing. Overt and indirect discrimination against women doctors who work 'part-time' should be firmly prevented. Women who wish to specialize in general practice should be assured of full maternity rights. Simply improving the ratio of female to male doctors is certainly not a radical reform, nor does it necessarily ensure the spread of explicitly feminist health care within the NHS. It would, however, at the very least, give more women patients the choice of seeing a women doctor, and a general improvement in career prospects for women in medicine might create more space and opportunities for feminist doctors to begin to put their principles into practice.

Second, feminists should demand a greater role for nurses and other health workers in relation to patient care. If nurses were given more responsibilities and autonomy within the health care system, it might begin to break down the rigidly hierarchical nature of mainstream health care institutions. The training of both doctors and nurses should emphasize the advantages of developing nurse practitioners, particularly within primary health care teams.

Third, health authorities should offer GPs a financial incentive to set up and run a Well Women Clinic within their own practice. Clearly a danger of this strategy is that some GPs would set up clinics run on very traditional patriarchal lines. Nevertheless, at the least such financial incentives could give some practical encouragement to those doctors who would like to try out new, less patriarchal, forms of health care, but who at present are given no practical help to do so.

Finally, it is very important for feminists wishing to reform health care services to emphasize the particular needs of women living in deprived areas. Health care providers in such areas will need extra resources if they are ever to do more than simply cope in a fairly traditional way with the high levels of demands made upon them. If health services in deprived areas do not receive positive discrimination within the NHS, there is a danger that middle-class women will begin to receive a health care service which is at least somewhat responsive to their particular wants and needs, but that those women most in need of a sensitive, caring health service will continue to be given a particularly under-resourced and therefore less sensitive service.

Given the general conservatism of the medical profession, we certainly cannot expect rapid progress within mainstream health care towards any radical model of feminist health care practice. Separate Well Women Clinics have at least provided us with a working alternative model of health care for women. Even if they do not prove to be the long term solution to women's dissatisfaction with conventional, male-dominated health care, they will have played an invaluable pioneering role. Without wishing to devalue their contribution, however, I will conclude by tentatively suggesting that the time may now be ripe for feminist health workers and campaigners to place much more emphasis on the very difficult and long term task of achieving significant changes within mainstream medical services starting, perhaps with a major campaign, to improve services for women within general practice.

NOTES

1 During 1987 the author interviewed fifteen women who were involved in the setting up and running of six Well Women Clinics in the North West of England. These unstructured interviews were then transcribed. Quotes from these interviews are unreferenced in the text of this chapter. Some material in this chapter first appeared in the *Journal of Social Policy*, vol. 18, pt 3, July 1989.
2 See note 1 above.

REFERENCES

Aitken Swan, I. (1977) *Fertility Control and the Medical Profession*, London: Croom Helm.
Allen, I. (1988) *Any Room at the Top? A Study of Doctors and their Careers*, London: Policy Studies Institute.
Armstrong, J. (1987) 'The Manchester experience II, Withington Well Women Clinic', in J. Orr (ed.) *Women's Health in the Community*, Chichester: John Wiley & Sons.
Barrett, M. and Roberts, H. (1978) 'Doctors and their patients: the social control of women in general practice', in C. Smart and B. Smart (eds), *Women, Sexuality and Social Control*, London: Routledge & Kegan Paul.
Bieggs, A. (1979) 'A pig and a poke', *Scarlet Women*, No. 10, December, pp 8-9.
Cooke, M. and Ronalds, C. (1987) 'The Manchester experience III, Rusholme Well Women Clinic', in J. Orr (ed.) *Women's Health in the Community*, Chichester: John Wiley & Sons.

Eisner, M. and Wright, M. (1986) 'A Feminist Approach to General Practice', in C. Webb (ed.) *Feminist Practice in Women's Health Care*, Chichester: John Wiley & Sons.

Gardner, K. (1983) 'A Well Women Clinic in an inner city general practice' *Journal of the Royal College of General Practitioners* 33: 711–14.

Leeson, J. and Gray, J. (1978) *Women and Medicine*, London: Tavistock.

Manchester Community Health Councils (undated), 'National Guidelines for Well Women Centres', Manchester: Manchester Community Health Councils.

Oakley, A. (1984) *The Captured Womb*, Oxford: Basil Blackwell.

Richardson, J. (1987) 'Well Women Centres', (Unpublished Survey).

Ruzek, S.B. (1978) *The Women's Health Movement*, New York: Praeger.

Savage, W. (1986) *A Savage Enquiry*, London: Virago Press.

Smith, L. (1987) 'Women and mental health', in J. Orr (ed.) *Women's Health in the Community*, Chichester: John Wiley & Sons.

Spencer, B., Gray, J., Durham, M. and Jones, V. (1982) 'An evaluation of the Manchester Well Women Clinics, (Unpublished Paper) Community Health Council, St Anne's Square, Manchester, CHC.

Thornley, P. (1987) 'The development of well women clinics', in J. Orr (ed.) *Women's Health in the Community*, Chichester: John Wiley & Sons.

6 Putting on an Act for children?

Miriam David

INTRODUCTION

The care of children or child care is an odd aspect of social or public policy. It is generally buried amongst a variety of other issues such as the family and has therefore not been seen as properly a topic for public or general concern. Traditionally in social policy, the questions about children have tended only to focus on children's needs 'for care' when the family or parents are seen as, in some senses, inadequate or not capable of providing adequate care. In other words, the assumptions that have generally held are that child care is properly the concern of the family, to be carried out in its privacy. Only when the family fails or breaks up/down, should the state be involved in providing some alternative care. Of course, this argument assumes a 'normal' family and the state is therefore at least indirectly involved in defining what the normal standards of family and parental care are and should be and when the rules are breached (David 1985). Nevertheless, child care in the social policy and social services literature has come to mean the care of children in contexts other than the privacy of the 'normal, nuclear family'.

In this chapter, I shall review the recent debates about child care, both those culminating in the Children Act 1989 and surrounding the *causes célèbres* about child protection and child sexual abuse, and the feminist critiques of child care and family policy. I take feminist to mean social investigations which do not render women and girls invisible but which seek to highlight social issues from the standpoint of women (Smith 1988). Despite almost two decades of feminist organizing and campaigning, as well as academic work on questions of gender and social policy, women's studies and feminist sociology, the public policy debate in Britain seems assiduously to ignore these issues on topics where gender is central if not crucial. This can best be illustrated by reference to the recent debates about child care policy. Why women's issues remain excluded may also be explained by the nature of the feminist critiques offered, which I shall attempt to present in the second half of this chapter.

CHILD CARE LAW REFORM

Current debates about child care in England and Wales, excluding Scotland, where the law and policies on child care have been developed differently and separately, have culminated first in a series of consultation papers reviewing aspects of the law, second, a series of public inquiries about particular issues of child abuse and, third, the Children Act, which reached the statute book by the end of 1989. What is important about the Act, first and foremost, is the attempt to bring together, in one comprehensive piece of legislation, most of the disparate issues relating to the care of children. However, there are some notable and noteworthy exceptions such as the health care and education of children, which serve to illustrate how the Act is in some senses a tidying up exercise for social welfare and family lawyers rather than an Act that deals comprehensively with the care of children. However, the Act does seek to clarify the notion of *parental responsibilities* generally, but particularly in respect of key areas of children's welfare, namely either where children are seen as 'at risk' in their current home circumstances or where the family unit has broken up as a result of marital breakdown. Traditionally, these two areas of the law relating to children have been kept separate. Indeed, historically, it is only with respect to the former 'public' law that social workers involved in local authority social service departments have been involved with child care. The involvement of social welfare workers with cases of private family law, namely marital breakdown and the consequences for the care of children, is of more recent origin. The traditions of the various agencies of the state – local authorities, the courts and the social and welfare workers – are very different, although all cling to some notion of a conventional family form and the necessity of its model in alternatives to the family of origin for child care. It is, I believe, because of this common concern to preserve at least the model of the conventional nuclear family and with it parental responsibilities, that the impetus for a fresh piece of legislation on child care derives. Indeed, Professor Brenda Hoggett, a Law Commissioner, responsible for helping to draft the legislation, argued explicitly at a 1989 conference to discuss child care law reform[1] that the *key* concept of parental responsibility can be the same for parents by virtue of being mothers or married fathers, for non-marital fathers and grandparents to acquire by agreements, for local authorities through court orders and for guardians who might acquire responsibilities for children by a signed agreement. It is through this concept and the allied concepts of care and residence orders, that the public – child care – law and the private – family – law systems are brought together into one comprehensive piece of legislation. In her words, the concerns of the law reformers are with concepts of parental responsibility and orders which settle the arrangements for where, and with whom, a child lives.

CHANGING 'FAMILY WORLDS'

The origins of the concern to clarify and codify the public and private family law systems are, however, more than just an ideological concern about the functioning of the family and its reproduction in settings which may appear to be different from the conventional family form: foster-parents, guardians, custodians, local authority or voluntary children's homes, lone-parent families created by divorce, separation or choice, or reconstituted families (unions of parents and step-fathers or half-parents, etc.). They are to do with the social and demographic changes which have transformed the traditional nuclear family from its apparent dominance to a complexity of 'family worlds', to use the term coined the authors of an OECD publication (CERI 1982). As they state:

> The family microcosm is extraordinarily differentiated and, even limiting the description to those families with children, the typology that can be constructed immediately becomes complex. . . . Now if this typology is combined with other parameters, for example socio-economic status or number of active persons, the immense diversity of situations experienced by children is immediately obvious. In other words, there is an *enormous number of different family worlds* in which they may grow up [author's emphasis]. There are not only the parents and the siblings, or one of the parents, but also grandparents, uncles, aunts, cousins, grandchildren, servants, boarders, married brothers and sisters, with or without children. It must also be remembered that households undergo changes over time. Of particular interest are the changes of environment for the child whose parents have divorced and remarried. Such families are often 'corporations' including a mixture of adults and children from two families. These observations are important, because very often the variety of 'realities' is underestimated. Through stressing the role of the parents, one ends up forgetting about all the others, as if the majority of families consisted of one couple and their children. Certainly, this is the majority situation, in the sense that it applies to a great number of children, but a good number of other situations exist alongside it.
>
> (CERI 1982: 19–20)

Whether or not the nuclear family as the biological breadwinning father and the biological housewife/mother ever assumed the pre-eminent position afforded it in ideology, clearly there have now been substantial economic and social changes whereby it is no longer even so statistically important. The effect of these social changes is to produce a variety of family forms either by force or by choice. The choices to divorce or separate may be made by either spouse, whereas mothers may have through force of economic or social circumstance to rear children in situations not of their choosing: in poverty, in liaisons with potentially violent or difficult men, in derelict homes.

Not only are the family worlds in which children now grow up clearly more varied than was assumed to be the case in some bygone era, so, too, are the activities of the parents in such family worlds. As Peter Moss (1988/9: 21) argues:

> Over the last 10-15 years, *differential unemployment rates* for men with and without dependent children have developed. In 1973, the rate was similar, at three per cent. By 1980, *fathers had edged ahead*, with five per cent compared to four per cent. *By 1985* the gap had widened *to 10 per cent compared to five per cent*. Unemployment was highest among men with a child under five, 12 per cent compared to 9 per cent for men with a youngest child aged five to nine and six per cent for men with a youngest child aged 10 or over (OPCS, 1987: Table 6.19) . . . though the impact of unemployment on men with children is far less than the impact of leaving the labour force on women with children (author's emphasis).

He goes on to argue the contradictory point that, however,

> men's earnings are likely to increase while they have dependent children. Average gross weekly earnings for men increase with age up to 50. Manual workers in their thirties earn on average 24 per cent more than workers in their early twenties, while for non-manual workers the difference is 65 per cent (Department of Employment, 1987: Table 125). . . . Any increases in men's earnings are unlikely to offset the loss of earnings experienced by their partners. The initial effect when a first child is born, and when most women leave full-time employment for a period of unemployment, is a massive fall in household income. (ibid.: 22).

In traditional two-parent households, then, as Moss argues, there is now likely to be substantial unemployment (one in ten) amongst fathers, and, in the early months of child-rearing, low household income, although this may rise quickly, in part due to long hours of father's work.

Since the 1940s, there has been an increase in the number of mothers in employment. By 1985, 30 per cent of women with children under 5 were employed, and 60 per cent of women with a youngest child aged 5–9

(OPCS 1987: Table 6.11). Most of these employed mothers work part-time, a large proportion for very short hours. As Martin and Roberts (1984) show, 75 per cent of mothers with a youngest child under 5 and with a youngest aged 5–9, work part-time, which contrasts with 58 per cent of employed women with a youngest child aged 11–15 who work part-time (Table 2.18). The rates of part-time employment for lone mothers are lower, although the rates of full-time employment for lone mothers are the same as in two-parent households (OPCS, 1987: Table 6.6). Lone-parent households where the parent is not employed have the lowest equivalent income level of any households with children, with the exception of two-parent households where both parents are out of work (Moss 1988/9: 26).

The picture that now emerges of the family is that the parents in the union are not necessarily any longer breadwinner father and housewife mother. In a substantial minority, the father may be unemployed. He may not be the biological father, but rather a step-parent. On the other hand, he may be forced to work long hours to make ends meet or to make a good household income. In a substantial minority, too, the mother may be a lone parent, rearing children alone, often in conditions of poverty (Glendinning and Millar 1987; and Chapter two in this volume). The vast majority of mothers are in paid employment, whether in two-parent or lone-parent households; albeit that employment is of a short, part-time variety and may involve a substantial number of changes. Mothers' chances of long-term, permanent paid employment, whether in lone-parent or two-parent house-holds are quite slim, and the costs for women quite considerable (Joshi 1987). In other words, the apparent changes in family forms have had a major impact on women's working lives, despite the fact that their lives still do not mirror those of fathers. 'The costs of caring', as Joshi (1987: 130) notes, fall most heavily on women, given 'the social expectations about the female caring role'.

THE NEW RIGHT AND THE FAMILY

It is these social expectations that are addressed by the child care law reformers, albeit indirectly and obliquely. Changes in family patterns occasioned by the liberalization of divorce laws in the late 1960s and 1970s have prompted many politicians and social commentators to mourn the passing of the nuclear family and hope to reinvoke it, by various measures. For example, Ferdinand Mount, one time editor of the *Spectator* and organizer of the Family Policy Group within the Cabinet Office wrote a passionate text about the naturalness of the family and its survival through history, based on gender-differentiated roles within the family.

The defenders of the family . . . assert always the privacy and independence of the family, its biological individuality and its rights to live
according to its natural instincts. It is for this reason that, even in
societies where male supremacy is officially total, the family asserts its
own *maternal* values [author's emphasis] . . . We may hope and expect
that as a result the spirit of civic equality may seep through into the
private world of marriage and blot out the patches of inequality and
consequent resentments that disfigure it. But we should also recognise
that these inequalities originally seeped through into marriage from the
outside, from the public world. For it is *within* marriage that the notions
of equality and openheartedness have existed long before they became
part of a political programme. . . . The old ideals . . . are opposed to
egotism, whether male or female. They assume a biological ethic – a
series of duties of nest-gathering, nursing, feeding, protecting and teaching, all involving the sacrifice of self.

(1983: 240–1)

Digby Anderson, too, of the Institute of Social Affairs has also argued
against these changes in family patterns, especially those which leave
women independent of men, rearing children alone. He called his journalist
piece 'Ripe for a British moral majority', arguing for 'the cause of the
normal family . . . husband and wife living with their own children, the
husband the major earner, the spouses intending and trying to stay together'
(*The Times*, 15 October 1985: 12). He contrasted this with the anti-family
lobby which he claimed is 'merely disposed to help casualties of the
traditional family, such as abandoned wives or children brought up by one
parent.'

The effects of some of these social commentaries have been to reinforce
notions of 'parental responsibility' built into divorce procedures, especially
those of divorce conciliation. As Piper (1988: 478) argues:

whilst an unknown quantity in many countries only 10–20 years ago,
conciliation has rapidly colonised divorce settlements until it is now a
fashionable topic among interested academics and practitioners in a
variety of fields. Significantly, throughout this period of growth and
across national boundaries, virtually all the literature has made a connection between conciliation and the operation of parental responsibility.

But, as Piper herself asks, what is meant by parental responsibility? She
shows, through her research, that:

there is a particular concept of parental responsibility which prioritises
joint decision-making and *harmonious co-parenting* [author's
emphasis] but masks inequalities of input into caretaking and assumes

pre-separation expertise in joint parenting . . . To the extent that care-taking before and after parental separation is the responsibility of mothers, and to the extent that conciliators are able to impose the ideology on parents, then conciliation *will* operate against the interest of women.

(ibid.: 491–2)

In other words, the concept of parental responsibility built into previous family law and procedures is not, in fact, a gender-neutral term, although there is an attempt to achieve equal responsibilities within divorce settlements. Mothers remain those with the major caring responsibilities, and, therefore, as Joshi (1987) has noted, not with the same access to paid employment as fathers, either in divorcing or two-parent families. Of course, Piper may not be correct to consider that this is necessarily 'against the interests of women', although the mothers in her sample may have felt burdened by the pressures to achieve co-parenting in divorce and the need to find paid employment. Other writers and pressure groups such as 'Families Need Fathers' have noted the difficulties that the social expectation of the female caring role places on fathers' access to child care (New and David 1985: chs 8 and 9). What *is* against the interests of women is not child care itself but the question of adequate financial support for both children and mothers in divorcing families.

The concern about divorce and its effects, curiously, has largely centred on parents rather than the children in the families. As Wadsworth and Maclean (1986: 147) point out:

child support received very little attention in statute, or common law decision-making. But although divorce in England has become easier, with the introduction of legal aid, the abolition of fault, and the delegalization of divorce through the special procedure for undefended cases, nevertheless, the legal interest in the child's position has remained residual, providing no more than a safety net by demanding that the court should be satisfied that arrangements made for children are adequate. There has been no attempt to define what these arrangements should be or how they should be enforced. In 1984 the Matrimonial and Family Proceedings Act stated for the first time that the interests of children must be considered first in making financial arrangements.

But they go on to show, through their research, that there are long-term consequences for children of parental divorce. They conclude that:

in view of growing concern for the 'new poor' in female-headed households, following what L.J. Weitzman has termed 'The Divorce Revolution' with its 'unexpected social and emotional consequences for women and children; (Weitzman, 1985) . . . the aftermath of divorce may involve inter-generational effects. The children of divorcing parents currently in their mid-thirties that were studied in the National Child Development Study had significantly underachieved compared with their peers from intact families, and from families broken by death. This effect remained, though mitigated, when the custodial parent remarried.

(ibid.: 157)

The kinds of 'underachievement' with which Wadsworth and Maclean were here concerned were generally educational and emotional: a serious consequence for children of divorcing parents. Their research, however, is quite unusual and, although they make a plea that 'the issue of children's life chances should find a place in the agenda when the policy issues surrounding divorce are under discussion', this request has gone unheeded. Nevertheless, the general question of child care, albeit not children's life chances, has become a key concern in the current policy debate surrounding divorce. On the whole, however, this is to bring together questions of child care for children in even more unfortunate social circumstances than those in families where the marriage is ending. In a sense, then, the Children Act could be seen to be a levelling down of, rather than an improvement in, children's situations.

CHILD ABUSE CASES

Indeed, the other kinds of children's life chances that have occasioned the child care policy debate have been the series of child abuse cases that have resulted in a child's death at the hands of its parents. There have been a number of local authority inquiries of particular cases of children's deaths which, as Brenda Hoggett argued, were important sources for the drafting of the Children Bill. These were the three inquiries into the deaths of Jasmine Beckford (in Brent), Kimberley Carlile (in Greenwich) and Tyra Henry (in Lambeth). All these cases received a great deal of public scrutiny and consideration, with the Blom-Cooper report on Jasmine Beckford (London Borough of Brent 1986) perhaps receiving the greatest amount of attention and most important in informing the legal and public policy debate.

Interestingly, however, what has only rarely been noted in the media is the fact that *all* the children who were the subjects of abuse and public inquiry were little *girls* and all the perpetrators of the actual physical abuse and violence, *men*, usually their fathers, step-fathers or men co-habiting with their mothers. In the inquiries, however, what was the key issue was not the inter-generational *gender* relationships but the inter-generational relationships, *per se*, with the mothers receiving as much critical attention as the perpetrators of abuse. In fact, in the court cases that preceded the inquiries, the mothers also received very serious sentences and rebukes, usually for child neglect, rather than for the actual death of the child. The public inquiries themselves focused largely on the inadequacies of both the families and their social work support. In particular, the mothers were seen to be inadequate at protecting their daughter from the violence and abuse of their co-habitees. For example, the Carlile Report (London Borough of Greenwich 1987) in its judgement of Pauline Carlile's role in Kimberley's death attaches as much blame to her for failing to protect her daughter as to Nigel Hall. Mrs Carlile was also held responsible as she was seen as being 'fatally attracted to violent co-habitees' (p. 111).

This notion of child protection, however, was one initiated in the seminal Blom-Cooper Report as 'a new activity' for social workers, according to Parton and Parton (1988/9: 38). Indeed, in all the reports, the social workers were the most heavily criticized. It was Blom-Cooper, however, who first attempted to redefine and codify social workers' roles in relation to families and child abuse: 'We are strongly of the view that social work can in fact be defined *only* in terms of the functions required of it by their employment agency operating within a statutory framework' (London Borough of Brent 1986). This 'new activity of child protection' initiated by the Blom-Cooper Report has led to a greater degree of scrutiny and assessment by social welfare professionals of the degree of risk or danger of child abuse in families brought to their attention. It has led to a tighter definition of families at risk and notions of dangerousness and parental responsibility. It is this trend in legalizing notions of parental responsibility for child protection which is the occasion for child care law reform.

The specific impetus, however, in terms of child abuse cases, comes from the Cleveland Inquiry into child sexual abuse. The social services department in Cleveland, it was reported, relied heavily on the Blom-Cooper concept of child protection.

The public criticism of social workers for failing to act promptly and positively to secure the protection of children . . . had the effect in Cleveland of creating a renewed sense of determination to ensure that if serious risks to children were seen, effective steps would be taken to intervene. Social workers were becoming more aware of child sexual abuse and they had been led to believe that the scepticism of the past had resulted in significant numbers of children being left in situations of continuing abuse. They had been reminded by the Beckford Report of the importance which social workers should attach to their child protection responsibilities. Social workers and their managers were anxious not to have been seen to fail the children involved by leaving them in situations of risk.

(Butler-Sloss Report 1988: 84, s.4.189)

Butler-Sloss herself, in the conclusion to the Report, was sympathetic to this dilemma for social workers and invoked the principle of child protection.

It is however important to bear in mind that those who have a responsibility to protect children at risk, such as social workers, health visitors, police and doctors have in the past been criticised for failure to act in sufficient time and to take adequate steps to protect children who are being damaged. In Cleveland the general criticism by the public has been of over-enthusiasm and zeal in the actions taken. It is difficult for professionals to balance the conflicting interests and needs in the enormously important and delicate field of child sexual abuse. We hope that professionals will not as a result of the Cleveland experience stand back and hesitate to act *to protect the children.* [author's emphasis] . . . It is a delicate and difficult line to tread between taking action too soon and not taking it soon enough. Social Services whilst putting the needs of the child first must respect the rights of the parents; they also must work if possible with the parents for the benefit of the children. These parents themselves are often in need of help. Inevitably a degree of conflict develops between those objectives.

(Butler-Sloss Report 1988: 244, paras 15–16)

Butler-Sloss reiterated the concept of child protection, and even went further in arguing for courtesy in the treatment of children: 'There is a danger that in looking to the welfare of the children believed to be the victims of sexual abuse the children themselves may be overlooked. The child is a person not an object of concern' (ibid.: 245). The implication of this statement, however, is that a child is a person *in law* rather than a person subject to care and concern. It follows then that, as a lawyer, Butler-Sloss would be particularly eager for the concepts of child protection and parental rights and responsibilities, as well as the roles of the many agencies involved, to be redefined in law. She urged the implementation of the proposals in the White Paper on Child Care and Family Services (ibid.: 252). The White Paper had been published in 1987 whilst the crisis over child sexual abuse in Cleveland was at its height. Interestingly, the Children Bill was not published until after Butler-Sloss had reported on her inquiry into the Cleveland cases, although the White Paper had covered substantially similar grounds.

In some senses, it could be argued that the issue of child *sexual* abuse deflected concern about child protection and parental responsibility. Although the three child abuse inquiries were about little girls being abused and murdered by their step-fathers or mothers' co-habitees, the issues were never publicly raised as to whether or not there was a *sexual* element to the nature of the abuse. The issue was couched in terms of protecting children, as genderless persons, from parental violence. Implicitly, of course, it was acknowledged that the parents were gendered and that the forms that their actions took differed on gender lines: men perpetrated the violence, women failed to protect against it, or even colluded with it. So parental responsibility was clearly being breached here by both parents: mothers and fathers (or co-habitees) alike. In the cases of child sexual abuse, in Cleveland, the question of the nature of the harm, violence and, therefore, danger to the child is more opaque (especially given that it did not result in death). Butler-Sloss herself is at pains to give parents the benefit of the doubt and therefore to continue to afford them some rights, at very least to courtesy and information about the legal procedures. She is also at pains to deny any gender element to the cases, despite the fact that there is acknowledgement of it being sexual abuse. The definition provided in the report is:

> 'Sexual abuse is defined as the involvement of dependent, developmentally immature children and adolescents in sexual activities that they do not fully comprehend and to which they are unable to give informed consent or that violate the social taboos of family roles'. . . . In other words, it is the use of children by adults for sexual gratification.
>
> (Butler-Sloss 1988: 4)

In the description of the cases under consideration in the inquiry there is some passing acknowledgement that there is a gender dimension.

> From the evidence presented to the Inquiry a majority of children sexually abused in the UK are girls but there are significant numbers of boys. . . . It would be impossible to say how many sexually abused children in Cleveland were boys. But there were some boys sexually abused during the period and significant proportions in respect of whom allegations were made.
>
> (ibid.: 6)

Curiously, the reference here is to the lack of knowledge about how many boys, not how many girls were abused! However, the report is more direct about the abusers:

> Much of the abuse is contained within the family, and such facts as are available, many of them anecdotal, show a preponderance of fathers,

then step-fathers, uncles, elder brothers. There is a view held that the sexual abuse of a step-daughter is not as heinous as abuse of a daughter. There were examples in Cleveland of abuse by father, step-father, boy-friend, uncle, cousin, elder brothers, baby-sitter and neighbour. There may be a single perpetrator or several abusers in one family. At least one girl in Cleveland was likely to have been abused both by her uncle and her father.

(ibid.: 7)

Yet again, the report is at pains to appear to be gender-neutral and so we are offered the following, by way, presumably, of balance:

Sexual abuse of children by women has been reported but this was only alleged in the case of one child considered by the Inquiry. There were examples of children coming within the other definitions of abuse at the hands of mothers during the period investigated.

(ibid.: 7)

This returns us to the rather less difficult issues of physical or emotional child abuse, where the guidelines seem easier to apply. It also returns to the gender-neutral language of child protection and parental responsibility. However, one issue which is briefly touched on but then neglected in the subsequent recommendations is 'the long-term effects on the abused child'. It is acknowledged that there are effects on intergenerational relationships as well as adult sexual relationships, but again all couched in gender-neutral language, masking the particular effects on girls into womanhood and motherhood. Yet, it was this question of the long-term effects of children's life chances that Wadsworth and Maclean pleaded for inclusion in the policy debate on divorce. It should be noted that they, too, couched this in gender-neutral terms, despite acknowledging the particular financial hard-ships of female-headed households, especially formed through divorce. It is particularly pleasing that Mavis Maclean and Diana Kuh have looked at the impact on the daughters of divorcees (see Chapter 9 of this book). They have not compared these effects with those on the daughters of abusers, whether sexual or physical child abuse. It would be interesting to compare the various emotional effects, on intergenerational and sexual relationships.

LEGISLATING FOR CHILD PROTECTION

Given the relative lack of public knowledge about this, and the fact that the policy debate about child care has become more juridical rather than concerned with social welfare and social relationships, it is not perhaps surprising that these concerns are ignored in the policy proposals for child care included in the Children Act. Yet the bill was seen as a pressing issue given both the spate of child abuse inquiries, the Blom-Cooper concept of the inadequacy of social workers' definitions of their role and the growing complexity of the law with regard to divorce settlements. The specific pressure, however, came from those concerned about defining legally rights and duties for parents, children, local authorities and others involved in providing child care. In other words, it was pressure to ensure that those families which did not conform to the traditional nuclear family would as nearly as possible imitate or mirror it in their legal and consequent social responsibilities. Hence, the centrality to the law reform of the concept of parental responsibilities whether for parents or those given responsibility *in loco parentis*.

As a corollary, the other general principle in the Act is 'the child's welfare'. But this is defined in an incredibly narrow way to cover the child only in regard to care and contested family proceedings, when deciding any question of upbringing or property. The court, it is stated, may not make an order 'unless it considers that doing so would be better for the child than making no order at all'. A 'welfare check-list' of seven points is provided. These are:

(a) the ascertainable wishes and feelings of the child concerned (considered in the light of his (*sic*) age and understanding);
(b) his (*sic*) physical, emotional and educational needs;
(c) the likely effect on him (*sic*) of any change in his (*sic*) circumstances;
(d) his (*sic*) age, sex, background and any characteristics of his (*sic*) which the court considers relevant;
(e) any harm which he (*sic*) has suffered or is at risk of suffering;
(f) how capable each of his (*sic*) parents, and any other person in relation to whom the court considers the question to be relevant, is of meeting his (*sic*) needs;
(g) the range of powers available to the courts under this Act in the proceedings in question.

These considerations will be used to determine which of four sorts of court orders to apply in family proceedings, namely, one a residence order (where children will live); two a contact order (who will have access); three a specific steps order (determining the exercise of parental responsibility, and four, a prohibited steps order (steps not to be taken without leave of the court). Local authorities, however, also retain other responsibilities for children in need and where consistent with this, to promote their upbringing by their families. To do this they have a duty to identify the children and publicize their services, to take reasonable steps to prevent neglect or abuse, to provide home help, holidays, family centres with counselling and other services to keep children in their families 'as they consider appropriate'. This latter term is also used for local authority provision of day care for the under-fives in need, facilities for child-minders and for older children. However, there are no resources associated with these provisions and, in general terms, local authorities are expected now to give assistance in kind, or, in exceptional circumstances by a recoverable loan.

The emphasis, then, in the Act is on clarifying court proceedings for a child's welfare, not for providing generally for social welfare. There is a clear shift to legalizing the procedures in courts and for social workers. Social workers will clearly become more involved in assessment of children at risk and defining the kinds of ways such children can be helped. But as Parton and Parton (1988/9) argue, there is:

> a new approach to children and families which is qualitatively different in rationale and approach. Much of this is symbolised by the emergence and emphasis on the notion of child protection. In essence the approach argues that, for those families identified as high risk or dangerous, it is suggested their children be removed on a long-term, preferably permanent, basis. For those deemed to be low-risk, at the so-called 'soft-end', the role of preventative, supportive work becomes a minimal one, reserved for the few families where assessment is problematic. Such a residual, individualistic policy, it is argued, would not only enable social service departments to use scarce and expensive resources more effectively but would minimise state intervention and intrusion into family life.
>
> (1988/9: 39)

It is certainly the case that the Act emphasizes the privacy of the family and the limited legalistic role that social work intervention should take. The emphasis is on parental and children's rights, in gender-neutral terms, rather than on the resources available to families. There is a clear shift from the social welfare model to a more justicial one. The ideology underpinning it seems to have been well stated by Mount:

> The family's most dangerous enemies may not turn out to be those who have openly declared war. It is so easy to muster resistance against the blatant cruelty of collectivist dictators. . . . It is less easy *to fight against the armies* of those who are 'only here to help' – those who claim to come with the best intention but come armed, all the same, with statutory powers and administrative instruments: education officers, children's officers . . . welfare workers and all other councils . . . which claim to know best how to manage our private concerns (author's emphasis).
>
> (1983: 173)

CHILD CARE AND HOME VISITING

Indeed in the 1980s, schemes of 'armies' of helpers have developed apace as the state system has been cut back. The schemes themselves began in the late 1960s and early 1970s influenced by programmes set up during the 1960s in the USA as part of the War on Poverty, which sought to provide educational opportunities for pre-school children from disadvantaged families through the use of positive discrimination (David 1980). In particular, the Headstart Programme focused on home intervention and saw a key role for the children's parents as well as early childhood education (Bronfenbrenner 1974). In Britain, pre-school home visiting as a means of intervention took off in the early 1970s with an Educational Priority Area scheme in Yorkshire (Smith 1975). The problems of deprivation and disadvantage were seen to be located primarily in the individual and collective characteristics of those suffering the problem and preventative strategies were looked to as a means of countering them. But over the years there has been a marked shift from the early educational emphasis on a child's cognitive and social performance to a focus on family support and parental participation to underpin the part that parents are to play or should play in their children's development: 'There has been a realisation that the work is most effective when it is directed as much to the parents as to the children' (Poulton 1983: 25). All such pre-school home visiting schemes use 'visitors' who visit families with a child or children under 5 in the family's own home:

> The strength of home visiting is that this task is carried out in the security of the families' homes, where both the parents and the children can use familiar aspects of their own environment as pegs for learning.
>
> (Poulton 1983: 23)

Families who are felt to be 'in need' of a visitor are referred to the schemes by health visitors, social workers, school teachers, even by friends of the family itself. Families are then initially visited to assess whether home visiting is the best form of help to meet their needs. Poulton states that by the mid-1970s the role of home visitor could be defined:

> She [*sic*] was frequently required to offer support to mothers in their childrearing. She was certainly involved in trying to improve the quality of mother-child interaction. She was often modelling adult-child behaviour for mothers to observe and possibly develop for themselves. . . . She was acting regularly in liaison with other agencies' field co-ordinators with 'problematic' families.
>
> (ibid.: 2)

The development of home visiting schemes has been well documented and criticized for the ways in which it has imposed on families with need for social work help, white, middle-class standards of child care (Finch 1984a; David 1985; New and David 1985). The schemes have not just been aimed at families in need despite the gender-neutral rhetoric. They have also been aimed specifically at mothers to give them help with their child-rearing practices, assuming that such mothers are disadvantaged, inadequate, incompetent and potentially neglectful of their children or live in areas of multiple disadvantage. Indeed, the helpers, be they volunteers in schemes such as the pre-school home visiting schemes like Homeplus, befriending schemes, family centres, community centres and so on are almost invariably women; chosen for their female 'caring' qualities, to pass on their skills to less 'naturally' equipped women. Indeed, in some such schemes, the women volunteers themselves are vetted before they are entitled to help poorer mothers. The vetting has taken the form of checking out the adequacy of their own homes in terms of cleanliness, housekeeping, etc. Indeed, in many such schemes they are meant to help with domestic chores and family budgeting as well as child care. Some schemes prefer non-professional to professional helpers, that is teachers, health visitors, etc., because it is felt that there are less likely to be barriers between them and the parents. Poulton, indeed, argues that 'in all of the schemes there has been strong support from the parents' (1983: 22) in that they have the same aspirations for their children as middle-class parents and that this provides the motivation for them to accept the schemes (Poulton and James 1975; Aplin and Pugh 1983).

As Edwards (1988) has argued, these schemes have several aims: prevention and parental participation, with prevention being of either educational failure or family breakdown. The Social Services Select Committee, in its examination of children in care felt that 'children sometimes have to be received into care because their parents simply lack parenting skills' (1984: xxv, para. 48) and saw home visiting schemes as a means of countering this.

> Several witnesses emphasized the value of giving families under strain practical help in their own homes . . . the value of such help cannot be over-emphasized: its prompt provision could avert a number of receptions into care.
>
> (para. 49)

The criticisms of the schemes do not just point to the reinforcement of motherhood as a social role. Intervention to prevent family breakdown and malfunctioning has also been criticized for its failure to take account of structural process at work with regard to parental inadequacies in child care:

> Irrespective of the nature and strengths of the pressure exerted by structural variables on the family, the analysis of family failure by those anxious about the family's future have been grounded at the level of individual behaviour.
>
> (Lewis 1986: 33)

However, the schemes are generally justified not only on grounds of prevention, but also about parental participation, giving parents greater confidence and involvement and consumer rights. For example, Smith (1988) argues that participation:

> carries notions of a service's responsiveness to its consumers, and of consumers' rights to organise the service as they think best or at least to have a say in how it is provided.
>
> (1988: 12)

It is certainly this kind of notion that has been the basis for the recent expansion of home visiting schemes. However, one recent research evaluation of one scheme found that this was the least developed side of the scheme. As Edwards argues:

> Mothers certainly did not see themselves as being 'educated' to replace the Visitor in her role but viewed the Project in a 'complementary' light. . . . The majority of mothers now feel more prepared to consult professionals if they have serious problems. However, the mothers' confidence in their own ability to tackle the real constraints they see as operating on their own lives remains untouched. . . . While this remains the case criticisms that the Project is just teaching mothers to be 'good little mummies' remain uncontested.
>
> (1988: last page)

Edwards, in other words, argues that the chief value is to give mothers a respite or break from the daily round of child care, hence reinforcing or enabling mothers to return to their 'normal' female caring role (1988; 1989). Indeed, Mount also makes this point in his critique:

> what is always affronting, offensive and distressing is the simple fact of their *intrusion* into our private space. Our feelings are mixed even in the case of the most helpful of all public visitors. The District Health Visitor who visits mothers with babies is often sweet and sensitive and genuinely useful. . . . But (mothers) cannot help being continuously aware that she is there as an inspector as well as an adviser . . . The

Visitor – grim, symbolic title – remains an intruder. . . . In all the revolts against big government and high taxes . . . resentment has played its part . . . the feeling that the state is intruding into private space more and more and ought to be stopped – is growing. The Visitor is being made to feel unwelcome. His or her claim to moral superiority is being disputed.

(1983: 174)

Mount's views appear to underpin the Children Act. There is very little emphasis on home visiting schemes and where there is, it is on voluntary arrangements. This then extends the notion of self-help schemes which had been started in the mid-1980s and invigorated by Edwina Currie, as Minister of Health, in October 1986 as part of the Government's helping the community to care in the self-help family centres project. In other words, the Act itself reinvigorates the notion of the privacy of the (genderless) family, coping on its own. Social work support for such families becomes minimized and instead social workers are expected to help to root out more serious cases of need and risk or dangerousness.

REINFORCING FAMILY PRIVACY

A further testimony to the way in which the privacy of the family is reasserted is through the lack of attention to the general kinds of support that *all* families need in order properly to care for children. There is no attention given to the question of resources necessary for children. Indeed, all the social security measures that exemplify the welfare state have been eroded or changed by the Government so that there are no universal significant measures of family support (Land and Ward 1986). The Act itself does not address this nor the question of child care services, such as comprehensive day care for the under-fives or after-school and holiday play facilities. It appears that the framers of the Act do not assume such facilities to be necessary for adequate family child care (New and David 1985). They are left, again, to the vagaries of market forces or self-help schemes. In recent years, however, private businesses and industry have begun to develop schemes of child care for under-fives, for the children of their women workers. Midland Bank has launched a scheme to develop a hundred workplace nurseries, over the next two years. But, given the Government's reluctance to see this as necessary to the conditions of work for mothers, and the punitive systems of taxation that were, until the 1990 budget, imposed on workplace nurseries, it is unlikely that this system will grow rapidly.

Child care for the under-fives has not been a major issue of concern for the women's movement, which may go some way to explaining why it is not currently on the agenda of the child care law reform. Feminists have, on the whole, been ambivalent about addressing public policy issues around motherhood and have focused rather on questions of women's position in relation to men, in public life or in paid employment. Curiously, concerns with the conditions of paid employment have not extended to the question of the care of children. This can be illustrated anecdotally by the quiet reception that the book I co-authored with Caroline New (1985) received in the feminist world, by contrast with its reception in the world of social work and social services. Entitled *For The Children's Sake: Making Child Care More Than Women's Business*, one might have expected at the very least critical attention, but it has barely been addressed. Sylvia Ann Hewlett reports more abusive responses to her book on a very similar theme in the USA.

> *A Lesser Life* was published in the States in March 1986. It received massive attention from both the quality and the popular media and provoked a series of fierce debates.
>
> One of the first reactions came from the women's movement. In the main feminists were feisty, riled up and hopping mad. Robin Morgan opened the offensive in a March issue of *Ms* magazine. In it she described my book as full of 'tediously familiar right-wing anti-feminism', and accused me of 'blaming the victim' because I point out that feminist organisations have neglected to support motherhood . . . I did have some feminist defenders . . . Elinor Guggenheimer (president of the Child Care Action Campaign) . . . supported one of my basic contentions that none of the feminist organisations has ever given meaningful support to mothers or children.
>
> The women's movement has given short shrift to child care. To date I know of no conference held by a woman's advocacy group where a major address on child care has been given, nor of any feminist publication whose major focus has been on child care . . . Despite hostility from the elite ranks of the women's movement . . . mothers of young children connected with particular passion with the themes of *A Lesser Life*. . . . If you listen to the voices of housewives, working mums, divorcees, widows, to a remarkable degree they tell the same tale. It is almost impossible to raise a family and earn a decent living in America.
>
> (Hewlett 1987: xvii)

Hewlett goes on to argue that 'the central problem of our age' is easing the problems of working parents, especially mothers, and ensuring a better start in life for our children. Sadly, these issues have still not been taken up and included in the public policy agenda, and certainly are not part of the child care law reform. Feminists in Britain remain ambivalent to public questions of child care. As Sheila Rowbotham puts it in an article entitled 'To be or not to be: the dilemmas of mothering', published in *Feminist Review* to celebrate twenty years of feminism:

> it is not just a matter of challenging how motherhood is portrayed in the external culture. Women bring to the decision whether or not to have a child a psychological image of motherhood as power and submission bound together. The problem for feminists is whether this is a fixed unalterable structure or whether it can be changed. If it can be changed, where should we concentrate our efforts: on psychoanalytic exploration, on attempting to represent mothering differently, on changing the relations in which we mother, or on transforming the social conditions of mothering? Not surprisingly there is no unified strategy. Feminists have buried themselves in all these areas. As the women's movement has become more fragmented it has been harder to consider even how the differing forms of activity and inquiry might interrelate.
>
> (1989: 88)

This form of fragmentation has meant that it has been difficult for the women's movement to integrate its concerns about motherhood with questions of violence against women and, more recently, the work on violence against children and child sexual abuse. Indeed, the women's movement response to the Cleveland crisis was a very muted affair, with the exception of Bea Campbell's book *Unofficial Secrets* (1988). Indeed, Campbell herself explains why:

> What the sexual abuse crisis of the 1980s has forced us to confront is that the perpetrators aren't dangerous strangers, lunatics exiled from settled communities. They're the men we all know, not so much the outcasts as the men *in* our lives, respectable dads, neighbours, stockbrokers and shop stewards, judges and jurors. They are men of all ages, races, religions and classes.
>
> Because *sexual* crime has not been seen as an expression of a *social* relationship, we have been left with the politics of crime and punishment, from which we all retreat when we are faced with these realities of sexual abuse ... The key words that come from when we talk about child sexual abuse are protection and punishment. Can we really protect children? And do we really want to *punish* the men involved? All these questions shadowed Cleveland's catharsis – and yet they were largely suppressed in the subsequent public debate.
>
> (1988: 5–6)

Indeed, the Children Act surprisingly, given its appearance in the wake of the Butler-Sloss Report, has very little to say specifically on these issues.

PAYING THE BILL FOR CHILDREN?

In conclusion, then, although heralded as a comprehensive reform of child care law, the Children Act is clearly now an extremely limited exercise in reforming those parts of child care law that relate to children who are deemed not to be in 'normal' nuclear families. The reforms themselves appear to reinvigorate notions of the privacy of the family, through re-inforcing the key concept of parental responsibility. They reduce state responsibility for child care, except to assess the extent of risk of dangerousness or need for support. In those respects, the law will leave mothers very much on their own, in the privacy of their own homes, without the general support of social services or social welfare, to care for children. No additional resources are to be devoted to our children who are our future. It seems that it is resources for child care to support parental responsibility that should also be the key concept in the Children Act – or the children themselves will pay the price.

NOTE

1   National Children's Home, Family Rights Group and Association of Directors of Social Services, Child Care Law Reform Seminar, 23 January 1989, Great Western Hotel, Paddington, London: keynote speaker: Professor Brenda Hoggett.

REFERENCES

Aplin, G..and Pugh, G. (eds) (1983) *Perspectives on Pre-school Home Visiting*, London: National Children's Bureau.
Bronfenbrenner, V. (1974) *Is Early Intervention Effective? A Report on the Longitudinal Evaluations of Pre-school Programmes*, Washington: Office of Child Development, US Department of Health, Education and Welfare.
Butler-Sloss, Lord Justice E. (1988) *Report of the Inquiry into Child Abuse in Cleveland 1987*, Cm. 412, London: HMSO.
Campbell, B. (1988) *Unofficial Secrets*, London: Virago.
Centre for Educational Research and Innovation (CERI) (1982) *Caring for Children*, OECD.
Children's Legal Centre (1989) 'A bill for children', *Briefing* 7–10.
David, M. (1980) *The State, the Family and Education*, London: Routledge & Kegan Paul.
—— (1985) 'Motherhood and social policy – a matter of education?', *Critical Social Policy* 12: 28–43.
Department of Employment (1987) *New Earnings Survey 1986*, Part E, London: HMSO.
Edwards, R. (1988) 'Pre-school home visiting projects: a case study of mothers' expectations and experiences', unpublished MSc dissertation, LSE.
—— (1989) 'Pre-school home visiting projects: a case study of mothers' expectations and experiences', *Gender and Education* 1, 2: 165–183.
Finch, J. (1984a) *Education as Social Policy*, Harlow: Longman.
—— (1984b) 'The deceit of self-help: pre-school playgroups and working class mothers', Journal of Social Policy 13:1.

Glendinning, C. and Millar, J. (eds) (1987) Women and Poverty, Brighton: Wheatsheaf.

Hewlett, S.A. (1987) *A Lesser Life: The Myth of Women's Liberation*, Harmondsworth: Penguin Books.

Joshi, H. (1987) 'The cost of caring', in C. Glendinning and J. Millar (eds) *Women and Poverty*, Brighton: Wheatsheaf.

Land, H. and Ward, S. (1986) *Women Won't Benefit*, London: National Council for Civil Liberties.

Lewis, J. (1986) 'Anxieties about the family and the relationship between parents, children and the State in twentieth century England', in M. Richards and P. Light (eds) Children of Social Worlds: Development in a Social Context, Cambridge: Polity Press.

London Borough of Brent (1986) *A Child in Trust: The Report of the Panel of Inquiry into the Circumstances Surrounding the Death of Jasmine Beckford*, Brent Town Hall.

London Borough of Greenwich (1987) *A Child in Mind: Protection of Children in a Responsible Society: The Report of a Commission of Inquiry into the Circumstances Surrounding the Death of Kimberley Carlile*, Greenwich Town Hall.

London Borough of Lambeth (1987) *Whose Child? The Report of the Public Inquiry into the Death of Tyra Henry*, Lambeth Town Hall.

Martin, J. and Roberts, C. (1984) *Women and Employment: A Lifetime Perspective*, London: HMSO.

Moss, P. (1988/9) 'The indirect costs of parenthood: a neglected issue in social policy', *Critical Social Policy* 24: 20–37.

Mount, F (1983) *The Subversive Family*, Harmondsworth: Penguin Books.

New, C. and David, M. (1985) *For the Children's Sake: Making Child Care More Than Women's Business*, Harmondsworth: Penguin Books.

OPCS (1987) *General Household Survey 1985*, London: HMSO.

Parton, C. and Parton, N. (1988/9) 'Women, the family and child protection', *Critical Social Policy* 24: 38–49.

Piper, C. (1988) 'Divorce conciliation in the UK: how responsible are parents?', *International Journal of the Sociology of Law* 16.

Poulton, L. (1983) 'Origins and development of pre-school home visiting', in G. Aplin and G. Pugh (eds) *Perspectives on Pre-school Home Visiting*, London: National Children's Bureau.

Poulton, L. and James, T. (1975) *Preschool Learning in the Community: Strategies for Change*, London: Routledge & Kegan Paul.

Rowbotham, S. (1989) 'To be or not to be: the dilemmas of mothering', *Feminist Review: Twenty Years of Feminism* 31: 82–93.

Smith, D.E. (1988) *The Everyday World as Problematic*, Milton Keynes: Open University Press.

Smith, G.A. (1975) 'The West Riding project', Educational Priority, vol. 4, London: HMSO.

Smith, T. (1980) *Parents and Pre-school*, London: Grant McIntyre.

Social Services Select Committee (1984) *Children in Care*, London: HMSO.

Wadsworth, M. and Maclean, M. (1986) 'Parents' divorce and children's life chances', *Children and Youth Services Review* 8: 145–59.

Weitzman, L.J. (1985) *The Divorce Revolution: The Unexpected Social and Economic Consequences for Women and Children in America*, New York: Free Press.

White Paper (1987) The Law on Child Care and Family Services, Cm. 62, London: HMSO.

7 Women and community care
Reflections on a debate

Sally Baldwin and Julia Twigg

INTRODUCTION

No man – or woman – is an island. We depend on each other for survival. But some of us – small children and people disabled by physical or mental incapacity or by frailty in old age – are more dependent on others for our basic human needs to be met. In most societies at most times, the sexual division of labour has given responsibility for the care of people who are frail or vulnerable to women – within families and on the basis of love or duty. The archetypal images are of women as nurturers and carers, and men as financial providers and protectors. It is startling, then, to reflect that it is only in the past fifteen years or so that the meaning for women of their role as carers, and its consequences for their life chances has begun to be examined systematically – and policy makers to be confronted with questions about the justice and acceptability of what has emerged.

This shift, from caring as a taken-for-granted and unquantified aspect of women's lives to its identification as *problematic* – warranting conceptual analysis and empirical investigation – resulted from the debate and scholarship generated by the women's movement of the early 1970s. Liberal feminists had earlier engaged with the position of women in society generally, leaving the relations of men and women within families largely unquestioned. For the new wave of feminists, these relations and their connection to women's oppression in the wider society were a primary focus. The sexual division of labour within the family was the fulcrum around which analysis of gender relations swung. Crucially, the definition of women's unpaid activity within the home as *work* opened the way for critical appraisal of the relations between women and men, both within the family and in the public sphere. A pioneering stream of research – by Gavron (1966), Oakley (1974), Pahl (1980), and others – rigorously analysed what went on in the domestic sphere: raising and answering questions about who did what for whom, to whose benefit and cost. A parallel stream of work by feminists interested in social policy pointed up the connections between these domestic divisions of labour and Government policies – notably those promoting the care of elderly and disabled people 'in the community'.

In its original form, community care policy had envisaged a significant role for public services in maintaining highly dependent people outside large institutions. By the late 1970s, this was less clearly the case. Under the twin pressures of fiscal crisis and an ideologically driven commitment to reducing the role of the state in service provision, the original vision was replaced by a much stronger emphasis on the provision of care by 'the community' itself (Parker 1990). At this point, gender emerged for the first time as a key variable in the analysis of community care policy in a paper presented by Janet Finch and Dulcie Groves to the Annual Conference of the Social Administration Association, and subsequently published in the *Journal of Social Policy* (Finch and Groves 1980).

Finch and Groves' paper transformed the existing debate on community care in two ways. It cut through the euphemistic language of 'community' and 'family' to argue that community care was essentially about the care provided by women; and it discussed the effects of caring on women's life chances in terms of equality of opportunities with men.

The authors argued that community care policy stood to intensify the inequalities women already experienced by virtue of the care they provided – both for children and for relatives with physical or mental disabilities. The demanding and continuous nature of this work and the fact that it was unpaid meant that women's access to time and money of their own was much less than that of the men in their families. Caring responsibilities also reduced women's opportunities for entering the labour force on an equal footing. Policy in the field of community care was based on the assumption that such exploitation would continue, and indeed increase. The irony that government was simultaneously committed, however weakly (via equal opportunities and anti-discrimination legislation), to pursuing equal opportunities for women in the labour market gave particular force to the authors' argument.

In the decade since Finch and Groves' paper, the debate on community care and its exploitation of women's labour has continued and developed – fuelled principally by the research and scholarship of feminists in the field of social policy. In this chapter we review the current state of the debate, outlining the impasse which it now seems to have reached, and suggesting ways of moving it on. In reviewing the current state of the debate, we will refer in particular to two authors: Janet Finch and Gillian Dalley. Both draw extensively on feminist analyses. Their related but differing viewpoints will be used as a springboard to discuss the current tensions within community care policy, particularly in regard to the role of women.

SAYING NO TO COMMUNITY CARE

In 1984, Janet Finch published an attack on community care policy (Finch 1984). The paper caused considerable controversy – principally because of its argument for the rejection of community care and its replacement by an expansion of care in institutions. Finch's critique turned around the central issue of whether a non-sexist version of community care was possible, or whether the concept was, as Wilson (1982) and others had argued, essentially gendered, and of its nature exploitative of women.

The question raised by Finch is important and timely for two reasons. First, she rightly identifies unresolved ambiguities in feminist thinking with regard to informal and community care. The problem, as she sees it, is that we know what we are *against*, but do not clearly know what we are *for*.

> We are clear what we want to reject: we reject so-called community care policies which depend on the substantial and consistent input of women's unpaid labour in the home, whilst at the same time effectively excluding them from the labour market and reinforcing their economic and personal dependence on men. But what do we want to promote as an alternative? . . . It seems to me that no clear answer to this question can be found in recent feminist writings on community care, and also that we *need* an answer if we want the message about community care to make a deeper impact upon other people who engage with social policy.
>
> (Finch 1984: 6)

The second reason why Finch's comments are so pertinent lies in the continuing and accelerating trend towards community care, and the support for it found across a spectrum of opinion that extends from the 'new right', across liberal reformers, to radicals and socialists. This last group are particularly significant for Finch since they represent a constituency who can otherwise be regarded as broadly sympathetic to feminist issues. The recasting of community care that writers like Walker (1982), for example, present, thus offers a potentially sympathetic way forward. Walker's support for the policy has, as its basis, the conviction that community care has the potential for greatly increasing the control people can exercise over their lives, reducing the power of professionals and bureaucrats and making service delivery more democratic and more accountable. However, Walker's account and that of others on the left who seek to reform community care, raise the fundamental question of whether such developments

can only be advanced at the expense of women. Walker argues for a policy
. that would not depend primarily on female kin; that would entail the
expansion of services and allow the cared-for greater control in the determination of their needs. He nevertheless envisages the family as the prime
locus of social care. Here, for Finch, lies the rub. How *can* community care
be reformed when it continues to rest on an institution identified by
feminists as profoundly sexist?

Finch's critique draws on the growing body of work – both empirical
and theoretical – exploring the incidence and character of care-giving. As a
result of this work, we now have a much clearer understanding of the nature
of informal care. Before examining Finch's argument in detail, we will
briefly review the main elements that make up this new understanding.

The first element is a perception of informal care as primarily care
provided by women. As noted above, terms like 'community care' and
'family care' systematically obscure this simple reality. Recent research,
however, for example data from the 1985 General Household Survey
(Green 1988; Arber *et al.* 1988), has slightly dented the assurance with
which this statement is made. Men are more involved in care-giving than
had previously been supposed, and further work is needed to explore
adequately the incidence and characteristics of informal caring by men. It
appears likely that the greater involvement of men is largely explained by
the particular role of the spouse-carer, which to some degree overrides the
gendered division of labour in the provision of care. One of the most
significant developments in the recent carer literature has been the trend to
disaggregate the category of carer and explore how its dynamics operate
differentially in regard to different relationships. Much of the feminist
literature has been concerned with the unequal burdens of women in
relation to the care of elderly people, of disabled offspring and other kin.
This emphasis may have obscured important differences that obtain where
the dependent person is one's spouse and where considerations of gender
are less clearly dominant (Parker 1989).

Having noted this, however, it does still appear that women are more
involved than men in the heavy end of care-giving (Green 1988). And thus,
although the simple equation of informal care with care by women needs
some amendment, the general understanding of caring as a predominantly
female activity remains.

The unequal sharing is further reinforced by the tendency for one person
to be assigned the full responsibility of caring. There is still debate as to
whether this pattern has been exaggerated by research methodologies that
focus on a single carer rather than a wider network (Smith and Cantley
1983). However, the trend of evidence supports the view that genuinely
shared care is relatively rare. There appear to be dynamics in the caring

relationship that lead to one person taking on all, or the majority, of the tending work. Where tasks are shared in the kin network, they tend to be the more remote and less arduous activities such as entertaining the dependent person, taking them to hospital, doing the garden or paying for treats. Men tend to be more involved in these types of support, rather than in the more intimate tasks of personal care, with the frequency and consequent restriction these involve.

The unequal sharing of the burden of caring applies particularly within families that share a household. Nissel and Bonnerjea, for example, studying households consisting of couples caring for an elderly person who lived with them, found that a number of the husbands were only peripherally involved in their wives' caring activities, even where the elderly dependant was their own parent. Some, indeed, were hostile to their wives' caring activity, seeing it as a deflection of attentions that should come to them. Others were supportive, but indirectly – through emotional support rather than the sharing of tasks. Thus, in terms of time spent, the husbands averaged 8 minutes per day, in contrast to the 139 minutes of their wives (Nissel and Bonnerjea 1982). Ungerson's study makes similar points concerning the unequal distribution of the burden of care (Ungerson 1987). A growing body of research points to the effects of these responsibilities on the psychological and physical health of women carers (Parker 1990).

There is also evidence that male carers receive more help from statutory services than female, though the evidence is somewhat fragmentary. Wright's study of single carers did show such a pattern, but it was based on a relatively small number of cases (Wright 1986). Arber *et al.*'s analysis of General Household Survey data on the receipt of home help and district nursing support did not endorse a simple gender bias, but did demonstrate a bias in the provision of support against carers who were married women (Arber *et al.* 1988). It is not yet clear how far this pattern is the result of discriminatory allocation by service providers, of the internalized values of carers themselves or, as Parker's recent research suggests, of a failure to develop the kinds of help women carers are likely to perceive as useful – help with household maintenance and repairs, for example, rather than housework (Parker 1989).

The imbalance between men and women does not apply only to the physical and emotional burdens involved. It also has material consequences, both in the short and in the longer term, arising from reduced employment prospects and forgone pension rights. (See, for example, Baldwin 1985; Hirst 1986; Nissel and Bonnerjea 1982; Glendinning 1989.) The financial losses and long-term vulnerability consequent on caring affect both men and women who are substantially involved. However, there is reason to believe that women are affected to a greater degree: more of them are affected and they are more likely to give up employment to care or to delay re-entry to the labour force. Again, the issue is a complex one. Recent work by Glendinning (1989) highlights the difference in effect between households with single carers and those where the dependant lives with two or more adult relatives. It seems that married women carers may be protected financially, to a degree, in that some will receive future and current benefits from their husbands' paid employment. Against this, their access to money of their own is conditional on a husband's decisions, and there is no guarantee that divorce will not remove access to pension rights gained through a husband's contributions. The greater earning capacity of most male employees is frequently used in this context to legitimate the gendered pattern of caring (Becker 1981), but its explanatory power remains dubious in the context of powerful cultural assumptions.

Some of these cultural assumptions have been explored in recent work that has sought to explain *why* caring is seen as women's work. The explanation of women's identification as carers is clearly complex. One of the roots lies in normative expectations of kinship obligations. Qureshi and Walker (1989), for example, have explored the ways in which cultural assumptions lead to a preference being given to female rather than male kin in the support of frail elderly people. Thus, daughters are more likely to be assigned responsibility for caring for a parent than are sons. This pattern holds, moreover, where the relationship is that of in-law; men appear able to discharge their obligations to frail kin through the labour of their wives. The pattern is complicated, and gender is not the only factor. The existence of a spouse relationship or co-residence with the elderly person can override the gendered pattern. It remains the case, however, that gender is a major element in the distribution of responsibility. Kinship obligations for care are discharged mainly by women.

Kinship obligation is clearly only part of the answer as to why caring is assigned to women. In attempting to understand why it is so and why this is accepted by women, accounts conceptualizing care primarily in terms of structurally assigned tasks have had to give way to more complex accounts that recognize the particular mix of obligation, love, opportunity and physical labour that characterizes women's experience of caring for others. Above all, it is important to understand the ways in which care-giving is congruent with other aspects of women's work and lives.

Thus, informal care shares many of the characteristics of the work that women undertake in both the paid and unpaid sectors. It tends to be flexible, and performed without relation to status or training. It often involves responsiveness to the needs of others, in ways that override the subject's own interests. Caring work is often repetitive and carried out over long hours. Indeed, there are usually no limits circumscribing its performance;

the obligations are continuous and open-ended. To a degree then, caring is best understood in the context of all the work women do in holding together their families, the economy and society – the 'crazy quilting' so vividly described by Balbo (1987). Often involving physical contact of an intimate character, its defining qualities – ideally at least – are emotional warmth and self-sacrifice. The dominant cultural perception of caring sees it as involving essentially female qualities. This perception, which is shared by many women, is used to explain and justify the gendered division of caring. It thus appears more 'appropriate' for women to be the ones who wash, toilet, feed and care for people who are ill or frail. (The strong parallels with child care that permeate the whole subject serve further to underwrite perceptions of caring as an essentially female activity.)

Two writers in particular have explored some of the deeper ways in which the association of caring with femaleness is structured. Ungerson's argument concerns the cultural rules that might proscribe men from – or allow them to avoid – dealing directly with human excrement or certain forms of nakedness (Ungerson 1981). Since the personal care of dependent people often involves both of these, this cultural pattern, she argues, effectively precludes men from being involved or imposes tensions that make the situation unstable. There are problems in Ungerson's argument, notably around her use of the concept of incest and the fixity with which these cultural 'taboos' are endowed. Empirical work, including Ungerson's own (1987), indicates that they are less strong than she had previously suggested, though such patterns do emerge in large-scale survey data (Arber *et al.* 1988). Ungerson has therefore identified a significant dimension of caring which might indeed limit the extent to which the burden is likely to be shared between women and men.

Graham's work has been particularly important in attempting to integrate women's experience of caring as both labour and love (Graham 1983). Drawing on the work of Chodorow (1978) and Baker Miller (1976), she explores the ways in which female self-identity is constructed around the giving of care. This caring, she suggests (in both the sense of caring *about* and caring *for*), underwrites women's self-identity at a profound level. Men, by contrast, achieve a sense of self-worth through activity and the achievement of goals in relation to themselves. These distinctions at the psychological level are linked to the wider sexual division of labour within society. As far as women and informal care are concerned, they help to explain not only why women continue to provide care in spite of the many disadvantages involved, but also why many experience satisfaction in doing so.

It is important to distinguish these understandings from biological determinism – the idea that women are somehow genetically programmed to care. None of the evidence concerning what caring actually involves supports such a view.

To summarize, the work on informal care carried out over the last decade shows:

- that the care of non-spousal dependent people falls primarily to women;
- that it is unshared to a significant extent by relatives, statutory or voluntary agencies;
- that it creates burdens and material costs which are a source of significant inequalities between men and women;
- that many women nevertheless accept the role of informal carer and, indeed, derive satisfaction from doing so;
- that the reasons for this state of affairs are deeply bound up with the construction of female and male identity, and possibly also with culturally defined rules about gender-appropriate behaviours.

Given this understanding of the nature of informal care, what, for feminists, is the way forward? Here we return to Finch's analysis. Finch (1984) believes the prospects for non-sexist forms of community care are not encouraging. Care by 'the family' is transparently sexist. Moreover, if we look at new developments within community care, we find that they also draw strongly – and exploitatively – on the character of caring as women's work.

Finch points first to the expansion of schemes that use volunteers to underwrite the community care of dependent people. A range of schemes operate on this basis, and the great majority of the volunteers involved are female. Some of the tensions around the use of such workers have been explored, though within a less strongly feminist framework, by Leat and Gay (1987) and Thornton (1989). Finch refers particularly to the Kent Community Care Scheme which has been widely influential in the development of such flexible, quasi-informal roles (Davies and Challis 1986; Challis and Davies 1986). Not all such schemes employ purely voluntary labour. Some operate on a quasi-voluntary basis, making token payments. Others use paid workers. Where they do, however, the pay rates are typically low, and the workers predominantly female. The flexible character of such schemes is one of their major virtues, and it explains their potential importance in the reform of community care. Flexibility is a quality that is particularly demanded of women workers, but it is one that operates to their detriment in the male-structured world of paid employment. It is clear, furthermore, that these schemes draw heavily on the expectation – well-founded in practice – that women will not only work flexibly for little reward, but will, in addition, develop close affective relations with those for whom they care, albeit as part of a job (see chapter 8 of this volume).

·Turning to attempts to support informal carers through benefits such as invalid care allowance, or support from services designed to help carers go on caring, Finch once again adopts a critical stance. Such moves to support carers, however laudable, do not affect the fundamentally gendered character of community care and only serve, she argues, to lock women more firmly into discriminatory and sexist ways of life. (There are clear parallels here with the wages for housework issue, and the criticisms of that approach as potentially limiting the opportunities of women by tying them to the domestic sphere, albeit in waged rather than unwaged labour (Fairbairns 1985).) Finch is willing to support such developments on a humanitarian basis, but sceptical about their role in any longer-term strategy.

Finally, Finch turns to the work of Ungerson and Graham. Here again, the message is a pessimistic one. The social and cultural assumptions that lock women into caring are structured at a deep level. We do not have to subscribe to the belief that they are natural patterns to appreciate that they are deeply rooted and hard to change. Graham's argument in particular, she believes:

> pushes us away from any slick solutions to the problem of women-as-carers. We may profoundly disapprove of women's social identity being so significantly defined by their relationships with other people, but while that remains the case, the prospects for non-sexist forms of caring remain bleak.
>
> (Finch 1984: 15)

Community care, Finch concludes, is a fundamentally gendered concept. Reformers like Walker may, she argues, be aware of the issue of gender and include some discussion of it, but they do not really face up to how deeply entrenched the problem is and how radical, therefore, are the changes needed to overcome it. The status quo seems set to persist.

At this point, Finch makes a dramatic leap, suggesting that the only answer to this impasse lies in the expansion of institutional care. This is the part of her article that provoked the greatest objection, particularly, as Finch has herself noted, by male writers (Harris 1985 and, albeit also writing in defence of the interests of people with disabilities, Oliver 1986). It is important to ask at this point *why* she makes this leap, since the preceding argument does not lead smoothly up to it and the conclusion is presented with very little development.

The argument is primarily a polemical one: community care is un-reformable. We must get rid of it. It is about finally *saying no* to the exploitation of women and finding the means to underwrite that saying no. Implicit in the statement is an idea that institutions will somehow make visible the collective responsibility that exists for the care of dependent people. Neglect of this is possible in the community, partly because needs are hidden within the privacy of people's homes, but also because families – or rather women – step into the breach. Thus, Finch seems to be saying, the only way to ensure that the assumption of responsibility by women, against their own interests, can be broken is the physical removal of people who cannot manage without extensive support. Institutional care is the only way women have effectively to say no.

While we share Finch's concerns, we do not accept her conclusion. We will argue that the polemical polarization that she sets up between family and institutional care is unhelpful. What we should continue to aim for is community care provided on a non-sexist basis. This is still the strategic way forward, despite the tactical danger of subverting the ideal through partial implementation. We return to these issues later in the chapter.

THE RE-ASSERTION OF THE COLLECTIVE?

We argued above that Finch's call for a return to institutional forms of care is best understood as polemic. It is about saying *no* to the exploitation of women carers, and refusing to be diverted from this by putting the needs of dependent people first. As such, institutions are not presented by Finch as having a value of their own – though they are not without attractions for socialists. By contrast, Gillian Dalley's work (1983, 1988) begins from the premise that collective forms of living *do* have value – for those who live in them as well as those they liberate from 'family' responsibility. Her starting point is a preoccupation with the question of why – after a brief flowering in the 1960s – the valuing of collective ways of living has given way to a re-assertion of familial lifestyles and responsibilities.

In fact, Dalley's critique shares much with that of Finch. Both draw on the feminist critique of the family (as central in the oppression of women), and both locate informal care within that ideological and social construct. Dalley, however, is concerned to raise larger issues about how we live our lives. In doing this, she argues that many of the problems of community care are engendered by a false emphasis on the family – in both our descriptive analyses of society and our prescriptions for care. Thus, while Finch enjoins institutional care as a – somewhat dramatic – solution to the exploitation of women carers, Dalley suggests a revaluation of the principle of collec- tivism. The opposite of family care is not necessarily institutional care. There are, she believes, other ways of living.

Dalley identifies two ideological constructs as having central import-ance: familialism and possessive individualism. Like many feminists, she argues that the pervasive familialism of modern society provides the inter-nalized ideological structure that underwrites our perception of caring as women's work. It is in the relationships of the family that such assumptions are forged. Men are seen as natural 'providers', women as natural carers. Government policies build on and reinforce this picture, presuming the availability and altruism of women – though, as Land and Rose (1985) have argued, it is a compulsory altruism.

The hegemonic nature of familialism, Dalley argues, means that it is the standard against which all forms of non-family living are judged – and deemed deviant or irrelevant. So pervasive is the ideology of the family that people internalize its valuations, even when these run counter to their own experience or interests. Different ways of living are thus devalued or ignored.

The second, and related, construct is possessive individualism. For Dalley this is a gendered concept, applying in its fullest sense only to men. It is by ignoring this that new right thinkers are able to resolve the tension between their radical individualism and the strong value they place on the family. Men are the real subjects in these sentences; their families occupy a subordinate and secondary role, representing the emotional and private *parts* of men's lives rather than possessing individual subjectivity in themselves.

Taken together, Dalley argues, the dominance of these two ideological strands, and particularly their recrudescence in the last fifteen years, has led to a devaluation of the collective. In a search for alternative models, she reviews the literature in relation to three areas in which she believes greater prominence has been given to collective values.

First, she examines the anthropological literature which demonstrates that possessive individualism has not always been the dominant mode that it is in the modern west, and that family and related social structures have themselves been very varying. She recognizes, however, that more collective, or at least non-nuclear, family forms are not necessarily benign in regard to women.

The second area is the collectivist tradition which flourished largely in nineteenth- and twentieth-century Britain and America. This encompasses a range of ventures – religious, political and utopian – setting up communal forms of living. Dalley notes the problems and instabilities of such attempts, rightly identifying the central problem posed to them by the pair bond. And again she acknowledges the ways in which these communitarian forms of living typically do not enhance the freedoms of women. Unless gender issues are confronted head-on, collective ways of living simply replicate the gendered division of labour in new forms. Moves towards egality and fraternity are of little use if the 'natural' nature of women and their tasks remains unchallenged. Interestingly, Dalley does not identify the major sources of strength in such institutions. These, we would argue, are their radical separation from the world – reinforced by strong physical and symbolic boundaries – and the existence of a powerful ideology to provide the uniting force.

Third, Dalley turns to the history of the dominant western tradition. Her argument here is that the value of collective responsibility for dependent people has always been present. There is a well-established tradition of collective responsibility for the vulnerable; less residualist than some commentators suggest. We misread the past if we believe that the only support provided for such people was by the family.

Dalley's objective in drawing on these three areas is partly to remind us that more collective forms of living are possible, and she clearly succeeds in this. What is less clear, however, is how these understandings derived from other societies and other periods can directly influence our thinking about the ways care for dependent people in contemporary Britain should be organized.

Insights from other societies do help us to see that particular social forms and their related ideologies – in this case nuclear families and possessive individualism – are not inevitable. But this perception does not allow us to co-opt these different forms, or to detach them from the very different cultural settings that have produced them. Nor does the collective living tradition, at least in its communitarian, Utopian forms, offer much that could provide a sound basis for care. The roots of success in this field – isolation from the world and a powerful uniting ideology – do not generally apply to people who come together through disability. Equality between men and women is far from guaranteed by collective forms of living. The aspect of this tradition that seems to offer the most fruitful insights for the provision of care concerns the role of social groupings. This suggests that we should perhaps give greater emphasis to communal forms of living structured around social, cultural or religious identities. (The role of Jewish institutions and voluntary agencies provides one effective example.) The universalism of public provision in Britain means that we have probably paid too little attention to *differences* and to bonds that rest on communal exclusion.

The historical tradition of collective responsibility does have things to say that are of practical relevance to policy and to the feminist debate. However, this tradition underwrites collective responsibility, not collective provision. It thus brings us back to the problem of what collectively financed provision would look like, were it to be reformed along non-sexist lines.

Dalley's work is therefore difficult to incorporate directly into policy. Nevertheless it expands the scope of the debate considerably, moving us on from Finch's bleak polarization of care into that provided in 'institutions' (often depersonalizing, poor in quality, and a last resort for both carers and cared-for); and in 'families' (exploiting and impoverishing carers and reducing the autonomy of 'dependants'). The implication is that we need to look further at both collective and independent options; and in particular uncouple the link too often made between closeness, care, a holistic response to the vulnerable person and 'the family'.

WAYS FORWARD?

In thinking about what the way forward might be, we would begin by making four observations. The first, rather obvious, observation is that the sexual divisions in caring which currently disadvantage women are closely bound up with other aspects of their subordination – crucially with their status in the labour force, where low pay and part-time work strongly confirm the 'common sense' of identifying them as carers. This situation is not unchanging. Currently predicted changes in the structure of employment together with labour shortages caused by a decline in the numbers of younger workers may lead to a revaluation of women's place in the labour force. Already policies are being designed both at government and employer level to help women with children to enter the labour force. Such developments could well work to the advantage of carers who in many ways face similar employment problems to those of women with children.

The second is that the feminist debate has, so far, neglected the common interests carers share with the people they look after. The emphasis has been on ties of affection and obligation, with the emphasis on the carer. This ignores important aspects of the dependent person's experience: the fact that they *are* cast as dependent and the meaning this has for them. It also ignores the political interests carer and cared-for have in common.

A third point concerns the variety of people with disabilities and their carers. Feminist discussion of informal care tends to focus on very dependent elderly people cared for by daughters or daughters-in-law. Clearly these represent a large group, although the dependent population is extremely heterogeneous. It contains disabled children and teenagers; adults with physical and mental disabilities; people cared for by parents, spouses and siblings. The limited research that has been done indicates that they want and need different things. Young adults, for example, are less likely to favour staying at home, cared for by relatives. Spouses are likely to find anything else unacceptable. Carers' preferences are equally varied and likely to depend as much on the nature and quality of their relationship with the dependent person as the type and degree of care needed or the time for which this will persist. Solutions to the problems of carers have to take this variety on board.

The final point is that the terms of the debate have shifted since Finch's 1984 paper, as the momentum behind community care policies has increased. Spurred on by the availability of social security for 'board and lodging', a wide range of hybrid, in-between types of living arrangement have developed.

For older people these include a variety of schemes to adapt housing to make it possible for people to stay put in their own homes as long as possible; sheltered and very sheltered housing for those who need support closer at hand and, increasingly, 'retirement complexes' where it is possible to receive varying levels of support on one site as the need for it arises. People who are mentally ill or handicapped can, according to the degree of support they need, find accommodation in hostels, group homes and assisted lodgings. For people who are severely physically disabled, housing associations and voluntary organizations have begun to develop schemes specially designed to make independent living more possible. This is not to suggest that such facilities are widespread or easily available. Models do, however, exist.

Finch's dichotomizing of 'community' (female) versus 'institutional care' now seems less relevant. The means are more available than ever before to sustain very dependent people in their own homes, or in a variety of residential settings, with varying degrees of support from statutory, private and voluntary agencies. The debate now centres on the boundaries between individual, 'family' and collective responsibility for meeting needs arising from disability or old age.

Where does this take us in the quest for a way out of the double bind identified by Finch? Finch's own view is bleak. Community care is irredeemably sexist. Policies purporting to help carers simply lock them more tightly into caring. Only institutional care offers a true solution. But because the labour of care-giving is so intertwined with love and obligation, most women will resist this solution. Major social and economic change would be needed to change this. The only intellectually honest position may be to give up the quest for non-sexist forms of care until these changes have occurred and to accept in the meantime that women will go on caring.

We would argue that Finch's scenario is *too* bleak. Her analysis is most flawed in failing to take sufficient account of the perspective of the person cared for. Feminist analysis has understandably concentrated on the effects on women's lives of moving responsibility for care back into 'the family'. It is important to recognize that the effects are equally damaging for the person cast as dependent. Croft's (1986) paper recognizes the potential for community care policies to divide and rule, setting carers and cared for in opposition and deflecting attention from collective responsibilities. A strategy that directed itself to meeting their common needs would, we suggest, be the most effective approach.

Finch's scenario also seems over-pessimistic. It seems important to acknowledge that progress *has* been made, even if only to sustain us in what looks like a never-ending struggle. There has been a significant shift, for example, in the force with which policy makers argue explicitly that families must assume responsibility for dependent relatives. The language used is cast more often, nowadays, in terms of shared responsibility. There is more acknowledgement of the dependent person's right to exercise choice in decisions about where and how they live. The independent living movement is increasingly vocal in challenging the lack of provision to support disabled people in setting up their own homes. The Wagner Report (1988) has stressed the importance of helping people with disabilities to make positive choices about moving to residential care. In the case of older people, policy increasingly focuses on ways of enabling them to plan for and finance their own care. Public awareness of the situation of carers has also grown. There is evidence that the general public has quite complex views of family obligation and does not regard family care as invariably the right choice for all people who are very dependent (West 1984). There are also signs of improvement at the local level. A number of local authorities have established initiatives to identify carers and improve support to them. Carers are becoming more visible in legislation. The Disabled Persons Act 1986 gives carers the right to request an assessment of their dependant's needs and of their own ability to go on caring. The changes in the wake of the 1990 NHS and Community Care Act should create similar opportunities. Finally, as noted above, economic and demographic change will increase the demand for women in the labour force. This will inevitably affect their availability as carers.

None of this will dramatically transform the current situation, in which women's commitment to relatives is exploited by policy makers in both central and local government. But neither is it true that no progress has been made or that none *can* be made.

It seems to us quite possible to envisage a tactical approach that would improve the current situation of carers without jeopardizing the longer-term strategic aim of eradicating sexual divisions in caring. Such an approach would aim to shift responsibility for meeting the needs of dependent people both between the informal and formal sectors of welfare and between women and men. It would not depend on saying 'no' to community care, but on changing the balance of public and private provision.

This strategy, we would argue, should rest on two arguments. The first is the existence of a collective responsibility for people unable to survive independently. This can be delegated to an extent – but not to the extent that those discharging the collective obligation are prevented from leading relatively ordinary lives. Moreover, accepting that there *is* a collective obligation implies that carers (women) have rights to support and compensation.

The second argument concerns the rights of carers and people with disabilities to be treated *as* individuals – individual citizens with individual, and in some cases conflicting, interests. It is not acceptable that people who are very disabled should be forced to rely on relatives to have their basic needs met. The rights of each to a degree of choice and self-determination should be recognized. This does not mean creating disincentives to care for relatives, simply creating the possibility of choice – and supporting both people who decide to care for relatives, and disabled people who choose to live separately. (This principle can be seen in operation in the Nordic countries, and particularly in Norway, where families are not assumed to be responsible for the physical care of elderly parents and can be paid for providing care. In practice, very few women in Norway do provide large amounts of care to elderly relatives. Payment for care seems not, in practice, to reinforce the idea of caring as women's work.)

In practical terms, a strategy to improve the situation of carers while also weakening sexual divisions in caring would have three elements: policies to minimize dependency; the creation of frameworks to enable women to exercise real choices; and support for people opting to care.

A policy aiming to minimize the dependence of older people or those with physical or mental disabilities would require action on a number of fronts. This would include:

– housing (an increase in independent living and staying put schemes, sheltered housing, group homes and other forms of collective living . . .);
– health care (particularly rehabilitation services and the development and dissemination of new kinds of equipment and technology . . .);
– employment and employment training (including financial incentives to employers, employment counselling . . .);
– social security (including the level of benefits and ways of combining benefits with earnings from work).

It would also require a dramatic change in the culture which treats people with disabilities as passive recipients of services controlled by the able-bodied.

Ways of enabling women to exercise more choice about decisions to care require equally far-reaching changes. They stretch, at the more Utopian end of the continuum, from:

- changes in the education and socialization of boys and girls;
- changes in employment training for women to raise the level of their skills and the kind of jobs they aspire to;
- action to reduce inequalities in men's and women's pay;
- changes in employment policies to give men and women the possibility of 'caring breaks';

to, more practically:

- improvements in support to dependent people in their own homes; and
- improvements in the range and quality of residential provision.

Improving support to people choosing to look after dependent relatives would include:

- rights to a regular re-assessment of the situation;
- appropriate practical help;
- counselling and emotional support;
- regular breaks from caring;
- financial support during and after the period of care-giving;
- training in particular aspects of care-giving.

Clearly this is an ideal – and perhaps Utopian – prescription. It is presented more as an indication of the ways in which policy should be moving than as a blueprint for immediate action. The three main points that we would wish to stress are:

- that it is probably impossible to change the situation of carers without reference to the quality of life of the people they feel responsible for;
- that the most fruitful avenue for this may be in maximizing the potential people with disabilities have for independence;
- that achieving this is strongly linked to challenging concepts of 'family' responsibility by reasserting the principle of collective responsibility.

Above all, we would argue that there *are* ways forward; that it is entirely possible to make the immediate and smaller scale improvements in carers' lives which are so long overdue without compromising the longer-term goal of creating a society in which caring for and about vulnerable people is seen as men's, as well as women's, work.

REFERENCES

Arber, S., Gilbert, N. and Evandrou, M. (1988) 'Gender, household composition and receipt of domiciliary services by the elderly disabled', *Journal of Social Policy* 17, 2: 153–76.

134 Sally Baldwin and Julia Twigg

Baker Miller, J. (1976) *Towards a New Psychology of Women*, London: Allen Lane.

Balbo, L. (1987) 'Crazy quilts: rethinking the welfare state debate from a woman's point of view', in A. Showstack Sassoon (ed.) *Women and the State*, London: Hutchinson.

Baldwin, S. (1985) *The Costs of Caring: Families with Disabled Children*, London: Routledge & Kegan Paul.

Becker, G.S. (1981) *A Treatise on the Family*, Cambridge, Mass.: Harvard University Press.

Challis, D. and Davies, B. (1986) *Case Management in Community Care: An Evaluated Experiment in the Home Care of the Elderly*, London: Gower.

Chodorow, N. (1978) *The Reproduction of Mothering: Psychoanalysis and the Sociology of Gender*, Berkeley: California University Press.

Croft, S. (1986) 'Women, caring and the recasting of need', in *Critical Social Policy* 16: 23–39.

Dalley, G. (1983) 'Ideologies of care: a feminist contribution to the debate', *Critical Social Policy* 8: 72–81.

—— (1988) *Ideologies of Caring: Rethinking Community and Collectivism*, London: Macmillan.

Davies, B.D. and Challis, D. (1986) *Matching Resources to Needs in Community Care*, London: Gower.

Fairbairns, Z. (1985) 'The co-habitation rule – why it makes sense', in C. Ungerson (ed.) *Women and Social Policy*, London: Macmillan.

Finch, J. (1984) 'Community care: developing non-sexist alternatives', *Critical Social Policy* 9: 6–18.

Finch, J. and Groves, D. (1980) 'Community care and the family: a case for equal opportunities?', *Journal of Social Policy* 9, 4: 486–511.

Gavron, H. (1966) *The Captive Wife*, Harmondsworth: Penguin Books.

Glendinning, C. (1989) 'The financial needs and circumstances of informal carers', Unpublished research report, University of York: Social Policy Research Unit.

Graham, H. (1983) 'Caring: a labour of love', in J. Finch and D. Groves (eds) *A Labour of Love: Women, Work and Caring*, London: Routledge.

Green, H. (1988) *Informal Carers: A Study*, London: OPCS, HMSO.

Griffiths, R. (1988) *Community Care: Agenda for Action*, London: HMSO.

Harris, R. (1985) '"End points and starting points" some critical remarks on Janet Finch "Community Care: Developing Non-Sexist Alternatives"', *Critical Social Policy* 12: 115–22.

Hirst, M. (1986) 'Young adults with disabilities: health, employment and financial costs for family carers', *Child-care, Health and Development* II: 291–307.

Land, H. and Rose, H. (1985) 'Compulsory altruism for some or an altruistic society for all', in P. Bean, J. Ferris and D. Whynes (eds) *In Defence of Welfare*, London: Tavistock.

Leat, D. and Gay, P. (1987) *Paying for Care: A Study of Policy and Practice in Paid Care Schemes*, London: PSI.

Nissel, M. and Bonnerjea, L. (1982) *Family Care of the Handicapped Elderly: Who Pays?*, London: PSI.

Oakley, A. (1974) *The Sociology of Housework*, Oxford: Martin Robertson.

Oliver, M. (1986) 'Social policy and disability: some theoretical issues', *Disability, Handicap and Society* 1, 1: 5–17.

Pahl, J. (1980) 'Patterns of money management', *Journal of Social Policy* 9, 3: 313–35.

Parker, G. (1990) (2nd edn) *With Due Care and Attention: A Review of Research on Informal Care*, London: Family Policy Studies Centre.
—— (1989) *A Study of Non-Elderly Spouse Carers*, unpublished research report, University of York: Social Policy Research Unit.
Qureshi, H. and Walker, A. (1989) *The Caring Relationship: Elderly People and their Families*, London: Macmillan.
Smith, G. and Cantley, C. (1983) 'Pluralistic evaluation: a study in daycare for the elderly mentally infirm', unpublished report.
Thornton, P. (1989) *Creating a Break: Home Care Relief for Elderly People and their Supporters*, London: Age Concern Institute of Gerontology.
Ungerson, C. (1981) 'Women and caring; skills, tasks and taboos', in E. Gamarnikow, D.H.J. Morgan, J. Purvis and D. Taylorson, *The Public and the Private*, London: Heinemann.
—— (1987) *Policy is Personal: Sex, Gender and Informal Care*, London: Tavistock.
Waerness, K. (1984) 'The rationality of caring', *Economic and Industrial Democracy* 5.
Wagner, G. (1988) *Residential Care: A Positive Choice*, London: NISW.
Walker, A. (1982) 'The meaning and social division of community care', in A. Walker (ed.) *Community Care: the Family, the State and Social Policy*, Oxford: Martin Robertson.
West, P. (1984) 'The family, the welfare state and community care: political rhetoric and public attitudes', *Journal of Social Policy* 13, 4: 417–46.
Wilson, E. (1982) 'Women, the "Community" and the "Family"', in A. Walker (ed.) *Community Care: the Family, the State and Social Policy*, Oxford: Martin Robertson.
Wright, F.D. (1986) *Left to Care Alone*, Aldershot: Gower.

8 'What d'ya want if you don' want money?'

A feminist critique of 'paid volunteering'

John Baldock and Clare Ungerson

INTRODUCTION

'Paid volunteering' is an ambiguous and self-contradictory term. In our exploration of the phenomenon and its meaning for women, we have found that this essential ambiguity persists whatever criteria of evaluation are used. We are not the first to have found this by any means: Diana Leat, in a particularly telling series of pamphlets and articles, has herself explored many of the ambiguities (Leat and Gay 1987; Leat 1988). Like her, we have found great difficulty in settling whether paid volunteering is a step forward or backwards, is beneficial or exploitative, is a break with tradition or merely an extension of it, is good or bad for helpers or helped, for volunteering or for the welfare system. It is always both positive and negative in its implications.

However, the world of 'paid volunteers', as all the studies have found, is occupied almost entirely by women. In itself this is curious, since general studies of volunteering – deliberately defined as unpaid work – have not found such enormous differentials between the sexes, even where the beneficiaries of the work have been sick and disabled adults (General Household Survey 1981, Table 8.23). But the existing literature, while noting this, very rarely comments upon it at any great length, and certainly, until now, there has been no overt feminist analysis of the phenomenon. In this chapter, we ask the question 'why do women, as women, enter this hybrid world?' and, inevitably, we seek to apply a feminist perspective to this growing phenomenon. But before turning to a gendered consideration of the issue, we will place the development of this form of work within the context of general change in the way in which services for those in need, particularly the elderly and dependent, are being organized and delivered. We argue that paid volunteering, while still a minor part of the provision of social care, is a distinctive signifier of dramatic shifts which are taking place in social policy and the actual provision of social welfare.

Second, we argue that paid volunteering is tightly bound up with the development of case-management as a method of public care. Here, too, the ambiguities abound. This is one of the rare social work developments that experimental research has shown to work and to enhance welfare. At the same time, it is a method which is easily appropriated by those whose primary wish is to limit spending on social services and who question the universalist core of the British welfare state.

Third, we examine the benefits and costs to the paid volunteers themselves. We find these are inextricably tied to the fact that the volunteers are almost always women and that paid volunteering thrives on the disadvantages that define the subordinate position of women in our society. Finally, we turn to trends in the caring capacity of the community and suggest that it is just possible that these embryonic payments which do, at least, recognize the work involved in caring, may eventually develop into a more conventionally organized form of properly paid work, not just for volunteers, but for informal carers as well.

A SIGNIFIER OF FUNDAMENTAL CHANGE?

The use of paid volunteers has emerged during the 1980s as a distinct strategy for agencies responsible for the provision of personal care services in the community. It is particularly associated with innovative and experimental schemes aimed at providing care 'in the community' for people who previously would have been placed in an institution. The titles given to these schemes usually contain within them a clue as to what they do and how they are perceived: thus there are 'good neighbour' schemes which generally aim to provide care at home for dependent people by a neighbour (much studied by the late Philip Abrams and his co-researchers – see, for example, Abrams *et al.* 1981; Bulmer 1986); 'helper' schemes which are similar to the 'good neighbour' schemes and have been much studied by the University of Kent Personal Social Services Research Unit (see, for example, Challis and Davies 1986; Qureshi, Challis and Davies 1989); 'foster' schemes which involve placement of dependent adults and young people other than children within other households (see, for example, Leat and Gay 1987); 'respite' schemes which involve paying someone small sums to relieve the informal carer for short periods – of these the best known is probably the Crossroads Care Attendant Scheme (Bristow 1981) and other schemes have followed suit (see, for example, Thornton, 1989). Most of these schemes are orchestrated by local authority Social Service Departments (although Housing Departments are often involved in 'visiting warden' schemes, particularly where the people looked after are their own tenants). Increasingly, too, the large voluntary organizations such as

Age Concern, Help the Aged, and Mind, are becoming involved in paying their 'volunteers'. This arises directly out of the growing tendency of local authorities to contract out their social service provision to such well-established voluntary organizations which, in turn, find that a considerable budget combined with a contract to guarantee service delivery act as an inexorable push towards some kind of payment to the 'volunteers' actually providing the service.

To anyone bred on the ideologies of expansionary years of the post-war welfare state, the term 'paid volunteer' is an uncomfortable one. The cause of the discomfort is more than the semantic dissonance that comes from juxtaposing two contrary ideas; payment and gift. It is because the term is part of a new discourse about welfare that has emerged in the 1980s. This new discourse is self-consciously tough-minded, practical, economistic and untroubled by linguistic niceties. It is represented in the blunt and anonymous writing of the documents that are making the running in the social policy debate these days: the reports of Government auditors (Audit Commission 1985; Audit Commission 1986) and social service inspectors (1987), the Griffiths Report (1988) and the NHS White Paper (1989). The new discourse we term 'managerialist' – a term with which we are sure the authors themselves are comfortable. In contrast, the old discourse was self-consciously humanitarian, even Utopian, concerned with need rather than cost. It worried a great deal about meaning: stigma, equality, universalism, relative deprivation and so on. However, there is one empirical reality that is conspicuously missing from the documents of the new managerialist discourse. Although they are about personal care services, they say little about the mechanics of care, the tending tasks themselves. This may be because this is a reality that is difficult to change. The essence of the care of the dependent remains immutable and timeless – rooted in the human condition. The dependent need to be washed, toileted, fed, dressed, lifted, transported, entertained and, above all, loved. These basic tasks cannot be fundamentally altered. There are few new technologies to be exploited, no obvious productivity gains to be made in the production of care at the level of the individual person. One can only change who does the caring and where it is done.

The point here is that the literature which is supporting, justifying and driving policy towards the substitution of home care for institutional care, is almost entirely concerned with organization and management issues and says little about the craft of caring. It is merely concerned with its availability and cost. Paid volunteers have emerged as a potential source that scores well on both these counts. But by leaving the actual content of the craft of tending unspecified, but failing to unpack and analyse this part of the production of home care, it tends to ignore its centrality to the success or failure of the whole enterprise and to downgrade the skills of those who do it and to ignore their welfare. This is not only a form of exploitation (well known to students of the place of women in the family), but also a hostage to fortune because it leaves unexplained a make-or-break linchpin in the whole enterprise. It means that the replication or universalization of a scheme which relies on paid volunteers or on low-paid part-timers is gambling on the assumption that this factor will remain the same and perform as before. This may of course be a reliable assumption, but even if it is, we should know why.

This difficult reality, that the labour content of care of the dependent has not been reduced by progress, but has rather been increased by it as acceptable standards have risen, is reflected in many of the modern accounts of care innovations and experiments. It is reflected in a studied avoidance of the issue. One has to search hard for a detailed account of the business of caring. The immense literature generated by the Thanet community care experiment in the care of the elderly, and its successors in Gateshead (Challis *et al.* 1988) and Darlington (Challis *et al.* 1989), give little space to the routine mechanics of caring. The published account of the Newham and Ipswich experiments in the home care of the confused elderly does not tell us how the care workers actually managed to get through the days and keep some of the very disabled old people at home. Occasionally, in the reports of these innovations and experiments, we are told that the helpers were given a short training, rarely for more than a few days, but what this training consisted of is less clear. Only the Normanton experiment in patch-based community care (Hadley and McGrath 1984) and detailed reports of the Dinnington project (Bayley *et al.* undated) are notable exceptions; from them one does begin to accumulate a feel for the texture of the caring business.

None the less, in many of the accounts, there are clues to the centrality of caring skills. The helpers recruited often have a background in nursing, residential care or in tending a relative at home. We learn that allowing them to meet together to compare their experiences was helpful or in some instances that care was more easily sustained if more than one person routinely worked on a particularly heavy case (Darlington, Normanton). But the technicalities of caring are never at the core of the accounts. It is as though one were reading recipes that only mention the ingredients but which say little about how to mix them.

Moreover, just as there has developed a new literature on the management of caring (which is countermanded by another set of literature that looks at the same issues but from a feminist perspective), so there have been very rapid changes in the actual delivery of caring services. The idea of paid volunteers is part of a broad range of shifts in the nature of the welfare state and the way in which its obligations to the dependent are defined. These shifts have in part been forced by a deep crisis in the care of the dependent. The severity and extent of this crisis is not reflected in public awareness or political salience. Rather it manifests itself publicly in the occasional media scandal over old people dying alone or of hypothermia, ill-treatment in institutions, the mentally ill left to wander the streets or ending up in prison. The crisis is partly the product of raised definitions of the minimally acceptable and partly due to political decisions not to raise public spending in these areas as fast as the growth of numbers in need. Whatever the causes, this crisis is about the collapse of some of the core universalist guarantees of the post-war welfare state. Anyone who today finds themselves responsible for a handicapped child, a physically disabled or mentally ill adult or a dependent old person will have found that there is no universal minimum level of state support that can be relied upon. Rather there are unpredictable, contingent, regionally variable and rather unreliable possibilities of help. This has been called the 'Lebanonization' of social care. As in Beirut, the best exists a short distance from the worst. You need energy and your wits about you to survive. There are no clear standards to appeal to and, at any moment, there is a chance that what you have will be shot to pieces.

Conventionally, the alternative to universalism is selectivity and, in principle, the new welfare state will be one with myriad criteria of selective entitlement, all justified by a careful calculation of marginal benefit and opportunity cost. Nowadays, much paper is expended delineating the multi-faceted attractions of a pluralist system of care driven by market forces and competition on one side, and community spirit and 'active citizenship' on the other. 'Paid volunteering' is the mongrel progeny of this curious 1980s *mélange* of money-making and altruism.

PAID VOLUNTEERING AND CASE-MANAGEMENT: A SYMBIOTIC RELATIONSHIP

The language which describes universalism's replacement talks of a 'mixed economy of welfare', 'partnership' and 'co-ordination' between service sectors. 'Social care' once implicitly meant state service; now one must say which sectors are supplying it and the terms 'informal care' and 'private (for-profit)' and 'voluntary (not-for-profit)' care help describe the new welfare world. Hence, not surprisingly, the spread of the idea of paid volunteering is closely tied to the development of the role of 'case-manager' as an appropriate function for public sector professionals. Traditionally (since the late nineteenth century), the state has *not* offered service management for those at home but rather a selection of actual services to be used 'off the shelf'. Where total management of the care package was required, the state provided this in some sort of residential home or hospital. Now, largely as a result of the run-down of public institutions for the chronically dependent, there are not enough places and beds to fulfil that implicit public commitment. The public sector is therefore faced with the, at least theoretical, obligation to provide quasi-institutional care *in people's own homes* – an obligation it very unevenly fulfils. The debate about how this should be done (Barclay, Griffiths) appears to be culminating in the view that the state will provide the case-management of a plurality of personal care sources. The voluntary sector is an obvious source of service to be case-managed into home care; moreover, paying volunteers helps ensure the accountability required by case-management (Leat and Gay 1987). Paying an individual volunteer to do a care job is little different in principle from contracting a whole voluntary organization to provide a care service (for example, Age Concern to provide day care). In each case, the purpose of payment is very largely to engineer control by the paying authority and commitment, by the organization or volunteer, to continuous delivery of the service.

The argument can be pushed a little further. If community care is in many cases to mean essentially the moving of twenty-four hour care regimes from public institutions into private homes (and this may be desirable in the sense that it is what people desire), then the increased use of voluntary carers, paid or not, takes on a more insidious aspect. Appallingly paid as many women were as residential care workers, are they now to be even more partially paid, or not paid at all, as the labour providing residential care in people's own homes? 'Home care' is a mantle of legitimacy which might well hide lowered standards for both care-recipients and care-givers alike.

The public case-management of private and voluntary welfare signifies and requires a substantial redefinition of the traditional relationship between these sectors. Whereas until now the doing of tasks was a public function (home help, care assistant, district nurse, meals-on-wheels) and their co-ordination and integration in an overall care-plan was a private function, now the public sector proposes to do the co-ordinating and the private, voluntary and informal will do the actual caring work. This has an obvious logic (intellectual and economic), but it does amount to a rather dramatic reversal of public/private roles. It is important to note, therefore, that 'paid volunteering' is part of the new image and new vocabulary and thus an ideologically-loaded term which should not be considered outside the wider pattern of fundamental change of which it is a part.

SEX AND GENDER AND PAID VOLUNTEERING

So far we have not brought the question of sex and gender into much of our discussion. However, questions of sex and gender have, by implication, thrown a long shadow over the previous section: for example, we argued that much of paid volunteering is contiguous with, and very similar to, care-work which takes place within the more conventional labour market. But the conventional labour market is notoriously sex-segmented in Britain, with women very much predominant in the low-paid personal service sector; hence this contiguity with low-paid work in the conventional labour market applies almost entirely to women rather than to men. Second, we suggested that, particularly in the managerialist caring literature, there is a black hole of non-recognition about the nature of the 'craft of caring'; instead, there is a general assumption in this literature that certain types of personality and ordinary people with certain types of work experience will make suitable 'helpers'. What we did not spell out, but what is strikingly obvious when one takes a close look at what is actually being said, is that an assumption is being made that women embody, as a sex, these personality attributes and this work experience. This is particularly clear in a section from Challis and Davies' book on the Kent Community Care Scheme:

> The team had few initial preconceptions about the attributes of a suitable helper, save a caring attitude and sound commonsense . . . the previous caring experience of the potential helper, whether on a formal employed basis or informal basis, was considered particularly important.
>
> (Challis and Davies 1986: 121–2, *passim*)

The 'craft' of caring – in other words, the skills involved – stays unrecognized because it constitutes a fundamental part of female socialization and women's paid and – more particularly – unpaid work experience.

These two themes – that what we are talking about bears very close resemblance to 'women's jobs' in the personal service sector of the conventional labour market, and that it is assumed that women, as women, contain the necessary characteristics to make them particularly suitable as care workers – are themes that we will continue to look at more closely. But the more specific questions that we wish to address here are:

- is paid volunteering exploitative of women, or is it in women's interests, since, first, it recognizes the work involved in volunteering and, second, it could perhaps be used as a springboard for further and fuller payment. Or
- is it a mechanism for engaging women in extremely low-paid work

while presenting their work as something other than work and more akin to pleasure and leisure? And,

- what do women themselves say about this form of care-work, and how can feminist commentators include within their feminist analysis an acknowledgement that the work is apparently *both* highly satisfying *and* highly exploitative?

EXPLOITATION OR RECOGNITION?

The notion of exploitation is, of course, extraordinarily difficult to agree on, let alone quantify. For our purposes, the very crude indicator that we shall use is a comparative one: is the work undertaken remunerated at the same level as directly comparable work elsewhere? Immediately, of course, we run into the usual difficulty that housework, child care, and caring for the frail, dependent, and elderly, are predominantly carried out for no remuneration at all, although, under carefully defined and constructed circumstances, payment in the form of wages, salaries and compensation for opportunity costs, are made for all three activities. Although we will have to bear this point in mind throughout this discussion, the point of comparison we shall use is existing payment for care-work that is presently remunerated financially through the conventional means of a pay packet.

The first point to make when considering rates of pay for care-work is that it is impossible to draw up truly comparative data because we are actually talking about rates of pay for two rather differently organized types of work. On the one hand, there is the work undertaken by local authority employees who have conventional working hours and methods of pay, conventional employment rights and social security cover, and wage bargaining procedures organized by national unions such as NUPE and NALGO. In contrast, there is the care-work carried out by 'ordinary people' (Leat and Gay 1987; Thornton 1989), many of whom have been recruited to provide caring services as quasi-volunteers, where, quite often, the remuneration is calculated on a person-by-person basis often designed to avoid loss of benefit through the operation of earnings rules or the imposition of tax (Challis and Davies 1986: 128; Tinker 1984: 27). However, despite these rates of pay 'tailor-made' for individuals, most of these schemes also have a 'bespoke' system running alongside, which has one common basis between them: they pay *not* according to time spent, but rather according to the number of cases undertaken, or tasks carried out and/or visits made. For example, the Kent Community Care Scheme (Challis and Davies 1986) generally pays the helpers according to the number of visits they make to the one person they are looking after; other schemes, such as visiting warden schemes described by Anthea Tinker

(1984), pay according to the number of people the warden agrees to visit. Nevertheless, there are some schemes we have come across that do pay according to the time spent caring: for example, the 'In Safe Hands' scheme run by Age Concern in York as a relief system for informal carers pays a maximum of £1.00 an hour up to a daily maximum of £8.00 and a weekly maximum of £56.00 for residential care (Thornton 1989), while a Home Support Project in Newham and Ipswich paid, in 1984, an hourly rate of £2.59 and £2.40 respectively, with no apparent limit operating (Askham *et al.* 1987).

Hence it is impossible to compare hourly rates of pay either between the two sectors of care-work employment described, or, indeed, within the 'paid volunteering' sector. The overall amounts that individuals receive on a weekly basis vary considerably: typical amounts of pay per week cited by Tinker in her study carried out in 1981–2 were £21–£140 for visiting wardens who kept an eye on twenty to thirty-five elderly people, between £11 and £20 a week for 'Good Neighbours' who looked after a similar number of elderly people in their neighbourhood, and up to £10.00 a week to 'neigh-bourly helps' for looking after one person in their neighbourhood. Even within a single scheme, individuals can negotiate very different amounts for very similar contracted tasks (Challis and Davies 1986; Qureshi *et al.* 1989). In contrast, there are full-time care-workers within local authority housing and social service departments earning at least three times as much and often, in multiples, a great deal more. For example, in Tinker's study, 'home-carers', with case-loads of eleven elderly people in any one week, earned a minimum of £115.00, and emergency telephone information officers, who answered emergency calls and, at regular intervals, telephoned elderly people for check-up, earned between £80 and £120 per week (Tinker 1984: Table 4.1).

Clearly, it is arguable that all these care-workers were doing rather different kinds of work, with large differences in case-load, face-to-face contact, responsibility for the overall welfare of an elderly person or persons; above all, it could be suggested that the amounts of time spent in caring by these different categories of worker are reflected in these pay differentials, particularly since the wages of more conventionally paid local authority workers are calculated on a full-time rather than part-time basis. However, even here there is a problem since the job descriptions of the conventionally employed workers often seem to have a close resemblance to the expected function of the quasi-volunteers. For example, the function of the 'home-carers' employed by the London Borough of Hammersmith studied by Tinker in 1981–2 and paid a minimum of £115.00 a week, was described as: 'to provide the sort of personal and domestic care a relative would give – i.e. wider than existing statutory services' (Tinker 1984: Table

4.1), while the function of 'neighbourly helps' employed by Cambridge-
shire County Council and paid up to £10.00 a week was described in
somewhat similar terms: 'to give help to one elderly person (usually a close
neighbour) on a flexible basis i.e. as and when needed in conjunction with
statutory help e.g. home help if needed' (Tinker 1984: Table 4.1).

Already it should be clear that comparisons are analytically difficult
because there is a great deal of irrationality in the overall system of paid
care-work. The irrationality is further compounded when one moves
beyond consideration of the job descriptions to look at the work actually
undertaken. (Once again, the study used here is the invaluable compendium
of studies undertaken by Anthea Tinker.) For example, 107 visiting wardens, employed by Rotherham District Council, with case loads of between
20 and 35 and paid between £21.00 and £40.00 per week, claimed that they
had carried out the following tasks:

*Average percentage of visiting wardens who had ever helped with the
following tasks:*

Bathing	17%
Washing (personal)	50%
Taking to the lavatory	62%
Getting in and out of bed	60%
Feeding	22%
Shaving (men) Brushing and combing hair (women)	42%
Dressing	64%
Cutting toe nails	20%
Shopping	94%
Preparing or cooking meals	47%
Washing clothes	16%
Giving nursing care	32%

(Source: Tinker 1984: Figure 4.2)

The job description of these wardens was as follows: 'to speak to each
person (mainly elderly) on their list daily and to check they were all right
and to alert other people/agencies if they were not' (Tinker 1984: Table
4.1). This is just one example of a group of care-workers working well
beyond their brief; similar results were found by Tinker in case-studies of
other named categories of workers including, and especially, 'Good Neighbours'. Only home carers appeared to work to their brief, which was so
wide anyway that almost all of them claimed that they had carried out every
kind of caring task delineated by the survey.

However, before coming to the conclusion that all these care-workers
were doing very similar kinds of work for hugely different rates of pay, it

is important to point out that it is almost certainly the case that these different categories of worker were doing rather different things most of their working day. The Tinker surveys show that, in terms of time spent, there were quite some differences between, for example, the visiting wardens – most of whose visits were fifteen minutes or less – and the home care workers and the neighbourly helps – most of whose visits were between thirty minutes and two hours (Tinker 1984: 35–6). But what is striking about all these surveys, and other studies looking at conventionally paid care-workers and the 'paid volunteers', is the frequency with which workers take on work which falls right outside their brief, even to the extent of involving their own spouses and children in delivering services (see, for example, Tinker 1984: 45). Additional examples can be quoted from most studies of these kinds of scheme, but the example of the helpers in the Kent Community Care Scheme is the perhaps best known because it is exceptionally well documented:

> The social workers saw helpers as having a separate and distinct contribution to make to the care of the elderly. It was not simply care to meet basic instrumental needs of daily living, however important this was, but care with an affective basis which in many respects resembled that of informal care . . . interviews with helpers who had been involved with a client for a considerable time indicated that the importance of the contract had diminished (Qureshi *et al.* 1983). For these people, a relationship had developed with the elderly person whom they helped and the tasks and activities undertaken had broadened out, albeit within the original planned approach.
>
> The development of this relationship, where the original formal approach grew into a personal exchange between helper and helped – in short the move towards informal care – could be observed in four ways (Qureshi *et al.* 1983). First, helpers undertook tasks which were not required in the original contract. They tended to do more and different tasks for their clients. Second, helpers developed strong attachments to individual clients and were unwilling to change, even when for other reasons this might have been convenient for them. People would retain contact with clients even after leaving the scheme. Third, in many cases a feeling of personal responsibility emerged, a feeling which some helpers likened to their responsibility for dependent members of families such as children. Fourth, helpers with families tended to involve them in looking after the elderly person. Husbands would do odd jobs in people's homes, young children visited and elderly people were taken for meals to helpers' homes.
>
> (Challis and Davies 1986: 142)

A further important implication must be drawn out: as the above quote makes implicitly clear, the very fact that care-workers (particularly those paid nominal amounts) commonly take on considerable additional work, can be absorbed into the structure and rationale of payment in such a way that it emerges as a quite explicit intention of the nominal and tiny pay. The idea is that such very small amounts of pay, particularly where the amount paid has been deliberately divorced from the time spent, encourage the helpers to use as their reference point *not* the 'formal' delivery of services normally associated with 'professional' carers who have been trained to care and whose work is organised within the public domain, *but rather* the reference of informal care which uses experience as the training ground, altruism and obligation as the sources of motivation, and the family as the *locus* of care. In this way, it is thought, love becomes the motivation rather than greed; and from love, it is assumed, follows better quality of care.

Here lies the nub of the difficulty of deciding whether or not these forms of pay constitute exploitation, or an embryonic and potentially enlarging form of recognition for caring work. If one looks closely at the rates of pay prevailing in the more conventionally organized and paid for care-work – even taking into account that this is amongst the lowest paid sectors of the conventional labour market – one cannot but find that paid volunteering involves payments that are ridiculously small and actually extremely exploitative. But if one considers these payments in relation to the fact that most care-work is actually carried out for no payment at all, then one is driven to the conclusion that these payments, however small, are an improvement on the usual position of informal carers. There is also an argument supporting the system of paid volunteering that suggests that the quality of care delivered is better than the more conventional systems of care. The key word, which recurs again and again in the literature, is 'flexibility'. The suggestion is that nominal amounts of pay, which divorce time and motivation from money, mean – logically and in practice – that helpers are prepared to expand the time they spend in care-work until, like many informal carers, they are caring up to and even beyond the point where the cared-for's needs are wholly satisfied, and that their motivation springs from love rather than mercenariness. Such a system of care has a distinctly attractive air to it. Would not we, like many of the carers (n.b. the *carers*) in the Tinker surveys, be delighted to find ourselves, at the end of our independent lives, looked after within such a system?

It seems to us, however, that there are three arguments which can be used to suggest both that paid volunteering is a form of exploited labour and that the suggestion that this is *the* way to underwrite high quality extensive and intensive care is nonsense. The first argument has been used by one of us before (Ungerson 1990a) and maintains that those who support paid volunteering as a way of delivering high quality flexible care are positing a false dichotomy between the apparent attributes of so-called 'formal' care on the one hand, and 'informal' care on the other. The proposed dichotomy – in its crudest and most extreme form – is that the 'formal' system substitutes skill for tenderness, is contractual, hierarchical, subject to rigid divisions of labour laid down through collective bargaining procedures, with bureaucratically managed resources in scarce supply; in contrast, it is suggested, the 'informal' system is spontaneous, loving, flexible, and un-trammelled by ideas of rigid divisions of labour (except, though this is rarely spelt out, the sexual division of labour). But, as one of us has pointed out elsewhere, there is plenty of evidence that workers within the 'formal' sector frequently work beyond their brief because they become involved with their clients on a personal level (Ungerson 1990a); moreover, the evidence from the 'informal' sector indicates that the quality of care is very variable and that the work is so intensive and extensive that 'love' as the initial motivator is often sorely tried and eventually undermined (Ungerson 1987). Finally, the idea that paying less means that more work will be undertaken with a more willing and loving spirit seems to be an argument only applied to the least well paid occupations within the health and welfare system; it is impossible to imagine persuading the medical profession that a reduced income means that they will provide better quality of care because they will be working for love rather than for money . . .

The second argument that paid volunteering constitutes a form of exploi-tation is a 'double jeopardy' argument. The assumption that paid volun-teering is more like informal care than formal care and that *therefore* it should not be paid the rate for the job contains the built-in premise that just because informal care is not normally remunerated now, it should not be remunerated in the future. As Hilary Land implies in Chapter one in this volume, the idea that there should be payment for informal care is one that should be carefully considered: indeed, such payment is practised elsewhere – not just in the anti-sexist welfare states of Scandinavia (Lingsom 1988), but also in some of the more pragmatically minded states of America (see, for example, Keigher *et al.* 1988, on payment for informal carers in the states of Michigan and Illinois).

The third argument that paid volunteering is exploited labour is a much more general argument that moves beyond the world of care-work into consideration of the wider context in which people, particularly women, operate within the paid labour market. We will argue that it is only possible to recruit people to do such work for such small amounts of pay because of the overall position of women, and because of the way in which the social security earnings rules and taxation thresholds work to depress the earnings motivation of two groups in particular: women, and active pensioners. But before turning to that argument in detail, it is extremely important to consider why schemes which pay such tiny amounts have, apparently, little difficulty in recruiting volunteers and, second, why the helpers commonly report very high levels of satisfaction. It may be paradoxical to suggest that high levels of reported satisfaction are themselves an indicator of exploitation, but, in our view, the restraining context within which most women operate in itself is a large part of the explanation of satisfaction. Hence, in the next section of this chapter, we look at the evidence of satisfaction among helpers and consider the wider context of their position.

SATISFACTION WITH HELPING – A GENDERED APPROACH

There have been only a few studies of paid volunteers themselves, but those that exist generally find that the helpers enjoy the work, and, in their responses to surveys, stress particularly the way in which the work can be fitted around their personal commitments and the sense of autonomy they gain from being expected to respond 'flexibly' to the needs of individual clients (Tinker 1984: Table A4.4; Abrams *et al.* 1986; Thornton 1989: ch. 8). The most comprehensive and recently published study of helpers emanates from the Thanet community care project, which ran for four years from 1977. This project was not only a pioneering innovation in the systematic use of paid volunteers to generate a new service, but it has also produced the most thorough account of paid volunteering available: *Helpers in Case-Managed Community Care* (Qureshi, Challis and Davies 1989). The central aim of the Thanet projet was to maintain very dependent elderly people in their own homes by using a mix of services – each of which had been shadow-priced – 'case-managed' by social workers. Built into the experiment was the insistence that the actual cost of the services provided to each elderly person should be no more than two-thirds of the marginal cost of maintaining an elderly person in permanent residential care. It was clearly necessary, therefore, either to reduce services to considerably less than twenty-four hour cover, or to find a way of providing something very like day and night cover, but at a very reduced cost. The answer, as it turns out, and one which was only stumbled upon in the early stages of the experiment, was paid volunteering. Each 'helper' was contracted to carry out certain tasks for an elderly person living close by: for example, getting them up and dressed, providing a meal, putting them to bed, etc. Payment was arranged by the visit, and, at first, payments per visit were individually negotiated.

The evaluation of the Thanet experimental project has produced a number of important research studies, all of which use the 'production of welfare' approach to the analysis of social care provision (see, for example,

Knapp 1984). This approach is essentially based in the discipline of economics, and the Qureshi, Challis and Davies book on the helpers is no exception. The book begins by outlining the substantial economics literature examining women's position in the labour market (Qureshi *et al.* 1989: 16–18). It seems that the supply of women's labour is very responsive to increases in the amount of pay offered and it is implied that this 'elasticity of supply' operates at very low levels of remuneration (Arrufat and Zabalza 1986). It is also stated that the potential loss of benefits is a sharp disincentive to those (wives) affected (Dilnot and Kell 1987). The implied conclusion is that very small amounts of pay will bring forth much female labour and, if they are small enough, will avoid the loss of benefits effect. The experience of paid volunteering in Britain would appear to confirm this.

One has to deal with the economistic argument here. Economists see the market response as a neutral indicator of people's preferences. It is the aggregation of numerous individual decisions. The reasons behind the choices may be very varied and be based on very different situations. It is risky to make judgements about why women respond as they do, but a very plausible feminist response – and one that we support – is that, whatever the reasons, they are generally rooted in forms of gender-based disadvantage. The economistic reply is that none the less, the women will be choosing to move to a higher level of welfare. They gain, the cared for gain, and the world is a better place. To criticize paid volunteering would appear to be saying that it is better people remain for the moment at a lower level of welfare. This is the old problem for those who would reform society. How high a price do they ask the already disadvantaged to pay for the vague promise of a better future?

The Qureshi study analyses why the thirty-seven women (and three men) made the choices they did. The reasons are indeed quite numerous and varied, depending particularly on age, class and family circumstances. It is to some extent contrary to the spirit of the economistic account to generalize, but it is perhaps legitimate to draw some conclusions about how the helper's preferences were structured – while still recognizing their variety. Relatively few of the Kent helpers indicated pay was an important motivation (40 per cent) for entering the project. This is not because these people did not value money, but rather that they were seeking other rewards as well. For example, the women in their fifties and sixties, particularly the widows, wanted to fill spare time and reduce social isolation. Younger women, although often heavily loaded with family responsibilities, sought independence and status outside their roles as wives and mothers. People in their twenties and early thirties were likely to be seeking work experience and skill that would help them into careers.

That people seek rewards other than pay from work is not unusual. But it is almost a defining characteristic of those who are disadvantaged in the labour market that they have to trade off these non-pecuniary gains against pay. In contrast, the relatively advantaged find the material and non-material satisfactions come together, and are positively related. Women's experiences of the strictures, obligations and isolation of their domestic labour can make them particularly anxious to obtain non-monetary rewards like social contact, independence, external recognition and status and the accumulation of skills. The paid jobs available to them and which they can fit with their family obligations – repetitive work in factories, night cleaning, residential care – do not offer these rewards. Women are not the only group that face this dilemma. The three men in the sample of Kent carers were either young unemployed (two) or disabled. Educated and professionally trained feminists, who have access to jobs which are both well-paid and personally satisfying, should be careful not to underestimate the returns from volunteering for tasks which carry a degree of autonomy, responsibility and social esteem.

The Qureshi study (1989: 78) demonstrates that a high proportion of the helpers in the Kent project did indeed find the non-monetary rewards they were seeking. For the most part, they had not, consciously, been led into a false bargain. However, the point is perhaps not that these women were exploited in the sense that they were left worse off than when they started but that they could have been even better off had they been properly paid for their work. This is the value dimension that is not captured by economic analysis. The question is not just whether the use of paid volunteers adds to the total sum of welfare enjoyed in a community. The evidence is that it does and that both the helped and the helpers are net gainers. The question is also whether it is justifiable for a public authority, particularly a social service, to seek to pay labour less than the accepted rate for the job and deliberately to search out those who, because of their socially-induced handicaps (in this case largely gender-based), are willing to accept exceptionally low payment. This is, of course, a political and financial question. We argue, too, that it has a moral dimension: a very important reason for public welfare systems is to mitigate those market outcomes which are agreed to be unacceptable. One of those agreements is that the dependent should not go unhelped for want of money. Another is surely that employers, particularly the state, should not take advantage of people's handicaps when setting rates of pay.

The majority of the motivations deduced from the sample in *Helpers in Case-Managed Community Care* is explicitly traced to a social disadvantage suffered. The volunteers in this account are almost always seeking to alleviate their own painful need. The bulk of the account, supported by hundreds of quotations, elaborates in blunt detail how this volunteering was a much sought-after escape for these women. They chose it despite knowing that the task might at times be difficult and unpleasant. The widows (37 per cent) were looking for friendship ('affiliation needs'), relief from lonely boredom ('time to spare') and to restore a sense of selfworth ('usefulness') after a lifetime of serving husbands and families. The housewives wanted an escape from the routine of housebound chores ('diversionary activity') and to accumulate skills ('human capital building') that might be marketable enough to bring them some autonomy ('independence') in the future.

This was an experiment that clearly emphasized the ethic of voluntariness (one of the three case-managers did not even tell potential helpers about the possibility of payment). 'Hundreds of old people struggling to remain in their own homes' read the advertisement used to recruit the majority of helpers (Qureshi *et al.* 1989: 94). None the less, after a year, nearly 80 per cent of the volunteers mentioned pay as a motivation or reward (80). It is clear that many of them thought they should have been paid more but realized they would have to trade off money against their other needs. We consider that the whole context here – very dependent old people, an innovative experiment, the flexible hours, the emphasis on care and developing emotional attachments – serves to mask the truth of exploitation. If all the helpers had been imported Filipinos, or the partially-sighted, the reality would be plainer but not different. These were women, largely from distinctly disadvantaged subgroups, living in a depressed part of the country at a time of economic recession, who keenly needed the benefits, including pay, that we all routinely seek in employment and who found this was the best that they could get.

In arguing that there is evidence that paid volunteering exploits the needs of particular groups of women, we have avoided the larger issue of whether it might exploit them as members of the working class. This is a complex question, not least because of the changing nature of Britain's class structure and the perennial difficulty of fitting women into categories largely designed for men. However, in the literature on paid volunteering, the issue of class is a constant theme, if a background one. First, it is regularly noted that the women's labour called forth by payment is working class. As Diana Leat puts it in her overview of the large Abrams study of neighbourhood care schemes:

> If we compare schemes where some form of payment was given to helpers (full-time wage and token payment) with those where helpers received no payment then the results indicate the influence of social class . . . in the paid schemes 87 per cent of helpers were working class

while in the unpaid schemes only 44 per cent of helpers were working class.

(Abrams *et al.* 1986: 56)

This pattern leads other writers to more bluntly managerialist conclusions:

Some method of payment . . . has already proved its worth in a number of schemes, particularly those involving working class helpers, but more experimentation is needed to test the effects on recruitment and the impact on care of different forms of payment.

(Bulmer 1987: 206)

Goldberg and Connelly put another managerial goal rather bluntly:

Since common experience and the results of several studies suggest that people of similar backgrounds and habits of living get on better than those living in very different social circumstances, ways of drawing in more working class volunteers will have to be found.

(Goldberg and Connelly 1982: 178)

Behind these views is a long-established concern about the low level of volunteering in working-class communities. There is an implicit conventional wisdom here which would appear to argue that geographical mobility and the need for women to take waged work have destroyed the caring working-class community based on strong informal neighbourliness. This has perhaps led to a too simplistic assumption that working-class volunteering can be recreated by introducing nominal payments related to working-class women's labour market opportunities and the social security regulations. However, as Philip Abrams and, after him, Martin Bulmer have shown, it is empirically doubtful whether the caring communities postulated by this conventional wisdom have ever existed. The evidence is that neighbourliness, at its best, provides help in emergencies, but that personal care on a regular basis is almost entirely a consequence of kinship and close proximity over long periods (Bulmer 1987: 157–61). It seems to us that while the use of money to attract working-class women into the voluntary provision of regular personal care may be justified in terms of community-building, in reality it reflects a less romantic association of caring with working-class domestic service of the nineteenth and early twentieth centuries. This is 'appropriate' work for working-class women, neatly conflated with the more middle-class values of organized volunteering and social service. A need for money will, unsurprisingly, be more likely the more working class the volunteer. Not only is there an element of exploitation in carefully constructing schemes so as to obtain the right amount of help while spending as little as possible, by exploiting the voluntary motivations first, but it is also a form of discrimination against working-class women.

A final irony is that as well as discovering unexpected aspects of the job that they liked, particularly the gratitude of the old people, the helpers in the Thanet experiment were surprised by unpleasant aspects – incontinence, confusion, lack of support from other public services – but felt they could not withdraw because of the suffering they knew this would mean for their clients (Qureshi *et al.* 1989: 90–7). Other studies have found similar evidence: despite the fact that most of the helpers in Tinker's study enjoyed the work, 70 per cent of them thought the elderly people they were caring for would be better off in an old people's home (Tinker 1984: Table A4.2). As other researchers have shown (Lewis and Meredith 1988; Ungerson 1987), this, the emotional pull of guilt tied to feminine identities built round duty and kindness, is the classic method by which our culture entices women into informal and quasi-informal care.

POLICIES AND TRENDS FOR THE FUTURE

In the previous section, we argued that it is women's subordinated and isolated social position and the economic constraints on their labour market activity and remuneration that leads them into accepting – and gaining considerable satisfaction from – nominal payment for hard caring work. Community care schemes designed to provide extensive and intensive services for carefully targeted groups in the population are also, but in a far more hidden way, targeted towards the recruitment of a particular source of labour who, by virtue of their sex, are rendered vulnerable to the blandishments of such schemes. But at the same time, there is entirely another gloss that could be put on the same data: namely, that these schemes – through payment, however small – are an embryonic recognition of the fact that caring is work, and, as a result, the work as 'helpers' could, in future, develop into more conventional and properly-paid occupations. In this respect, it is interesting to note that the Darlington community care scheme, which was based on case-management principles and in other important respects was a copy of the Thanet community care scheme, employed helpers who were fully-fledged employees of the local authority with all the rights that followed therefrom. This ability to employ properly-paid helpers almost certainly derived from the fact that it was a well-funded scheme, aided by central government as one of their 'Care in the Community' demonstration projects (Knapp *et al.* 1990).

Thus, it may not be an inherent part of case-management that schemes are designed to recruit the most vulnerable in the labour market and, using an ideology of femininity closely tied to 'care', pay them almost nothing.

On pragmatic and financial grounds, such schemes *may* prove to be a springboard for a shift from unpaid and almost free care-work to paid care-work. There are demographic and social policy changes currently taking place that could provide the planks for the springboard. First, there is increasing concern, in government, that the decline in the numbers of young people coming on to the labour market in Britain should be offset by the entry and retention of married women, and particularly mothers, in the labour market. To that end, employers are being exhorted to introduced crèches at work, and 'career-break' schemes which entitle mothers to return to their previous jobs without loss of pay or status after the birth and early upbringing of their children (Fowler 1989; and for a discussion of these exhortations, see Ungerson 1990b). If such exhortations work and women find it somewhat easier to combine motherhood and conventionally paid work, then it is just possible that an important source of labour for paid volunteering will begin to dry up.

However, some schemes have found a fruitful source of paid volunteers from the ranks of recently retired women, particularly one-time nurses and home helps. For example, the majority of helpers recruited in the 'In Safe Hands' respite scheme in York were women aged 60 to 69 (Thornton 1989). Schemes able to recruit the active elderly for nominal pay are unlikely to be in competition with the more conventional labour market. Nevertheless, there are demographic changes which also apply to this older, 'non economically active' group of women and will, if they wish it, create an opportunity for them to demand better remuneration. The gap in numbers between the active elderly aged between 60 and 69 and the incapacitated elderly aged between 80 and 90 has been, and still is, steadily increasing. It is a curiosity of the British demographic structure that during the forty years from 1970, the number aged over 80 will more than double while the number aged between 60 and 69 hardly changes at all and actually falls at times during the period (Craig 1983). Hence, there will be a growing shortage of active elderly to care for the frail and dependent elderly. Moreover, until recently, pensioners were unable to earn more than £75.00 per week without having their pension reduced pound for pound until they lost their pension altogether at earnings of £119.00. Since October 1989, this so-called 'earnings rule' has been abolished in another quite explicit move by government to keep the active elderly in the conventional labour market and help avoid the wage-inflationary effects of a labour shortage. The expectation has to be that those pensioners who wish to remain in work will not be seeking the nominal payments available in community care schemes, but will be in a position to seek and find more conventionally remunerated occupations.

Nevertheless, the earnings rule for women on income support or whose husbands and cohabitees are on income support remain punitively tiny at less than £10.00 per week. Unless these rules are changed, then we have to assume that even if women's opportunities for conventionally paid work expand over the next two decades, the operation of the social security rules will still mean that there will be a considerable pool of women willing to work as paid volunteers in order to gain the non-monetary rewards of such work outlined by Qureshi *et al.* It is this point that draws us back once again to the context within which women operate and the way this determines their willingness to enter care-work for no – or practically no – pay. While we may object, on moral grounds, to the way in which case-managed community care schemes have exploited the general position of women, we must also recognize that, if the position of women as care-workers is to improve, then it is the contextual factors – the lack of availability of satisfying work for most women, isolation in domestic labour and child care, the punitive social security earnings rules – which have to be changed.

REFERENCES

Abrams, P., Abrams, S., Humphrey, R. and Snaith, R. (1981) *Action for Care: A Review of Good Neighbour Schemes in England*, Berkhamsted: The Volunteer Centre.
—— (1986) *Creating Care in the Neighbourhood*, London: The Neighbourhood Care Action Programme, Advance.
Arrufat, J.L. and Zabalza, A. (1986) 'Female labour supply with taxation, random preference and optimisation error', *Econometrica* 54: 47–63.
Askham, J., Barker, J., Lindesay, J., Murphy, D., Rapley, C., Thompson, C. and Murphy, E. (1987) 'The home care of dementia sufferers in Ipswich and Newham: the Guy's/Age Concern Home Support Project', in E. Murphy (ed.) *Home or Away?*, National Unit for Psychiatric Research and Development at the United Medical Schools of Guy's and St Thomas's Hospitals.
Audit Commission (1985) *Managing Social Services for the Elderly More Effectively*, London: HMSO.
—— (1986) *Making a Reality of Community Care*, London: HMSO.
Bayley, M., Seyd, R. and Tennant, A. (undated) *Neighbourhood Services Project, Dinnington, Paper no. 12: The Final Report, volumes 1 and 2, mimeo*, University of Sheffield.
Bristow, A. (1981) *Crossroads Care Attendant Schemes*, Rugby: Crossroads Association.
—— Bulmer, M. (1986) *Neighbours: the work of Philip Abrams*, Cambridge: Cambridge University Press.
(1987) *The Social Basis of Community Care*, London: Allen & Unwin.
Challis, D. and Davies, B. (1986) *Case Management in Community Care*, Aldershot: Gower.
Challis, D., Chessum, R., Chesterman, J., Luckett, R. and Woods, B. (1988) 'Community care for the frail elderly: an urban experiment', *British Journal of Social Work* 18: 13–42.

Challis, D., Darton, R., Johnson, L, Stone, M., Traske, K. and Wall, B. (1989) *Supporting the Elderly at Home: The Darlington Community Care Project*, Canterbury: PSSRU Monograph.

Craig, J. (1983) 'The growth of the elderly population', *Population Trends*, 32, London: HMSO.

Department of Health (1989) *Working for Patients: The Health Service: Caring for the 1990s*, Cm. 555, London: HMSO.

Dilnot, A. and Kell, M. (1987) 'Male unemployment and women's work', *Fiscal Studies* 8: 1–16.

Fowler, N. (1989) 'The Rights of Women', speech made at the joint EOC/CBI conference on *Work and the Family*, held on 2 March 1989 at the Queen Elizabeth Conference Hall in London, *mimeo*, obtainable from EOC Press Office, London.

General Household Survey (1981) Office of Population, Censuses and Surveys, London: OPCS, HMSO.

Goldberg, E.M. and Connelly, N. (1982) *The Effectiveness of Social Care for the Elderly*, London: Heinemann.

Griffiths, R. (1988) *Community Care: Agenda for Action*, a Report to the Secretary of State for Social Services, London: DHSS, HMSO.

Hadley, R., and McGrath, M. (1984) *When Social Services are Local: The Normanton Experience*, Hemel Hempstead: George Allen & Unwin.

Keigher, S.M., Simon-Rusinowitz, L., Linsk, N.L. and Osterbusch, S.E. (1988) 'Payments to informal versus formal home care providers: policy divergence affecting the elderly and their families in Michigan and Illinois', *Journal of Applied Gerontology* 7, 4: 456–73.

Knapp, M. (1984) *The Economics of Social Care*, London: Macmillan.

Knapp, M., Cambridge, P., Thomason, C., Darton, R. and Beecham, J. (1990) *Care in the Community: Evaluating a Demonstration Programme*, Aldershot: Gower.

Leat, D. (1988) 'Using social security payments to encourage non-kin caring', in S. Baldwin, G. Parker, and R. Walker (eds) *Social Security and Community Care*, Aldershot: Avebury.

Leat, D. and Gay, P. (1987) *Paying for Care: A Study of Policy and Practice in Paid Care Schemes*, London: Policy Studies Institute.

Lewis, J. and Meredith, B. (1988) *Daughters who Care*, London: Tavistock.

Lingsom, S. (1988) *Paying Informal Care Givers*, mimeo, Institute of Applied Social Research, Oslo, Norway.

Qureshi, H., Challis, D. and Davies, B. (1983) 'Motivations and rewards of helpers in the Kent community care scheme', in S. Hatch (ed.) *Volunteers: Patterns, Meanings and Motives*, Berkhamsted: Volunteer Centre.

—— (1989) *Helpers in Case Managed Community Care*, Aldershot: Gower.

Social Service Inspectors (1987) *From Home Help to Home Care: An Analysis of Policy, Resourcing and Service Management*, London: DHSS, HMSO.

Thornton, P. (1989) *Creating a Break: A Home Care Relief Scheme for Elderly People and Their Supporters*, Surrey: Age Concern.

Tinker, A. (1984) *Staying at Home: Helping Elderly People*, Department of Environment, London: HMSO.

Ungerson, C. (1987) *Policy is Personal: Sex, Gender and Informal Care*, London: Tavistock.

—— (1990a) 'The language of care; crossing the boundaries', in C. Ungerson (ed.)

Gender and Caring; Work and Welfare in Britain and Scandinavia, Hemel Hempstead: Harvester/Wheatsheaf.

—— (1990b) 'Conclusion', in C. Ungerson (ed.) *Gender and Caring: Work and Welfare in Britain and Scandinavia*, Hemel Hempstead: Harvester/Wheatsheaf.

Part III

Research and progress

9 The long term effects for girls of parental divorce

Mavis Maclean and Diana Kuh

Although granting a divorce decree is a legal event, the divorce process has begun with what has been called the 'uncoupling' of the spouses sometime before (Vaughan 1986), and the emotional, social and financial consequences of this uncoupling will affect the spouses, their children, their kin network, their relationships with friends, and their work performance for a considerable period afterwards. Divorce the event and divorce the process together form a turning point, leading to an altered path through life for those concerned for the rest of their lives and beyond through the experience of their children.

In this chapter, using new data from the MRC National Survey of Health and Development, we examine the impact of parental divorce before the age of 16 on women's work and family lives in adulthood. We have looked in earlier papers (Wadsworth and Maclean 1986; Maclean and Wadsworth 1988) at the socio-economic impact of parental divorce on educational achievement and on men's earning capacity in later life. But as women's work histories are more complex and more closely related to their family situation, it is important to look separately and in detail at the women's experience.

The study of divorce has developed in depth and breadth since the early work in which it was conceptualized as a rare and painful event. The aim of the social and psychological research on this topic twenty years ago was to develop preventive measures at best, or at worst, to improve ways of dealing with such a crisis (see, for example, Dominian 1965). As the divorce epidemic of the 1960s and early 1970s gathered pace (the number of petitions granted rose from 25,000 in 1961 to 74,000 in 1971 and 160,000 in 1985), the academic debate broadened in perspective and it was accepted that there might be positive aspects of divorce (see Richards 1987). 'Good divorce' was presented as preferable to 'bad marriage' which might involve conflict leading to violence within the home. Concern with individual freedom of action, viewing marriage as a relationship between two people rather than a social institution involving children and others, and the liberating aspects of divorce and single parenthood were emphasized (e.g. Itzin 1980),. As changes in family structure accelerated (Dunnell 1980), family research developed to include studies of life after divorce (Hart 1976) and remarriage (Furstenberg and Spanier 1984) and of stepparenting (Burgoyne and Clark 1986). Gradually a longer term perspective began to develop, seeing divorce as one event in a process which continues over time involving major changes in the lives of all concerned (Richards and Dyson 1982, Wallerstein and Blakeslee 1989).

The development of understanding of the full impact of divorce has been impeded by lack of knowledge of the functioning of continuing married families. For example, we are only just beginning to study the relationship between family and work careers (Martin and Roberts 1984), the allocation of resources between the members of intact families, and those now living in separate households (Brannen and Wilson 1987).

The consequences of divorce for children are now being studied over a longer period (see Wallerstein and Blakeslee 1989, covering a fifteen-year period after divorce; and Kelly and Corbin 1986 looking at children of divorcing parents when they reach higher education, review by McLanahan 1985). In addition, Guidobaldi's multi-dimensional set of 'ecological' measures over a four-year period round out our view (Guidobaldi *et al.* 1987). These studies cover both the short term and medium term consequences for children of parental divorce and are beginning to differentiate between those children who react relatively well and relatively less well to the experience of parental divorce. Both Wallerstein and Kelly and Guidobaldi *et al.*, for example, found particular difficulties for adolescent boys, who perhaps (given that nine-tenths of children live with their mothers) felt that the absence of a parent of the same sex was a problem; boys also find it more difficult than girls to share and talk through their experiences with their peers.

It is also clear that divorce brings serious economic problems, particularly for the mother-headed family. Income falls with only one earner whose earnings are likely to be low, while commitments remain very similar to the level in the intact family. Seventy per cent of single parents in the UK live on welfare income. In France, Bastard and Voneche (1988) have studied the attitudes of custodial mothers towards seeking income from various sources, and found an interesting variation between the women who believe society owes them a living and those who welcome the opportunity to manage their household budget independently, even if the total income is at a lower level than during the marriage. But economic uncertainty faced all the custodial mother families studied in Britain (Eekelaar and Maclean), France (Bastard), USA (Weitzman), Australia

(MacDonald), South Africa (Burman), Belgium (van Houtte), West Germany (Willenbacher), Japan (Minamakata), Poland (Kurczewski), and Hungary (Che Sombathy) in Maclean and Weitzman *Counting the Cost of Divorce* (forthcoming).

In this chapter we review earlier analyses of the impact of divorce on children in adult life, and then report data about women's experience of parental divorce in a thirty-six year birth cohort study. First, we describe the data from UK cross-sectional and US longitudinal studies. UK data (Eekelaar and Maclean 1986) show clearly a move into poverty for female-headed families after divorce for a small but nationally representative sample of households who had experienced divorce within the decade before interview in 1981. In this small study, only one of the families had been on welfare income at marriage, compared with 11 per cent at separation and 29 per cent at interview. Among female-headed families where the mother remained alone, 56 per cent were on welfare at interview and 15 per cent where she had remarried. We found also a marked disparity in income levels in the one parent families (only 20 per cent were above our poverty line of 140 per cent of supplementary benefit entitlement) compared with 63 per cent of remarried parents and 60 per cent of non- custodial parents. Maintenance or child support payments played only a very small part in the family income of mother–child families and could only benefit the families when the mother herself worked more than part-time, since if she received supplementary benefit (now income support), any child support payments were automatically deducted from the welfare payment.

We also have substantial evidence of post-divorce poverty for mother-headed families from analyses of the 2,000 women members of the Michigan Panel Study of Income Dynamics. McLanahan (1985) found, in this study, poor school attendance at 17 years, and low educational achievement in mother-only families associated with economic deprivation and showed that this lack of achievement was a major factor in the subsequent likelihood of experiencing poverty.

BRITISH LONGITUDINAL DATA

Meanwhile, we can make a reliable estimate of the extent of the problems, if any, amongst children of divorcing parents by using data from the MRC National Survey of Health and Development, a study of 5,000 people born in the first week of March 1946. They comprise a social class stratified sample of one-third of all births in that week. Information on a wide range of medical, psychological, social and educational topics has been collected at least every two years in childhood and slightly less frequently in adult life, by health visitors, school nurses and doctors, teachers and youth employment officers, and professional interviewers. The most recent data were collected in 1982, at the age of 36 years when the response rate was 85 per cent (for a full account see Atkins *et al.* (1981) and Wadsworth (1984)). The next set of data is being sought in 1989 at 43 years.

Findings from this birth cohort echo other work in finding significant excess of emotional disruption among the children of divorcing parents in the short term and the long term as measured by the prevalence of bedwetting at 15 years, which was twice that of those bereaved or in continuing marriages, and of delinquency at 21 years, which was twice as high. Two sets of factors may have been involved. First, the emotional vulnerability of young children at the time of the separation may affect the development of emotional coping processes, and, at the time when this sample were children, such a process may have been reinforced by the adverse expectations about the future of children whose parents had divorced (Wadsworth 1984). Second, the material disruption involved for many children at divorce, e.g. moving house and moving school, may also contribute to the difficulties experienced (McLanahan 1985).

At 26 years (see Table 9), the educational attainment of boys and girls from manual and non-manual workers' families was adversely affected by parental divorce before the age of 15, and this effect was greater for those losing a parent through divorce than through death. Perhaps a parent who dies remains an emotional presence in the family in a positive sense – the loss is seen as involuntary, and discussion of the lost parent is likely to be emotionally positive, and to draw the extended family network together. In the case of divorce, the child may be presented with negative images of the absent parent, and lose touch with him or her and with that side of the family. But, in particular, the reason stated for loss is not well understood by the child, and often not discussed with the child who may even, at a young age, feel blame for the event (Mitchell 1985).

This educational underachievement was associated with lower economic activity rates and lower earnings at the age of 36 for men. For example, men aged 36 with divorced parents were more than twice as likely to be unemployed than men from intact homes, and twice as likely to be in the lowest income group (Maclean and Wadsworth 1988). We linked these associations to educational underachievement and lack of feelings of self-esteem among the men.

We hesitated to include women in this analysis as women's careers in the labour market are likely to be more intermittent and complex than men's as a result of marrying and having children. We have therefore looked more closely at the women's work experiences, aided by background data from the large sample of (5,000) women interviewed in 1980 (Martin and Roberts 1984).

Table 9a Educational attainment of women at 26 years according to social class of origin and experience of parental divorce or death

Girls

Social class of origin	Experience of parental loss whilst 0–15yrs	Educational attainment by age 26 years				
		None	Up to and including 'O' level	'A' level and equivalents	University	Total (= 100%)
Non-manual	No loss	19.5	36.1	34.2	10.1	888
	Parental divorce/separation	44.2	30.8	17.3	7.7	52
	Parental death	12.7	43.6	38.2	5.5	55
Manual	No loss	54.1	34.2	10.9	0.8	960
	Parental divorce/separation	68.1	26.1	4.3	1.4	69
	Parent death	66.3	24.4	8.1	1.2	86

Comparing those with parental divorce with no loss:
x^2 for girls from non-manual families = 19.35 with 3 d.f. p<.001
x^2 for girls from manual families = 5.58 with 2 d.f. (adding cols 3 and 4) p=.06
Comparing those with parental death:
x^2 for girls from non-manual families = 3.42 with 3 d.f. not significant
x^2 for girls from manual families = 4.80 (adding cols 3 and 4) p=.09

Table 9b Educational attainment of men at 26 years according to social class of origin and experience of parental divorce or death

Boys

Social class of origin	Experience of parental loss whilst 0–15yrs	None	Up to and including 'O' level	'A' level and equivalents	University	Total (= 100%)
		— *Educational attainment by age 26 years*				
Non-manual	No loss	20.4	23.4	32.4	23.9	958
	Parental divorce/separation	42.4	19.7	27.3	10.6	66
	Parental death	35.0	23.3	23.3	18.3	60
Manual	No loss	55.0	19.0	21.0	5.1	1049
	Parental divorce/separation	73.0	17.6	9.5	—	74
	Parent death	56.3	18.8	21.3	3.8	80

Comparing those with parental divorce with no loss:
x^2 for boys from non-manual families = 19.41 with 3 d.f. p<.001
x^2 for boys from manual families = 11.65 with 2 d.f. (adding cols 3 and 4) p<=.01
Comparing those with parental death:
x^2 for boys from non-manual families = 7.90 with 3 d.f. p=.05
x^2 for boys from manual families = .05 (adding cols 3 and 4) not significant

EDUCATIONAL ATTAINMENT

The level of educational qualifications achieved by members of the 1946 birth cohort by 26 years, according to the experience of parental divorce and death and their fathers' social class at birth is shown in Table 9. The educational disadvantages for men were clear both for those from non-manual and manual families of origin, and this may be one of the important links in the chain that results in economic disadvantages in later life for men whose parents were divorced when they were children (Maclean and Wadsworth 1988). For women from non-manual origins, those from divorced families were over twice as likely to have no educational qualifications than those from intact families. Although this pattern of educational under-achievement was also present within the manual group for women from divorced families of origin, the association with parental divorce and death was weaker than for the other groups. This may have been because barriers to educational achievement for the majority of women from manual back-grounds were so substantial that parental divorce was simply one amongst many problems with which to cope. The level of educational qualifications achieved by women was significantly higher for those from both non-manual and manual families of origin if their mothers had gone to second-ary school themselves, but women from divorced families still had a significantly higher risk of leaving school with no educational qualifi-cations even when the effects of mothers' education and fathers' social class, at the time of the child's birth, were taken into account ($x^2 = 5.85$, $p = .01$ with 1 d.f.). Educational underachievement in women from non-manual divorced families may be due to downward social mobility after parental divorce, as well as to the emotional trauma. In contrast, the effect of parental bereavement carried little excess risk of educational underachievement.

WORK HISTORY

For the men, educational underachievement led to lower earnings and lower labour force participation. We might expect to find a similar effect, perhaps modified by having children, for the women after parental divorce.

Various hypotheses may be offered to suggest that women from dis-rupted families have a different chance of returning to the labour market after childbirth compared with women who experienced no parental loss. For example, as for the men, their chances may be reduced because of their lower level of educational attainment. On the other hand, these women have been found to marry and start childbearing at an earlier age (Kiernan 1986) and they are on average one year younger at the birth of their youngest child (by 36 years) than those mothers who did not come from disrupted families. This would increase the chances of having returned to paid work by age 36 years. Finally, if women from disrupted families are less likely to be married to men with middle-class occupations, this could also increase their chances of being employed.

The occupation of the women at 36 years is given in Table 10, according to the experience of parental death or divorce before 15 years. As there were no significant differences in reasons for not being in paid work, housewives and those describing themselves as unemployed were grouped together. The majority of men who experienced parental divorce and who were not working nor seeking work in their mid-thirties had some history of illness or handicap (Maclean and Wadsworth 1988). It is not possible to distinguish an equivalent group from the large number of women aged 36 years who were not in paid employment. In the 1946 birth cohort there was a tendency for the women from divorced families, and to a lesser extent from bereaved families, to be employed in part-time jobs rather than to remain at home, while the proportions in full-time work were almost identical (see Table 10).

But is experience of parental divorce related to lower occupational status for the women who do work? Table 11 shows that the proportion of women whose parents divorced and who had achieved occupations in social classes I or II was only two-thirds that of those from intact or bereaved families, and a greater proportion of them were in manual occupations.

Table 10 Work status of women at age 36 years and its association with childhood experience of parental divorce or death (0–15 yrs)

Work status	No loss (1)	Parents divorced or separated (2)	Parental death (3)
Working full-time	27.8	25.0	26.3
Working part-time	34.1	44.0	39.5
Not in paid work	38.1	31.0	34.2
Total (= 100%)	(1448)	(100)	114
Unknown	(6)	(1)	–

Comparing cols 1 and 2: ($x^2 = 4.08$ with 2 d.f., p = .13)
Comparing cols 1 and 3: ($x^2 = 1.44$ with 2 d.f., not significant)

This association between the woman's own social class and her experience of parental divorce was still significant even after taking account of two other early life influences, the father's social class and the mother's

Table 11 Social class of working women at 36 years according to childhood experience of parental divorce or death (0–15 yrs)

Social class	No loss	Parental divorce	Parental death
I & II	31.5	18.8	28.8
IIINM	38.4	40.6	34.2
IIIM; IV; V	30.1	40.6	37.0
Total (= 100%)	887	69	73

Comparing cols 1 and 2: $x^2 = 5.69$ with 2 d.f. p = .05
Comparing cols 1 and 3: $x^2 = 1.51$ with 2 d.f. not significant

education ($x^2 = 3.83$ with 1 d.f. p = 5.0). Some, but not all, of this association was due to the different rates of part-time work (which we found earlier to be more common for women at 36 years from disrupted families). But most of the difference in social status was explained by earlier educational underachievement.

Women's own social class provides only a partial picture of their economic and social circumstances and can only be used for women who are at work. We therefore looked also at their husband's socio-economic status. Participation of the current spouse in the labour market did show a significant association with family disruption; men married to women from divorced families were more likely not to be in paid work (see Table 12). As the numbers were very small, individual case histories were examined. The majority of the men who were not looking for paid work suffered from ill-health which raised the question of whether women from divorced

Table 12 Work status of partners when survey members were 36 years, and its association with childhood experience of parental divorce or death (0–15 yrs)

Work status	No loss (1)	Parents divorced or separated (2)	Parental death (3)
In paid work	95.1	89.0	94.2
Looking for paid work	4.1	5.5	4.9
Not looking for paid work	0.8	5.5	1.0
Total (= 100%)	(1274)	(91)	103
Unknown	(10)	(1)	(–)
Not living with partner	(170)	(9)	(11)

Comparing cols 1 and 2: ($x^2 = 17.88$ with 2 d.f., p<.001)
Comparing cols 1 and 3: ($x^2 = .19$ with 2 d.f., not significant)

families of origin were more likely to marry more vulnerable men. The small numbers and the limited information available on spouses did not allow us to test this hypothesis.'

FAMILY HISTORY

For women even more than for men, educational and occupational achievements are interrelated with marriage and fertility patterns and it is not satisfactory to consider one without the other when looking at the consequences of family disruption. The influence of family disruption on this cohort in terms of a lower age at first marriage and starting childbearing, and a higher risk of own marital breakdown for those who married as teenagers has already been found (Kiernan 1986). In our current analysis, the incidence of divorce by the age of 36 in relation to family disruption is presented separately for men and women in Table 13. By 36 years, the excess risk of divorce was not as strong among women from divorced families as it was among men, and was similar to the influence of parental death, whereas men who experienced parental death were no more likely

Table 13(a) Men's own marital history at 36 years according to experience of parental divorce or death in childhood (men)

Marital history	No loss (1)	Parents divorced or separated (2)	Parental death (3)
(a) Never married	10.4	11.5	7.2
In first marriage	76.3	60.4	76.3
First marriage broken by divorce or separation	13.0	28.1	16.5
First marriage broken by death	0.3	–	–
Total (= 100%)	(1457)	(96)	(97)
Unknown	(3)	(–)	(–)
(b) Never married	10.4	11.5	7.1
Married once	81.8	71.9	86.7
Married twice or more	7.8	16.7	6.1
Total (= 100%)	(1461)	(96)	(98)

(a) For those in first marriages at 36 years and those who have experienced divorce or separation:
Comparing col 1 with col 2 $x^2 = 16.70$ with 1 d.f. p<.001
Comparing col 1 with col 3 $x^2 = .47$ with 1 d.f. not significant
(b) Comparing col 1 with col 2 $x^2 = 9.66$ with 2 d.f. p<.01
Comparing col 1 with col 3 $x^2 = 1.57$ with 2 d.f. not significant

Table 13(b) Women's own marital history at 36 years according to experience of parental divorce or death in childhood (women)

Marital history	No loss (1)	Parents divorced or separated (2)	Parental death (3)
(a) Never married	6.0	4.0	2.6
In first marriage	76.5	72.0	71.1
First marriage broken by divorce or separation	16.3	23.0	23.7
First marriage broken by death	1.2	1.0	2.6
Total (= 100%)	(1454)	(100)	(114)
Unknown	(–)	(1)	(–)
(b) Never married	6.0	4.0	2.6
Married once	84.9	79.2	82.5
Married twice or more	9.1	16.8	14.9
Total (= 100%)	(1454)	(101)	(114)

(a) For those in first marriages at 36 years and those who have experienced divorce or separation:
Comparing col 1 with col 2 $x^2 = 2.22$ with 1 d.f. p=.14
Comparing col 1 with col 3 $x^2 = 3.24$ with 1 d.f. p=.07
(b) Comparing col 1 with col 2 $x^2 = 6.93$ with 3 d.f. p=.03
Comparing col 1 with col 3 $x^2 = 5.92$ with 2 d.f. p=.05

than men from intact families to be divorced by 36 years. For the majority, parental loss through death was the loss of their father, and the different divorce patterns between the sexes may reflect the different meanings attached to that loss by boys and girls. But given the sex and social class differences in age at first marriage, this pattern perceived at 36 years may yet change. We may speculate about a role model effect for men whose fathers left home. Women whose fathers died may try to replace their fathers by marriage, which, in turn, may lead to greater marital instability in later years when their husbands fail to match up to the idealized father image.

In taking account of the early influence of fathers' social class, Table 14 shows that it was significant. Women from divorced non-manual families were significantly more likely than their peers from intact families to experience marital breakdown by the age of 36 years (see Table 14).

To explore further these marital, educational and social class differences between women from intact families and those from divorced families, data on emotional difficulties at 36 years were examined.

Table 14 Women's marital history by 36 years according to social class of origin and experience of parental divorce or death

Social class of origin	Experience of parental loss whilst 0–15 years	Still in first marriage (1)	Marital breakdown (2)	Widowed (3)	Never married (4)	Total (= 100%)
Non-manual	No loss	76.2	13.9	1.0	9.0	(714)
	Parental divorce/separation	60.0	31.1	2.2	6.7	(45)
	Parental death	74.4	20.9	2.3	2.3	(43)
Manual	No loss	76.9	18.8	1.1	3.2	(727)
	Parental divorce/separation	81.8	16.4	—	1.8	(55)
	Parental death	69.0	25.4	2.8	2.8	(71)

Comparing parental divorce with no loss and cols 1 and 2 only:
x^2 for women from non-manual families = 8.51 with 1 d.f. p<.01
x^2 for women from manual families = .13 with 1 d.f. (not significant)

Comparing parental death with no loss and cols 1 and 2 only:
x^2 for women from non-manual families = .80 with 1 d.f. (not significant)
x^2 for women from manual families = 1.53 with 1 d.f. (not significant)

EMOTIONAL WELL-BEING

The Present State Examination (PSE) was administered to cohort members at 36 years by trained research nurses. This is a measure of current emotional state and the score reflects the number of symptoms that are present across a variety of disorders including anxiety and depression. The maximum score for women at 36 years in the 1946 cohort was 38, although 40 per cent of women have no symptoms, and hence no score (see Figure 1).

The mean score for the group of women who had experienced parental divorce was 4.2, significantly higher than the mean score of women from intact families (3.0) (F = 6.68 with 1 d.f. p<.01). This relationship was not changed when taking account of fathers' social class, which was not strongly related to the PSE score. The relationship between parental divorce and emotional state at 36 years remained significant even after taking account of many other early life experiences, such as parents' mental and physical health (Rodgers 1990). Rodgers also found that the PSE score was higher the greater the number of negative life events reported in the previous year, but more negative life events were not reported by women from divorced families of origin and did not account for the association between the PSE score and parental divorce. In contrast, there was no association between parental death in childhood and the PSE score.

For some people, alcohol intake and smoking may increase as a response to stressful life events and we therefore looked at these aspects of behaviour in our sample of women.

At 36 years, cohort members were asked to keep a diet diary for a week (Braddon *et al.* 1988). The mean daily intake of alcohol among women who drank that week was 9.46g, similar to the average intake recorded by other national surveys (Blaxter 1987). For women from divorced families, mean daily intake was significantly higher than for women from intact families (see Figure 2). (F = 12.32 with 1 d.f. p .001.) The significance of this 'association' was not accounted for by the early life factors of social class and mothers' education. The difference in average intakes was highest for women with better educated mothers; in this group, women from divorced families had two and a half times the intake of those from intact families. In contrast, alcohol intake was not associated with parental death in childhood.

Patterns of smoking were also investigated as smoking has also been suggested as a response to stress and because of the social class gradient in smoking. Those who experienced parental divorce or separation were indeed more likely to be smokers at 36 years (45 per cent compared to 32 per cent of those from intact families of origin and 39 per cent from those who had experienced parental death) (x^2 = 8.38 with 2 d.f. p = .01),

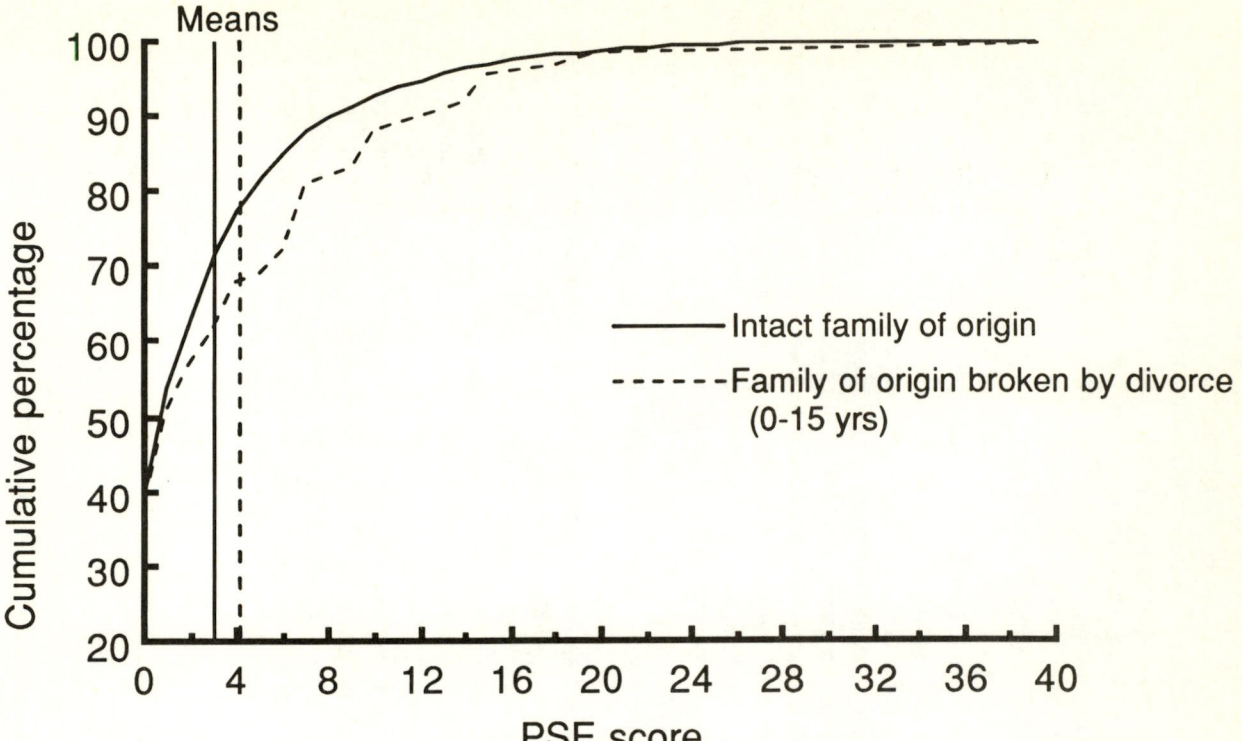

Figure 1 PSE scores at 36 years according to experience of parental divorce or separation when survey member 0–15 years (women)
Source: Reprinted by kind permission of the editor, *Journal of Biosocial Science*

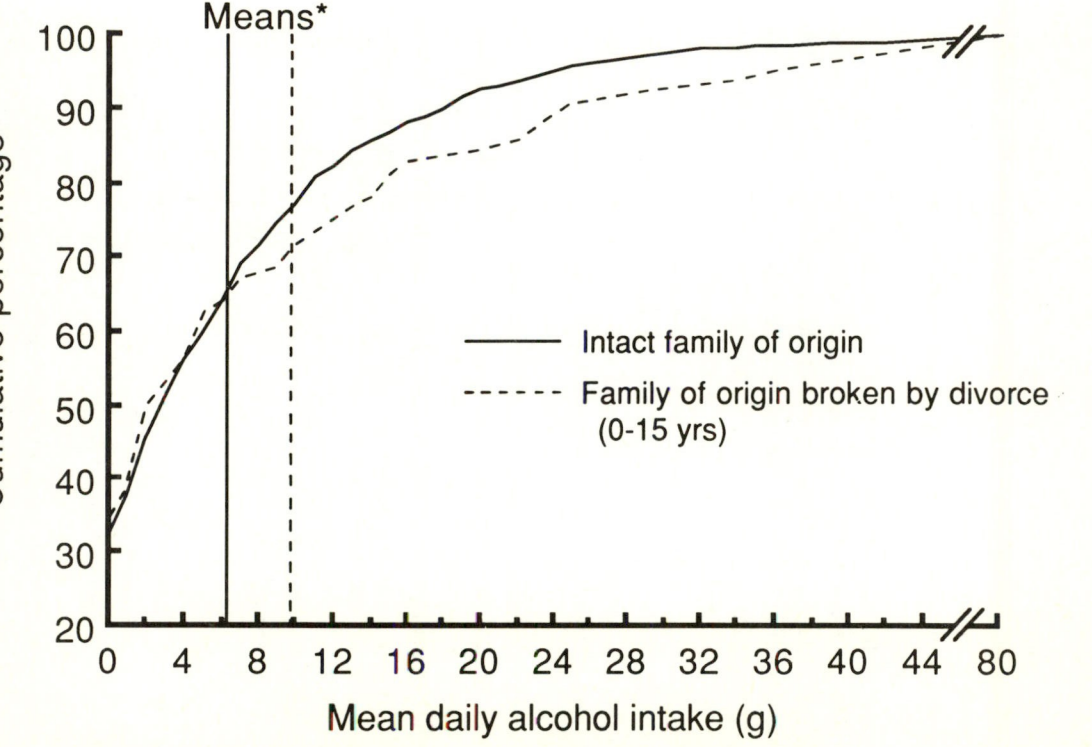

Figure 2 Daily alcohol intake at 36 years according to experience of parental divorce or separation when survey member 0–15 years (women)

Source: Reprinted by kind permission of the editor, *Journal of Biosocial Science*

although within the smoking group there were no significant differences in consumption patterns. Having taken account of social class origins, this relationship remained significant only for those from non-manual origins ($x^2 = 6.37$ with 2 d.f. p<.05). This may be due to downward social mobility after the divorce as the smoking rates resemble those from manual origins.

CONCLUSIONS

It is unlikely that these findings are limited to the effects of divorce. Data on the quality of parental relationships among families where separation did not take place might well have revealed a similar level of emotional problems and reduced educational and socio-economic attainment amongst those whose parents had poor relationships. Such a comparison would be particularly useful and would exclude the social and financial impact of divorce. However, the MRC survey does not include such data. It is also possible that these data may now be of only historical interest, rather than useful for current policy formation, as divorce now is more common and less stigmatizing for spouses and their families. However, it is unlikely that the emotional circumstances leading to separation have lessened in their impact on children – and the change in economic circumstances remains as great as ever. In this study, parental divorce had an impact not only in childhood but also in adult life, but the effects were different for men and women, and differed among women according to their social class of origin.

Women from divorced families seemed as likely as other women to work full-time, but they were more likely to work part-time than to remain in the home. This may be due to economic insecurity in childhood reinforcing a desire for economic independence, strengthened by having seen how mothers can work. It may also be related to their husbands' earning ability, in that these women appeared to marry more often un-employed men, and therefore perhaps needed to work.

The family histories of women from divorced families showed less disruption than for the men – perhaps because life with one parent of the same sex leads more easily to satisfactory family formation than life with one parent of the opposite sex.

That parental divorce leads to more long term emotional and socio-economic disadvantage than parental death confirms earlier suggestions that this is due to the more negative emotional impact of such an event as well as to the greater likelihood of downward social mobility in the remnant family after divorce (Wadsworth and Maclean 1986).

The overall picture is of measurable impact, with different levels of magnitude according to the woman's socio-economic class of origin. The girls from non-manual homes showed a sharper loss in educational and occupational attainment and marital stability as well as increased alcohol and tobacco consumption. This supports a view of women as beset by difficulties, of which parental disruption is only one and obviously only those a little further up the educational or occupational attainment ladder could fall back a rung or two. The increased stress shown by the women from higher socio-economic groups may well be due to the higher aspirations which they may have had, and their mothers may have had, and to the greater gap between aspirations and achievement at school, at work, and in family life.

REFERENCES

Atkins, E.C., Cherry, N., Douglas, J.W.B., Kiernan, K.E. and Wadsworth, M.E.J. (1981) 'The 1946 cohort study', in S.A. Mednick and A.E. Baert (eds) *An Empirical Basis for Primary Prevention*, Oxford: Oxford University Press.

Blaxter, M. (1987) 'Alcohol consumption', in B.D. Cox, A.W. Buckle, N.P. Fenner, F.A. Huppert and M. Wichelow (eds) *The Health and Life Style Survey*, London: Health Promotion Research Trust.

Bastard, B. and Voneche, L. (1988) *Les Familles Monoparentales Face a Leur Situation Economique*, Paris: Centre de Sociologie des Organisations.

Braddon, F.E.M., Wadsworth, M.E.J., Davies, J.M.C. and Cripps, R.A. (1988) 'Social and regional differences in food and alcohol consumption and their measurements in a national birth cohort', *Journal of Epidemiological and Community Health* 42: 341–9.

Brannen, J. and Wilson, G. (eds) (1987) *Give and Take in Families*, London: Allen & Unwin.

Burgoyne, J. and Clark, D. (1986) *Making a Go of It*, London: Routledge.

Dominian, J. (1965) *Marital Breakdown*, Harmondsworth: Penguin.

Dunnell, K. (1980) *Family Formation 1976*, London: HMSO.

Eekelaar, J. and Maclean, M. (1986) *Maintenance after Divorce*, Oxford: Oxford University Press.

Furstenberg, F. and Spanier, D. (1984) *Recycling the Family*, California: Sage.

Guidobaldi, J., Cleminshaw, A., Perry, J.D. and McLaughlin, C.G. (1987) 'Growing up in a divorced family', *Applied Social Psychology*, Annales 7, California: Sage.

Hart, N. (1976) *When Marriage Ends*, London: Tavistock.

Itzin, C. (1980) *Splitting Up*, London: Virago.

Kelly, J. and Corbin, J. (1986) 'Father child relationships after divorce', *Family Law Quarterly* 20: 109–29.

Kiernan, K. (1986) 'Teenage marriage and marital breakdown', *Population Studies* 37: 368–80.

McLanahan, S. (1985) 'Family structure and the reproduction of poverty', *American Journal of Sociology* 90, 4: 873–901.

Maclean, M. and Wadsworth, M.E.J. (1988) 'Children's life chances and parental divorce', *International Journal of Law and Family* 2: 155–66.

Maclean, M. and Weitzman, L.J. (eds) (forthcoming) *Counting the Cost of Divorce*, Oxford: Oxford University Press.

Martin, J. and Roberts, C. (1984) *Women and Employment: A Lifetime Perspective*, London: Department of Employment, OPCS, HMSO.

Mitchell, A. (1985) *Children in the Middle*, London: Tavistock.

Richards, M. (1987) 'Children, parents and families: developmental psychology and the re-ordering of relationships at divorce', *International Journal of Law and Family* 1: 295–317.

Richards, M. and Dyson, M. (1982) *Separation, Divorce and the Development of Children*, DHSS Review *mimeo* Cambridge Child Care and Development Group.

Rodgers, B. (1990) 'Adult affective disorders and early environment', *British Journal of Psychiatry* 157.

Vaughan, D. (1986) *Uncoupling*, Methuen: London.

Wadsworth, M.J. (1984) 'Early stress and adult health behaviour and parenting', in N.R. Butler and B.D. Corner (eds) *Stress and Disability in Childhood*, Bristol: John Wright & Sons.

—— (1987) 'Follow up of the first national birth cohort', *Paediatrics and Perinatal Epidemiology* 1: 95–117.

Wadsworth, M.E.J. and Maclean, M. (1986) 'Parental divorce and children's life chances', *Children and Youth Services Review* 8: 145–61.

Wallerstein, J. and Blakeslee, S. (1989) *Second Chances*, London: Bantam.

10 Sex and motherhood as handicaps in the labour market

Heather Joshi

WHY WAGES MATTER

No one tells you that you have to twist your psyche, your health and your money to fit into a society that seems to suffer from a kind of motherism, as opposed to 'sexism', racism or ageism.

(Hardie 1989: 58)

What Victoria Hardie calls motherism has also been eloquently described by Marina Warner (1989) in her 'CounterBlast' on the costs of childhood. The other contributors to Katharine Gieve's (1989) volume on the experience of motherhood also throw light on its various aspects. Sylvia Hewlett (1986) has written of the obstacles facing mothers in the US labour market. This chapter attempts to put numbers on some of the sources of mothers' financial sacrifices, one face of motherism. I argue that sexism still haunts the workplace, where sexism and motherism reinforce one another. I speculate about further consequences of the labour market's treatment of women and of mothers and end by indicating a direction for policies which could make it easier to be both a worker and a parent. The issue has long ceased to be whether motherhood and employment can be combined, but about the terms on which they are combined. Combined with steps to make life easier for children and their parents in general, 'family friendly' policies would be measures to moderate motherism.

In Britain, as elsewhere, women are at a disadvantage in earning cash for two main reasons. The labour market tends to pay men, all else being equal, better rates than women. Second, the domestic responsibilities of women, current and past, also affect directly how much they can earn. These two factors reinforce one another and are in turn both a reflection of the unequal division of labour. The expectation that male workers, but not females, have to support financially dependent spouses and offspring led to the idea of the 'family wage'. This, along with job segregation, and other forms of discrimination, is one of several reasons for the higher rates of pay for men.

These in turn, of course, perpetuate the expectation that women should undertake the bulk of the unpaid work needed to reproduce and maintain the population. These tasks would have even higher opportunity costs if undertaken by men.

I have written elsewhere about the opportunity costs of childbearing (Joshi 1987, 1989, 1990a, 1990b). Opportunity costs signify the alternative opportunities forgone or sacrificed to follow a particular course of action. In the case of motherhood, the opportunity cost on the labour market is typified by the earnings women forgo if they follow a typical employment pathway for a British mother rather than remain childless. An illustrative mother takes a break from paid work altogether while children are under 5, and works part-time while they are at school. Earnings are forgone for three reasons: absence from the labour market; reduced hours of work; and lower rates of pay per hour. There are, in turn, three factors lowering rates of pay: loss of experience or seniority; lower rates in part-time jobs than full-time jobs; and occupational downgrading on labour market re-entry. The last two factors often coincide, as it has been rare for part-time work to be offered at anything other than the lowest grades, and yet it is often the only form of employment feasible for mothers with no access to childcare outside school hours. Lost seniority, lost experience and lost training opportunities have a permanent though diminishing effect on a mother's earning potential: and, of course, low earnings imply low earnings-related pensions (Owen and Joshi 1990). My estimates of the total earnings forgone vary with a host of assumptions, at roughly around half of potential earnings after bearing the first of two children.

In some even rougher calculations, I suggested that the lifetime gap between the earnings open to a man (with or without children) and a woman who remained childless were of the same order of magnitude as those the woman would forgo to rear two children. This involved assumptions about the 'gender gap' between the pay of identically qualified and experienced men and women, conventionally taken as a measure of unequal treatment. My calculations were based largely on data on 32-year-olds in 1977-8. A widening premium of male pay over female as age increased, passed through an observed 32 per cent at age 32 and stabilized at 40 per cent after age 36 (Joshi 1989: 171) or 25 per cent and 29 per cent respectively, expressed as a percentage of men's pay, as most differentials will be in this paper. There are now further estimates of the gender gap, based on data for married men and women of all (working) ages collected in 1980 (Wright and Ermisch 1988). The gender gap I had assumed lies within the range of their estimates, though at its upper end. Even their lowest estimate, 16 per cent of men's (geometric mean) wages, should put an end to any belief that the equal opportunities legislation of the 1970s ended unequal treatment.

Indeed, given the continuing segregation of most employment into male or female workplaces, it is surprising that the Equal Pay Act achieved as much as it did.

Given labour market discrimination against women, there certainly ought to be gains for both men and women from a domestic division of labour. Yet the traditional domestic bargain does not work to the advantage of all women: it involves loss of earnings, future earnings potential and pension rights; it can involve social isolation, loss of autonomy and self and social-esteem; and perhaps most important, loss of security. Marriage contracts no longer have certain lifelong force. Current rates of divorce would lead to 37 per cent of all marriages contracted in the late 1980s ending in divorce (Haskey 1989). Courts have yet to perceive the erosion of their earning power that most wives have invested in their marriages. Even if the courts were to reverse the trend away from maintenance payments for wives, one may well wonder whether divorced women would ever get much compensation out of ex-husbands.

The relative pay of the sexes and their domestic responsibilities also interact in that improvements in women's relative earning power may also bring about further changes in the social structure: women catching up on men's educational attainments; women deferring, if not avoiding, taking on domestic responsibility and childbearing; women finding it financially easier to leave bad marriages; and men increasing their participation in the unpaid work in the home. All these things have been happening, to some extent, in Britain in the 1970s and 1980s (Ermisch 1990; Gershuny *et al.* 1986).

There have been improvements in economic opportunities for women. Women's hourly pay, relative to men's, rose in the mid-1970s (at the time the Equal Pay Act came into force) from a long unchanging level around 60 per cent of men's to a new plateau around 70 per cent. As yet, there is little sign that the Equal Pay for Work of Equal Value Amendment (1983) to the Equal Pay Act is having much of an upward impact on female wage rates. There have also been increased job opportunities for women over the 1970s, though almost all in part-time work. In the recession of the early 1980s, men's employment fell more than women's. Since a trough in 1983, female activity rates have resumed the upward trend that started around 1950. In the years from 1985, there are signs of female participation rates in full-time employment taking what may be a historically unprecedented upturn.

Before turning to future prospects in the final part of this chapter, let us look into the effects of sex and motherhood in the labour market of the 1970s, and try to untangle them. Though motherhood's major direct impact on women's status as earners is in keeping them out of paid work, and also in shortening the hours of those who do manage to combine some paid work with their domestic role, it is also important to study their rate of pay to get at the roots of economic disadvantage. We estimate and compare the pay penalties of motherhood with those of being female.

CASE STUDY OF ONE GENERATION'S LOW PAY FOR MOTHERS

> Seeing mothers in the same economically vulnerable position as myself underlined my own fragility. I did know mothers who managed lucrative careers, but they were exceptions. . . . It is interesting that not once has any of my husband's colleagues asked him how he manages to go to meetings . . . and evening functions when he has a family . . . . It is completely taken for granted that he is free to come and go as he pleases without any extra expense or any need for extra childminding allowance.
>
> (Hardie 1989: 64, 68–9)

These telling observations may seem to tell it all for some. This section offers supplementary evidence – a quantitative case study based on analyses I have done, with Marie-Louise Newell, of the 1946 birth cohort also cited in Chapter 9 of this book.

Data and methods

The National Survey of Health and Development has followed a sample of individuals born in Britain in 1946 (see Atkins *et al.* 1981; Douglas 1976; Joshi and Newell 1989, Appendix 1). We looked at the wages (rates of pay per hour) of the survey members, male and female, at two points in the 1970s when this information was collected. These were at age 26 in 1972 and on the eve of the survey members' 32nd birthday at the end of 1977 – at a stage of the life-cycle when many female survey members were moving between employment and full-time child care responsibilities.

Our studies investigated characteristics of both individuals and their jobs to see whether these explained the fact that the wages of male survey members were considerably higher than those of their female contemporaries in jobs. The answer to this was that the characteristics did not explain much, particularly in 1972 (Joshi and Newell 1989, or Joshi 1989: 164–9). This left the otherwise unexplained 'gender gap' cited above. We also used a similar approach to analyse the pay gap between women with children and those without (Joshi and Newell 1986, 1989, ch. 4).

At each of the contacts, about half the female cohort members were in the labour force (mostly not the same individuals), over half were mothers, rising from 61 per cent at 26 to 82 per cent at 32. The percentage of mothers among employed women was at each date smaller than in the cohort as a whole, 34 per cent and 71 per cent respectively. Our female regression samples (confined to civilian employees with known earnings and hours of work) consisted of 710 26-year-old women employed in 1972 and 462 who were employed at the time of the 1977 postal contact. The number of males in the regression sample from 1972 was 1,237, and at the next contact, 918.

The first step was to use regression analysis to fit explanatory models (sets of parameters) to the samples. One model follows the conventional 'human capital' category of explanations in terms of the individual's ability, education and employment experience. A second 'full' model also includes information about the characteristics of the job which adds statistically to the explanation of pay differences. This could reflect segmentation in the labour market such that identical individuals are not identically remunerated (see Joshi and Newell 1989; Main 1989; and Sloane 1985 for further discussion).

The next step was to see how the estimated models account for the differences observed between groups of workers. Between men and women, the parameters were quite different, indicating better pay for a worker with given characteristics if that person were male rather than female.

Noteworthy among the parameters are the effects of experience on pay, which these longitudinal data enabled us to estimate. In both 1972 and 1977, work experience is an important explanatory variable. According to the full model, used here to compare the subsets of women, in 1972, each year of work experience adds 4 per cent to the pay per hour, whereas in 1977, more recent work experience adds 1.6 per cent and more distant work experience 1.4 per cent. In the 'human capital' model, which is used here to compare men and women, the coefficients on work experience are slightly higher than in the full model. In this formulation fitted to males, a year of work experience marks pay up by 3 per cent (less than for women) in 1972, but by age 32 a year of recent work experience raised pay by 8 per cent. This term accounted for a substantial part of the estimated labour market advan- tage of being male at age 32 in 1977. 'Male advantage' is another way of describing the 'gender gap' cited in Part 1. It summarizes the difference between the sexes for the whole set of parameters. At age 26, when the gender gap was bigger, it was more than accounted for by a bigger constant term for males, offset by small female advantages on other terms such as work experience. Altogether, the pay gap left to be explained by gender amounted to a markdown on average male pay of about 25 per cent, at age 32, after the Equal Pay Act had come into force. Before that, in 1972, the gender gap was equivalent to 34 per cent of male wages.

We did not split the samples of male employees into fathers and others because there was virtually no difference between their rates of pay, before or after controlling for other factors. This is not surprising in view of the sort of attitude reported in the second quotation at the start of this section of the chapter; fathers are not expected to adjust their work to accommodate family needs for their time. In so far as fathers have been observed to adapt to their parental role, it is by increasing hours of overtime away from home. Note that the survey does not provide evidence on couples. The cohort members did not generally marry their exact contemporaries, fewer of the men than of the women had married at each stage. Those who had would tend to have wives born later than 1946 (Kiernan 1987).

Amongst the women workers, there were substantial differences between the pay of those who were and were not parents, but the parameters of a common model fitted both sub-samples equally well. It was quite surprising, at times in our own lives, unbelievable, that having children didn't have a direct downward effect on productivity and pay, independent of the other control variables. Perhaps too few of this generation were anywhere near high pressure career tracks – only 3 per cent of the female cohort were graduates. The common set of female parameters could be used to evaluate the contribution to pay differences of the differences in the two groups' attributes and job characteristics.

The explained differences between mothers and other women were divided up into those which are consequent upon motherhood and those which are independent of it, or at least determined at an earlier stage of their lives. This division was somewhat arbitrary. We assumed that the shorter employment experience and greater propensity to work part-time compared to non-mothers are routes through which motherhood affects pay. We assumed that downward mobility since childbearing was a consequence of motherhood. Though this might not always be so, current domestic constraints and the loss of skill or confidence over the break are plausible explanations for the mothers returning to jobs for which they appear to be overqualified (Newell and Joshi 1986; Joshi and Newell 1987). Our exercise hypothetically restored cases of downward movement to the level of job they held before their first birth. The remaining differences in the occupational structure between the two sub-samples are not treated as outcomes of their parental status. Neither did we treat mothers' relatively worse educational attainments as consequences of motherhood.

There are, of course, difficulties in dividing explanatory variables into those which are the consequences of motherhood and those which are its antecedents. We ignore those cases where pregnancy may have brought education to a premature end, for example. More broadly, it can be argued that it is anticipation of a conventional female role as adults that helped depress the attainments of girls as adolescents and similar expectations by the women and/or their employers which account for their relatively poor attainments in the labour market. But such arguments might, to some extent, apply to the women who as yet remained childless. The majority of these women did go on to have children. Seventy per cent of survey members childless at 26 (42 per cent of the cohort) had become mothers by age 36, which includes 52 per cent of the 20 per cent of the cohort still childless at 32.

Attributes compared

At both cross-sections, female employees without children were better paid than female employees with children, by 41 per cent of mothers' (geometric mean) pay in 1972 and 37 per cent in 1977. On virtually all personal and job characteristics, the childless women had scores worth more pay, at each cross-section. Mothers seemed to be somewhat less ambitious and less able (as measured at 15) than non-mothers and to have spent on average three-quarters of a year less at school between the ages of 15 and 18 than non-mothers. Mothers were more likely than non-mothers to have started their working lives before age 18 in the less well-paid types of jobs.

Mothers had, on average, substantially less work experience than childless women: 2.4 years less in the 8 years before age 26 and 4.3 years less in the 14 years before age 32. More childless women were resident in the south-east in 1972, and more of them had ever had any training on the job. In 1977, more childless women took some work home and more were likely to work in a firm with more than 25 employees. Large differences are found in the numbers in each sub-sample working part-time, with mothers being much more likely to be employed part-time. Rating occupation by our measure of the pay league of the current job, mothers tended to be found in the low and very low status categories and non-mothers to be dominant in the highest two status categories. Twenty-eight per cent of the mothers employed at 26 had experienced downgrading since the last job before the first birth, 33 per cent at age 32. (For details of the construction of the pay league of the job type, see Newell and Joshi 1986, Appendix B.)

As far as pay-enhancing characteristics of men are concerned, they were not, on balance, very different from those of childless women. This select minority of women were ahead of the average man in some respects, but behind him in others. They had higher scores on ability and ambition and more months of education to age 18, but their attainments in further education and occupational advance were inferior. They had almost as much employment experience as men, about one year less on average by age 32. Hence, the differences between the attributes of mothers and childless women also give a rough idea of those between mothers and men.

Wages of mothers and men

Table 15 shows that mothers among the survey generation who had paid work earned only about half the rate per hour of their male contemporaries at these two dates. How much of this gap was due to the fact that they were mothers, and how much to the fact that they were female? 'The wages of motherhood' revealed that some of the difference (ten percentage points of men's wages at age 26 and twelve at age 32) could be directly explained as the 'consequences of motherhood'. Part-time employment, job downgrading and lost employment experience accounted for roughly equal shares of this gap. As downward mobility affected only a minority who had thus far returned to work, it is not surprising that the other factors also come in. It is somewhat problematic distinguishing these effects, for as Brian Main has put it, job downgrading and lost experience are 'two sides of the same coin' (Main 1989).

The estimation of the consequences of motherhood for working mothers at each date are used hypothetically to restore them to their pre-motherhood job level, increase their employment experience to that of childless women and remove the hourly pay penalty involved in their working part-time. The result is shown in the second row of Table 15: making up to mothers for the direct consequences of parenthood, the mothers only reach 60 per cent and 67 per cent of men's pay. A different thought-experiment leaves mothers with their depleted earning assets, but values them at the rates paid to men. The pay advantages of being treated like a man in the labour market are greater, in 1972 far greater, than the gain to be made if all mothers avoided downgrading, employment breaks and part-time work. Being treated like men would put the mothers thirty-eight points ahead in 1972 and nineteen points in 1977–8. The impact of the Equal Pay Act is apparent in halving this measure of the gender gap for women with the mothers' characteristics.

The fourth line of Table 15 shows the joint effects of restoring mothers' earning assets lost to child care and then paying them at male rates. (The only attributes actually changed are the mothers' employment experience, because job type and part-time employment have no weight in the human capital model.) The difference between lines four and two is another way of measuring the gender gap, as it would be experienced by the mothers given the childless women's employment record. Combined with the men's rates of pay, this experiment brings the mothers closer, but not right up to, the levels of pay received by men. The remaining gap, 5 per cent at age 26 and 14 per cent at age 32, reflects the men's higher educational attainments, and

Table 15 The gap between men's and women's pay, for the 1946 cohort: an account of the gap between the pay of men and employed mothers

| | Hourly wage relative to men's actual | | |
	Age 26 1972	Age 32 1977–8	Account of each gap
	%	%	
Actual pay of mothers in paid work	50	55	Lost experience, downward mobility, extra part-time work
Wage mothers would receive if motherhood had no pay consequences	60	67	Difference from top line to third is gender effect for women with mothers' characteristics
Wage mothers would receive if paid as men	88	74	Mothers' lost employment experience valued at men's rates of pay
Wage mothers would receive if motherhood had no pay consequences and women paid men's rates	95	86	Value of men's greater educational attainments, etc
Actual wage of men	100	100	

Note: Wages women would receive if they were men are imputed using parameters of a human capital wage function fitted to male cohort members at each date, which then weight the women's work experience, education, etc.

The pay consequences of motherhood are taken as the average of the low and high estimates derived from a model including job as well as personal characteristics.

The full model is not used to compare men and women because (a) it arguably contains the outcomes of discrimination in job characteristics and (b) the measurement of job-type used to identify female occupational mobility is not available for males.

by 32, their higher average employment experience than even the childless women. The last bit of the gap in Table 15 is also bigger at 32 because the estimated premia for these attributes were higher.

The direct consequences of motherhood play a relatively minor part in accounting for mothers' low pay. Motherhood directly accounts for one-fifth of the pay gap between mothers and men at age 26 and one-quarter at age 32. Gender accounted for seven-tenths of the gap before the Equal Pay Act came into effect and four-tenths thereafter. The higher investment by males of that generation in further education accounts for much of the remaining part of the gap, one-tenth and three-tenths at 26 and 32 respectively. Although the pay penalty for just being female had fallen, at both points it appeared to be the major proximate source of women's disadvantage.

It is possible that the relative importance of the direct effects of motherhood in keeping rates of pay down could continue to increase over the life-cycle. At the point these data were collected, there had not been time for women with really long gaps in their work history to have returned to the labour market. At higher ages, it is possible that the re-entry of such women could pull down the average employment experience of employed mothers in the cohort, and hence drag down their average rate of pay. There was also still scope for those who were out of the labour force in 1977–8 to make downwardly mobile re-entries. On the other hand, there are possibilities of recovery as recent labour market experience is accumulated, cancelling the 'depreciation of human capital' thought to occur in breaks from paid work. It is also likely that job downgrading is transitory, though the NSHD data finished too early to detect any recovery.

Wages of childless women and men

Table 16 shows a similar but simpler exercise comparing childless women with men. Their actual pay was higher than the mothers but less than three-quarters of the men's. Their 'human capital' was broadly equivalent to men's but, as noted above, differently structured. Hence, when their attributes are valued at male rates rather than their own, virtually all of the gap is closed. For them the actual gap and the extent of unequal treatment is virtually the same. The gender gap at 26 was 29 per cent of men's pay, at 32, 22 per cent. These estimates of gender premia differ from those applying to mothers (less at 26, more at 32), because of changes in the parameters involved at the two dates and differences in average attributes in the four samples of women.

The low pay of childless women (compared to men) is nevertheless more than the mothers would earn if there were no 'consequences of motherhood' (row 2, Table 15). The mothers' attributes prior to childbearing were not worth as much on the labour market. The higher earning power of the childless women is consistent with an economic interpretation of fertility behaviour (Ermisch 1988). Those facing the greatest loss of earnings on motherhood seem more likely to have deferred it (Kiernan and Diamond 1983).

For both sets of women, the substantially higher earning power of men would tend to make partnership and 'domestic specialization' look like an attractive economic proposition. Perhaps those who had already made some sacrifice of (female) earning power in order to enter or maintain partnership with a male likely to get much higher rates of pay have done the smart

Table 16 The gap between men's and women's pay, for the 1946 cohort: an account of the gap between the pay of men and childless women

	Hourly wage relative to men's actual		Account of each gap
	Age 26 1972	Age 32 1977–8	
	%	%	
Actual pay of childless women	71	75	Better rates of pay, given worker characteristics for males
Wage childless women would receive if paid as men	100	97	Men's marginally 'superior' 'human capital' compared to women who remain childless
Actual wage of men	100	100	

(See note to Table 15 on p. 187)

thing. Whether they will have anything to regret depends on the duration of the partnership and its terms. Financial dependence makes people vulnerable. Financial independence also has its costs for women in the sort of labour market this cohort faced in the 1970s, especially when they were in their early twenties (peak marrying ages) and the gender gap was big. If you can't beat them, join them?

Motherhood or gender?

What does this case study suggest can be learned about the possibility of disentangling the influences of sex and motherhood on wages? Some might say that the interactions are so complex that the effects are inextricable, unamenable to partitioning. Comparing the employment aftermath of childbearing with what preceded it clearly does not capture all of the more generalized effects of gender on a person's fortunes in the labour market, but it is nevertheless one piece of the jigsaw. Though a relatively small component of the picture, these wage effects indicate conflict between women's paid and unpaid duties which may indirectly account for the gender gap.

Motherhood may have its effects indirectly, in, for example, inhibiting women's acquisition of earning assets, like education, before they ever have children. The prospect of motherhood and associated earnings interruption probably affects the choice of occupation and women's access to on-the- job-training. This would tend to result in larger parameters in the men's wage function. The mothers in these samples seem to have suffered from low assets and low parameters. The childless women were better equipped as earners than the mothers, but they faced the same low parameters. Relative to men with their high level of schooling, the childless women's qualifications and occupational attainments were modest. Perhaps the expectation that the childless survey members might become mothers was keeping their career paths subdued, and their rates of pay closer to those of women contending with domestic constraints than to those of their upwardly mobile male contemporaries.

CONCLUSIONS

Female autonomy is greatest where both society and the women themselves have little doubt about a woman's right to make decisions and to battle for her and her children's rights.

(Caldwell 1986: 202)

Are women low paid because they are mothers or because they are not men? The case study of young mothers in the labour market in the 1970s found that both factors lower women's pay. There were signs of the 'financial face of motherism', but these direct consequences of motherhood were smaller than those of gender. Differences between women's pay were overshadowed by differences between men and women. In a more general sense, the gender gap is probably the consequence of potential motherhood, given the prevailing domestic division of labour. Measures to support the equal treatment of men and women in the labour market cannot be effectively separated from measures to support the employment of mothers and promote egalitarian parenthood (Hewlett 1986; Bernhardt 1988). Furthermore, measures to support parents and measures of social support for children cannot really be separated. Rights of children and of mothers may in theory conflict, in practice they reinforce one another, as the quotation from Jack Caldwell above makes clear.

Though the evidence presented in this chapter was collected in the 1970s, it still seems to be telling a familiar story of a widening gap between men's and women's access to earned income as they pass through the ages of family formation. Facilities to help mothers combine parenthood with paid work were then, and remain, very limited. The facility which enables fathers also to be earners is, usually, the mother.

In the booming economy of the late 1980s, the demand for women to join, rejoin or remain in the labour force is higher than ever, particularly because of the growing shortage of new entrants to the labour force. This follows as a consequence of the 'baby bust', a drop in births by one-third from 1964 to 1977, representing a rejection of early childbearing (particularly by the middle class) and a retreat from large families of three or more. There is good evidence that this 'baby bust' was intensified by the improvements in pay opportunities for women around that time (Ermisch 1988). A generation later, in the late 1980s, the labour market seems set to offer yet another improvement of the terms on which women may participate in the economy. Relative wages may well rise again, employers are beginning to think about training for women and about facilities for those with domestic responsibilities.

It is a matter of interest, if not concern, as to how people will react. Family formation may well be deterred, family break-up possibly facilitated (Ermisch and Wright 1989). More to the point, will the terms on which women may combine employment with family roles be adjusted? Will roles within the family tend toward greater symmetry of men and women? Will the labour market recognize the need for adjustment so that men as well as women can adjust work to family responsibilities? Will men press for such changes?

Women's supply of labour to the paid economy has its unseen opportunity costs which are the other side of the coin to those of their domestic role. Increases in women's hours and efforts devoted to paid work could be realized without any of the adaptations outlined above, by either increasing the overload of those with unpaid responsibilities and/or reducing the input they are able to make to the care of children, the handicapped, the disabled, the elderly and, indeed, their husbands. Women have responded to economic change in the past by making compromises which have not removed their disadvantages in employment (Joshi 1990a and b). Will women really benefit this time from better opportunities in the 1990s? Or is Norman Fowler's 'Decade of the Working Woman' a trap? Will the perennial conflicts between 'domestic duties' and women's participation in the paid economy be better managed by a newly aware and 'reconstructed' generation of men and women, or will they indeed remain 'women's problems', to which the main adjustments are made by the women themselves?

These questions about the present and future combination of family and economic roles in something other than the traditional domestic division of labour are not just issues between individual couples, but involve policy for employers and unions, education, training, transport, health and social services, taxation and pensions for a start. I will not try to go into any great detail. The estimates presented above strengthen the case for reorganizing employment and child care so that women can avoid long breaks. Part-time employment should be more available at levels other than the lowest grade. The estimates also point to the need for more effective implementation of the legislation against sex discrimination in employment practice and pay. Men might take more of an interest in sharing child care if their wives could earn as much (or more) than they, and if working shorter hours were not as much penalized as now. I am not underestimating the likely resistance to such change, but the combination of market forces and greater government intervention than is envisaged at the time of writing could push things along.

I conclude that the challenge is to develop 'family friendly policies'. There are Scandinavian examples to follow. Ideally, such policies could not impose or presuppose any particular pattern of family division of labour or form of unit. They would assure the quality of child care, inside or outside the home. They would reduce the seclusion of children and their carers from the adult environment. They would reduce the tensions between the individual and the family. They would bring families more resources and options, so that the weak and dependent are protected without penalising whoever takes on the primary caring role. The undervaluation of mothers' unpaid work is as serious a problem as the underpayment in the labour market documented here. Motherism has not just a financial face.

REFERENCES

Atkins, E., Cherry, N., Douglas, J.W.B., Kiernan, K.E. and Wadsworth, M.E.J. (1981) 'The 1946 British Birth Cohort: an account of the origins, progress and results of the National Survey of Health and Development', in S.A. Mednich and A.E. Baert (eds) *Prospective Longitudinal Research*, Oxford: Oxford University Press.

Bernhardt, E. (1988) 'Fertility and employment', Contribution to Symposium on Population Change and European Society, European University Institute, Florence, Typescript, University of Stockholm.

Caldwell, J.C. (1986) 'Routes to low mortality in poor countries', *Population and Development Review* 12, 2: 171–220.

Douglas, J.W.B. (1976) 'The use and abuse of national cohorts', in M. Shipman (ed.) *The Organization of Social Research*, London: Routledge & Kegan Paul.

Ermisch, J.F. (1988) 'Economic influences on birth rates', *National Institute Economic Review* November: 71–81.

—— (1990) *Fewer Babies, Longer Lives: Implications of Demographic Trends*, York: Joseph Rowntree Foundation.

Ermisch, J.F. and Wright, R.E. (1989) *Entry to Lone Parenthood: Analysis of Marital Dissolution*, London: Birkbeck Discussion Paper in Economics 90/9.

Gershuny, J., Miles, I., Jones, S., Mullings, C., Thomas, G. and Wyatt, S. (1986) 'Time budgets: preliminary analysis of a national survey', *Quarterly Journal of Social Affairs* 2, 1: 13–39.

Gieve, K. (ed.) (1989) *Balancing Acts: On Being a Mother*, London: Virago.

Hardie, V. (1989) 'The world became a more dangerous place', in K. Gieve (ed.) *Balancing Acts: On Being a Mother*, London: Virago.

Haskey, J. (1989) 'Current prospects for the proportion of marriages ending in divorce', *Population Trends* 55, Spring, 34–7.

Hewlett, S.A. (1986) *A Lesser Life: The Myth of Women's Liberation in America*, New York: William Morrow & Co.

Joshi, H. (1987) 'The cost of caring', in Millar and Glendinning (eds) *Women and Poverty in Britain*, Brighton: Wheatsheaf.

—— (1989) 'The changing form of women's economic dependency', in H. Joshi (ed.) *The Changing Population of Britain*, Oxford: Basil Blackwell.

—— (1990a) 'The cash opportunity cost of childbearing: an approach to estimation using British data', *Population Studies* 44: 1 (also circulated as CEPR Discussion Paper 208).

—— (1990b) 'Changing roles of women in the British labour market and the family', in P. Deane (ed.) *Frontiers of Economic Science*, Proceedings of the British Association, Section F, Oxford 1988, London: Macmillan.

Joshi, H. and Newell, M.L. (1986) 'The wages of motherhood', Paper presented to the Annual Conference of the Regional Science Association, and also to the Bicentennial meeting of the Royal Statistical Society (March 1987) Typescript, London School of Hygiene.

—— (1987) 'Job downgrading after childbearing', in M. Uncles (ed.) *London Papers in Regional Science 18, Longitudinal Data Analysis: Methods and Applications*. London: Pion.

—— (1989) *Pay Differentials and Parenthood, Analysis of Men and Women born in 1946*, Coventry: Institute for Employment Research, University of Warwick (also circulated as CEPR Discussion Papers 156 and 157).

Kiernan, K.E. (1987) 'Demographic experiences in early adulthood: a longitudinal study', unpublished PhD thesis, University of London.

Kiernan, K. and Diamond, I. (1983) 'The age at which childbearing starts – a longitudinal study', *Population Studies* 37, 3: 363–80.

Main, B.G.M. (1989) *Women's hourly earnings over the life-cycle*, Coventry: Institute for Employment Research, University of Warwick.

Newell, M.L. and Joshi, H. (1986) *The Next Job after the First Baby: Occupational Transition among Women born in 1946*, London: Centre for Population Studies Research Paper 86–3, London School of Hygiene.

Owen, S.J. and Joshi, H. (1990) 'Sex equality and the state pension', *Fiscal Studies* 11: 1 (Also circulated as Birkbeck Discussion Paper in Economics 89/7).

Sloane, P. (1985) 'Discrimination in the labour market', in D. Carline, C.A. Pissarrides, W. Stanley Siebert and P.J. Sloane (eds) *Labour Economics*, London and New York: Longman.

Warner, M. (1989) *Into the Dangerous World* CounterBlast 5, London: Chatto & Windus.

Wright, R.E. and Ermisch, J.F. (1988) 'Gender discrimination in the British labour market: a reassessment', DP 278, London: CEPR (forthcoming in *Economic Journal*).

11 Feminist research and social policy

Janet Finch

INTRODUCTION

The concept of 'feminist research' – meaning not only the issues studied, but also the means by which research is conducted – has been a matter of some importance in the academic literature generated by second wave feminism. Ideas about the *ways* in which feminist research should be conducted have had considerable influence upon a range of social science disciplines. This is very obviously true in sociology, but it has happened also in other disciplines – political science, anthropology and psychology, for example (Smith 1974; Eichler 1980; Shapiro 1981; Gilligan 1982).

In social policy, however, the feminist intervention has been focused almost exclusively upon redefining the *content* of the discipline, and making issues of gender more central to it, but has paid rather little attention to issues of *method*. Although feminists have achieved some considerable success in these endeavours (as evidenced by other chapters in this book, *inter alia*), I believe that it is important to consider whether our impact upon the study of social policy might be advanced further by paying more attention to issues of method in feminist research. In my view, the central question which needs to be posed is this: Are there some ways of doing research in social policy which are more conducive than others to making visible (i) women's needs and interests and (ii) the importance of gender relations in welfare provision?

I am using this chapter to begin to address that question, but I make no claims to provide a fully developed answer. My intention is to highlight this as an issue for debate and discussion rather than to provide a blueprint for feminist research in social policy. I shall proceed by considering some of the main issues in the wider debate about feminist research, and suggest how these might have specific relevance for studies in social policy. Where there are connections with existing work, I shall try to point these out. Thus,

I hope to evaluate the prospects for consolidating a tradition of feminist research in social policy.

My discussion is structured around three themes which are prominent in the literature on methods in feminist research:

(1) What methods make gender issues most visible?
(2) Who is research 'for'?
(3) The relationship between the researcher and the researched.

Whilst all three are interrelated, it is useful to consider them separately in the first instance. They do not exhaust the range of issues about feminist research practice, but they offer a good basis for exploring the potential for transplanting these debates into research on social policy.

WHAT METHODS MAKE GENDER ISSUES MOST VISIBLE?

One of the main themes of the feminist debate on research methods has concerned the relative merits of quantitative and qualitative research, with a major emphasis being upon the value of small-scale, qualitative methods for research which seeks to make visible the needs and experiences of women.

Strong and influential arguments in favour of qualitative research can be found in a variety of places (Smith 1974, 1979; Oakley 1981; Graham 1983; Stanley and Wise 1983). The case depends not only upon the utility of qualitative methods, but also upon a critique of more conventional approaches, especially the large-scale survey. The case against survey methods, in particular, rests partly upon technical and partly upon episte-mological grounds. The technical arguments are concerned with the artificial nature of the way in which questions are asked in surveys, and with the meaning of the data collected by these means. These technical arguments are not really specifically feminist ones, although one of the most influential statements of this position is to be found in Oakley's (1981) work where she does cast this in the context of feminist debates. She argues that the survey researcher's belief that people can be interviewed in a totally 'objective' way, with no interventions on the part of the interviewer and keeping the data bias-free, just does not stand up to the reality of interviewing in practice. Similar points have been made by other writers on methodology who were not taking a feminist standpoint (Cicourel 1964; Denzin 1970).

However, when it comes to matters of epistemology, questions raised by feminists *are* distinctive. One of the most cogent statements is to be found in Hilary Graham's (1983) article on women and the survey method, which is given a title which neatly encapsulates her position: 'Do her answers fit his questions?' The argument here is that the knowledge base of social science disciplines has male bias built into it in a strong sense – it reflects the way in which men see the world, how they view their own and women's place in it, what they assume to be normal and abnormal ways of living. The feminist critique of the *content* of social science disciplines begins from this position; the argument of writers like Graham is that we should be considering how far this male bias has infected the process of generating data and the *methods* by which this is done.

A particular target of feminist criticism has been the survey method. Since it is also a method used commonly in social policy research, it is important to be clear about the nature of such criticisms. Again it is useful to distinguish between the technical and epistemological levels, although the two are, of course, linked.

At the more technical level, the case against the survey is sometimes made by feminists on the grounds that surveys typically study either households or individuals. If the household is the unit of study, this emphasizes the divisions between households rather than within them – a serious problem in any work which is about household resources, because it requires the researchers to make the (entirely untenable) assumption that all members of the household benefit equally from resources coming into it (Pahl 1984; Millar and Glendinning 1989). Where individuals are the unit of study, the web of relationships in which women are involved, and which are so central to the organization of many women's lives, are obscured. In either case, the significance of gender relations in social life is rendered invisible. Though a significant criticism against any survey which does obscure gender in this way, in a sense this point is more technical than fundamental. It does not call into question the basic concept of a survey and it is possible to take it on board in the process of survey design. In this context, it is helpful that major national surveys such as the General Household Survey and the Family Expenditure Survey – both of which are used extensively in social policy research – collect data in a form which enables it to be analysed either in household or in individual units.

A more fundamental criticism against surveys is epistemological rather than technical in nature. The argument here is that surveys try to find out about people's lives in ways which reflect women's experiences very inadequately. The survey method assumes that social life can be studied through measurement, and that the principal means of gaining measurable data is through putting experiences into words: 'What can't be put into words in an interview or on a questionnaire can't be recorded and can't be studied' (Graham 1983: 143). From a feminist perspective, it can be argued that women's experiences typically cannot be easily verbalized in this ultra-rational and objectified way and that social scientists who wish genuinely to understand women's experiences need to listen to women in a different kind of way (Smith 1974, 1979; Graham 1983; Stanley and Wise 1983).

The argument that quantitative methods in general, and surveys in particular, represent a distortion of women's experience has been very influential among feminists. However, it is by no means accepted universally that this should lead to a complete rejection of survey methods. Some feminists have made a strong case that quantitative research has positive value for feminists in certain contexts (Kelly 1978; Jayaratne 1983). There is no doubt that this is true. Clearly, a piece of research like the Women and Employment Survey (Martin and Roberts 1984) does ask questions informed by an understanding of women's lives and gives authoritative data about their distinctive and inferior place in the structure of employment. In that sense, it is extremely useful in making visible certain aspects of gender relations. It has been influential in writing on social policy, as elsewhere.

However, it is equally clear that such work does not exhaust the range of questions which feminists would wish to ask about women's experience of employment. A good illustration of how different methods can open out our understanding of gender issues can be found in Sheila Cunnison's (1986) study of the work of sheltered housing wardens – a topic which is highly relevant within social policy, since women working for low wages in effect sustain whole sectors of welfare provision. Her work arose out of an interest in trade unionism, and she was concerned to understand how it could happen that women working as wardens accepted terms and conditions which would have been out of the question in another setting such as a factory. They were on call twenty-four hours a day, received no extra pay if they were called out during the night and were expected to carry on their normal duties whatever else had happened. Not only did they accept these expectations, but they frequently went well beyond them, performing domestic and nursing tasks for residents which fell outside their job descriptions.

Cunnison poses the question 'Why do women consent to this apparent exploitation?' In answering that question, she contrasts two different concepts of the motivation for work, one industrially based (you only do what you are paid for) and the other based upon women's work in the family (you respond to other people's needs without consideration of gain). Sheltered housing wardens, she argues, experience their work in the latter rather than the former way, partly because it is literally based 'at home' (since most live on the job) and easily becomes an extension of their domestic role. She arrives at this conclusion via research which depended upon a range of methods, mostly qualitative: semi-structured interviews; further meetings with wardens and unstructured interviews; regular visits to housing schemes; and observation of various kinds, including following wardens around for a whole day.

Cunnison's work affords a good example of how systematic, detailed study of a qualitative kind is capable of making visible women's experiences, and of understanding what meaning those experiences have, in a way which cannot be addressed in a survey. Large-scale surveys are extremely useful for demonstrating that women's employment is concentrated in certain sectors – including low-paid sectors of welfare provision – but if you wish to understand *how* and *why* it is possible for our society to go on relying upon the exploitation of women's labour to sustain whole sectors of welfare provision, you really are asking a different kind of question and need different methods of investigation to answer it.

This example is just one of the many which I could have chosen to illustrate why feminists who work in the field of social policy might pay more attention to questions of method. I do not take the view that we should espouse a single 'correct feminist method'. But I do believe that it is important to consider the potential of the variety of techniques available for illuminating the kind of questions which we wish to ask, and to think more systematically about how they can be deployed.

In particular, I believe that there is space for a more sustained development of feminist work which focuses upon issues of experience and meaning in the context of social policy. Of course there are some precedents for this. In the inter-war period, feminists who were concerned about the living conditions of working-class women produced some very interesting work based upon informal interviews, diaries and letters – the very stuff of qualitative research (Pember Reeves 1913; Black 1915). Much more recently, work such as Clare Ungerson's (1987) study of informal carers or my own research on pre-school playgroups (Finch 1984a) explicitly tries to use qualitative methods to illuminate policy issues. However, such examples are relatively rare and authors tend to feel the need to justify their approach to a social policy audience. In addressing more explicitly questions of method, feminists could put this kind of research on a more secure footing.

WHO IS RESEARCH FOR?

The concept of feminist research implies renouncing any claim that social research can be an apolitical activity. The political commitments of the researcher are intrinsically woven into the activity of research – I implied that by posing my initial question about how research can make visible women's interests and women's experiences. The literature on feminist research uses as a key criterion of good work that the research should be 'for' women, in a strong sense.

This position is set out well by Harding (1987), in the introduction to her collection of articles on feminist methodology. The case starts from the recognition that – as I indicated above – all social science knowledge has tended to have a built-in male bias, and, consequently, our very understanding of the social world comes through men's eyes. The argument for counteracting this amounts to much more than an exercise in which women are 'added in', but the overall picture is left essentially unchanged. It is important that the whole picture should be redrawn so that social knowledge, especially of a kind which could be influential in shaping social policies and changing social institutions, should reflect the interests of women. As Harding puts it:

> Women should have an equal say in the design and administration of the institutions where social knowledge is produced and distributed for reasons of social justice: it is not fair to exclude women from gaining the benefits of participating in these enterprises that men get.
>
> (Harding 1987: 7)

Alongside these arguments about epistemology, there are overtly political issues about the role of the feminist researcher and the commitments of sisterhood. At a minimum, all feminists would agree that women are discriminated against, excluded and oppressed in our society. Anyone claiming the feminist label would be committed at a personal level to bringing about some change in that situation. But how far should such commitments enter into the professional business of conducting research?

Clearly, there are different possible views on this, and many feminist social scientists would reject a stance in which research becomes simply an extension of other political activities. On the other hand, few would feel comfortable about producing a piece of research which was actually going to damage the interests of other women. Presumably, somewhere between those positions is where most feminists would want to locate themselves, but working that out is not easy. Even meeting the minimum criterion of not damaging other women's interests can be more difficult than it seems, as I have discovered in my own research practice (Finch 1984b).

Again, these debates are not exclusive to feminist writing (Becker 1967; Cohen and Taylor 1977; Barnes 1979), but they are given a particular slant and importance in this context. They clearly are very pertinent to work on social policy, where research often is oriented towards some kind of policy change, and where therefore the possibility of damaging women's interests is a real one. More generally, the fact that it is more often women than men who are on the receiving end of social policy means that the idea that feminist research should be research 'for' women has particular resonance.

A good example of a piece of research which is specifically 'for' women is the community study of male violence, conducted by Hanmer and Saunders and their colleagues (1984). The researchers set out to uncover the extent of women's experiences of violence both inside and outside the home, and their work is geared to practical action and policy proposals. They chose the method of intensive study of seven streets in inner-city Leeds and, through patient exploration with sympathetic interviewers, documented just how widespread is women's experience of violence and the threat of violence. Their work had an interesting impact upon debates in criminology, since the levels which they documented were very much higher than those found in the British Crime Survey, which was being conducted at the same time.

This piece of work is very clearly 'for' women in a variety of ways. Not only does it make visible women's own experiences, in an aspect of their lives which normally is quite literally concealed, but also the researchers are committed to using their research to help women change their own situation. Their book thus contains simple, clear instructions to community groups on how women can conduct a similar survey in their own area and what they might do with the findings.

This approach to research may well feel comfortable from a feminist perspective, but, of course, researchers who take this route often find themselves subjected to criticism from colleagues who believe that research should be apolitical and value-free. These arguments about the nature of research are not specifically feminist ones, although feminist researchers need to be on top of them, and to know that the grounds on which we operate can be defended intellectually. I do not propose to discuss this issue here, although elsewhere I have explored it in relation to social policy research more generally (Finch 1986).

THE RELATIONSHIP BETWEEN THE RESEARCHER AND THE RESEARCHED

The idea that feminist research should be 'for' women leads naturally to a reconsideration of the relationship between the researcher and the people who are the subjects of the research. The key themes here are: personal identification, lack of exploitation, eroding the hierarchical relationship.

One of the most well-known feminist statements of this position is to be found in Ann Oakley's (1981) discussion of her research on motherhood, in which she argues that the idea that a researcher can maintain an objective distance from her subjects is not only unrealistic, but also – from a feminist perspective – politically unacceptable when women are the subjects of the research. Oakley rejects the conventional idea that a researcher should maintain social distance, should not be prepared to enter into informal discussion with subjects, and should retain complete control over the interview process. She argues that this creates a hierarchical relationship in which the researcher invests none of herself but expects other women to lay open their own experiences. A feminist should not be in the business of 'objectifying her sisters'.

Moving even further away from the idea that research should be an entirely objective activity, in which the process is not contaminated by interventions from the researchers, Liz Stanley and Sue Wise (1983) present a strongly argued case that feminists should use their own experiences as a key research resource. The case for so doing depends partly on recognizing that not only is all social knowledge necessarily constructed out of personal experience (men's as well as women's), but that women are in a distinctive position in having to construct new perspectives upon the social world, to counteract the orthodox views which reflect the life experiences of men. Sue Wise (1985) has provided an interesting example of using her own experience as a research resource in her discussion of becoming a feminist social worker. Another important exponent of a similar position is the Canadian feminist Dorothy Smith, who argues that the experience of being a social scientist is necessarily different for women and men, in a fundamental way, and therefore that women social scientists have to draw upon their own experiences and understandings of their world in order to be able to reshape social knowledge (Smith 1974, 1979).

The personal identification of women with the subjects of their research, and the use of their own experience as a legitimate way of pursuing it, are themes which have just begun to creep into the feminist literature on social policy. In Clare Ungerson's (1987) study of informal carers, an explicit attempt is made to link the researcher and the researched – an attempt which is reflected in the title of the resulting book *Policy is Personal*. In her introduction to this work, Ungerson writes of her experiences of informal care within her family, of her concerns about her own responsibilities in this matter, and about how this influenced her both to undertake research in this area, and to conduct it in ways which would make people's experience visible.

Ungerson's approach is notable because it is still rather unusual in the literature on social policy research. For the most part, these issues are not discussed, although one suspects that this type of research may be more widely practised than it appears. The importance of confronting these issues in the context of social policy research is obvious, however. The arguments for not objectifying your sister have particular relevance when research is being conducted on women who are in the weakest and most vulnerable positions – which is frequently the case in social policy research. At the same time, this alternative model of the relationship between the researcher and the researched does depart quite significantly from conventional notions of the research process and raises questions of politics and methods in their sharpest form. If this model is to become the orthodoxy in feminist work in social policy, it is important to be very clear about the intellectual, political and ethical grounds upon which research is being conducted.

FEMINIST RESEARCH AND THE DISCIPLINE OF SOCIAL POLICY

My main aim in raising these questions is to promote more debate among feminists working in the field of social policy about issues of method. In a short article, I have necessarily presented the issues in a rather attenuated form and, in reality, these are complex matters on which it would be quite inappropriate to take a simple view. It is quite properly a matter of debate among feminists as to whether we should be largely favouring qualitative methods, practising research which is 'for' women, and developing less hierarchical models of research practice in which our own experience is a prominent feature. These are all issues on which it is perfectly legitimate for feminists to take different positions. My main point is that they *should* be debated by feminists working in the field of social policy, rather more than they have been hitherto.

I would conclude with the observation that one of the main reasons why this has not happened so far is, I suspect, that social policy as a discipline – or area of study, for readers who prefer this formulation – in general has paid much less attention to methodological issues than have the social science disciplines upon which it draws. Although it has a strong empirical tradition, for the most part issues of method have been treated as technical questions rather than matters for intellectual debate. As a consequence, certain ideas about what constitutes 'proper research', and what should be its relationship to social policy, have held sway in a rather unexamined way. These ideas do not accommodate very easily the kind of feminist perspectives upon methods which I have been discussing (see Finch 1986 for further elaboration). In raising issues of method to a higher profile within the discipline, feminists would be making a contribution to its advance on a broad front.

REFERENCES

Barnes, J.A. (1979) *Who Should Know What? Social Science, Privacy and Ethics*, Harmondsworth: Penguin.
Black, C. (1915) *Married Women's Work*, London: G. Bell and Sons.
Becker, H. (1967) 'Whose side are we on?', *Social Problems* 14: 239–47.
Cohen, S. and Taylor, L. (1977) 'Talking about prison blues', in C. Bell and H. Newby (eds) *Doing Sociological Research*, London: Allen & Unwin.
Cicourel, A.V. (1964) *Method and Measurement in Sociology*, New York: Free Press.
Cunnison, S. (1986) 'Gender, consent and exploitation among sheltered housing wardens', in K. Purcell, S. Wood, A. Waton and S. Allen (eds) *The Changing Experience of Employment*, London: Macmillan.
Denzin, N.K. (1970) *The Research Act*, Chicago: Aldine.
Eichler, M. (1980) *The Double Standard: A Feminist Critique of Feminist Social Science*, London: Croom Helm.
Finch, J. (1984a) 'The deceit of self help: preschool playgroups and working class women', *Journal of Social Policy* 13, 1: 1–20.
—— (1984b) '"It's great to have someone to talk to": the ethics and politics of interviewing women', in C. Bell and H. Roberts (eds) *Social Researching: Politics, Problems, Practice*, London: Routledge & Kegan Paul.
—— (1986) *Research and Policy: The Uses of Qualitative Methods in Social and Educational Research*, Brighton: Falmer.
Gilligan, C. (1982) *In a Different Voice: Psychological Theory and Women's Development*, Cambridge, Mass.: Harvard University Press.
Graham, H. (1983) 'Do her answers fit his questions? Women and the survey method', in E. Gamarnikow, D. Morgan, J. Purvis and D. Taylorson (eds) *The Public and the Private*, London: Heinemann.
Hanmer, J. and Saunders, S. (1984) *Well-Founded Fear: A Community Study of Violence to Women*, London: Hutchinson.
Harding, S. (1987) 'Introduction: is there a feminist method?', in S. Harding (ed.) *Feminism and Methodology*, Bloomington: Indiana University Press.
Jayaratne, T.E. (1983) 'The value of quantitative methodology for feminist research', in G. Bowles and R. Duelli Klein (eds) *Theories of Women's Studies*, London: Routledge & Kegan Paul.
Kelly, A. (1978) 'Feminism and research', *Women's Studies International Quarterly* 1: 225–32.
Martin, J. and Roberts, C. (1984) *Women and Employment: A Lifetime Perspective*, London: HMSO.
Millar, J. and Glendinning, C. (1989) 'Gender and poverty', *Journal of Social Policy* 18, 3: 363–82.
Oakley, A. (1981) 'Interviewing women: a contradiction in terms', in H. Roberts (ed.) *Doing Feminist Research*, London: Routledge & Kegan Paul.
Pahl, J. (1984) 'The allocation of money within the household', in M. Freeman (ed.) *The State, The Law and The Family: Critical Perspectives*, London: Tavistock.
Pember Reeves, M. (1913) *Round About a Pound a Week*, London: G. Bell & Sons.
Shapiro, J. (1981) 'Anthropology and the study of gender', in E. Langland and W. Gove (eds) *A Feminist Perspective in the Academy*, Chicago: University of Chicago Press.

Smith, D.E. (1974) 'Women's perspective as a radical critique of sociology', *Sociological Enquiry* 44, 1: 7–13.

—— (1979) 'A peculiar eclipsing: women's exclusion from man's culture', *Women's Studies International Quarterly* 1, 4: 281–95.

Stanley, L. and Wise, S. (1983) *Breaking Out: Feminist Consciousness and Feminist Research*, London: Routledge & Kegan Paul.

Ungerson, C. (1987) *Policy is Personal: Sex, Gender and Informal Care*, London: Tavistock.

Wise, S. (1985) *Becoming a Feminist Social Worker*, Manchester University, Department of Sociology: Studies in Sexual Politics.

12 Will the abortion issue give birth to feminism in Poland?

Malgorzata Fuszara

In recent months, political and economic issues have provoked heated public discussion in Poland. One issue in particular has produced wide divisions in society and led to highly emotional debates. Here the divisions are largely independent of politics, however attempts have been made to use them for political purposes; it has been suggested that the debate was intended to distract attention from other problems. The event that gave rise to these divisions and discussions was a draft act 'on legal protection of the unborn child', proposing the introduction of a complete ban on abortion in Poland and of penalties for both having and performing an abortion.

The draft was submitted to the Seym by deputies of the former adminis-tration before the recent democratic elections to the Seym and Senate in June 1989. It provoked not only discussion and controversy, press articles and TV debates, but also street marches and demonstrations. Moreover, it gave rise to the opportunity for increased awareness of the situation and rights of women in Poland, and for some tentative attempts to organize movements in defence of those rights. When discussing the problems related to abortion in Poland, i.e. its legal regulation, the extent of the phenomenon, opinions about it, the new draft and the ideologies and attitudes of both the pro-abortionists and their opponents, it is essential to bear in mind the situation of women in Poland. This, however, is a very difficult task, not only because of the dimensions and complexity of the problem, but also because of the lack of reliable studies of Polish women's situation. The need for such studies could not even be discussed until recently. One of the many paradoxes resulting from the Communist system of government is that women ostensibly have equal rights combined with their actual exploitation. Under the banner of equal rights for women, the system burdened women with additional duties but failed to grant them any actual rights: this discredited the very slogan used and for some time has deprived the ideology of equality and the struggle for women's rights of its potency. We will now take a closer look at this paradox.

THE SITUATION OF WOMEN IN POLAND: PARADOXES

Many foreigners coming to Poland have the impression that women in Poland are truly free and enjoy equal rights. Indeed, one could believe this after a superficial examination of the Polish situation. Polish women receive education equal to that of men. There are now some statistics which suggest that they are even better educated than men. In 1987, 30 per cent of the adult population had secondary and higher education; amongst men the proportion was 27 per cent while amongst women it was 33 per cent (Statistical Yearbook 1988). Women's employment is also a mass phenomenon. In 1987, 75 per cent of women aged 25–29 were employed. In practice, however, this does not mean that all the employed women work from choice or want to satisfy their own ambitions or achieve self-realization through professional work. For many women, employment is simply an economic necessity. Their husbands' low wages are not enough to support their families and the women must take on paid work. The fact remains, however, that the vast majority of women are now employed in Poland, and the percentage of those in education is now greater than that of men. Women also have full electoral rights, and equal rights are protected under the constitution. The question arises, however, of how those equal rights came about and what opinions about them are today.

What was peculiar to the women's movement in Poland at its very beginning in the nineteenth century, was its connection with the struggle for independence. At the time, that struggle was of prime importance in Poland, and no group, including the women's movement, could avoid expressing an opinion on it. The first organized group whose aim was the improvement of women's status and education was that of the so-called 'enthusiasts', the best known of whom was the writer Narcyza Zmichowska. The group operated in Warsaw in the years 1840–50. The enthusiasts were engaged in the underground struggle for independence and for that reason suffered political oppression. Most of the activists were imprisoned and exiled by the Russian authorities, thus putting a stop to the group's operation.

In contemporary sources, information can be found about the rather specific role of women in nineteenth-century Poland. In the Russian sector, for instance, successive generations of men took part in insurrections for which they were imprisoned and exiled to Russia. The women who were left behind had to take over the responsibility of providing for themselves and their families. Such conditions did not favour the organization of women's rights movements.

But despite the division into male and female roles, the struggle for independence was a common national experience. In those days, women were already taking part in the struggle, joining underground movements and receiving their share of the persecution and repression suffered by those who struggled against the authorities. The division into countrymen and enemies mattered much more than that into men and women.

And yet the first signs of progress towards equal rights for women could be seen in the latter part of the nineteenth century. The first technical school for women was set up in the 1880s and women were granted the right to study at Polish universities in Cracow and Lvov in 1897. The Polish Society for Equal Rights for Women was established in 1907 and, amongst other things, it struggled for the right of women to vote. Women were finally granted that right in 1918 when Poland regained independence; in the first elections to the Polish Parliament they not only voted but also ran for and were elected to seats.

Over eighty different women's organizations were established in Poland between the First and Second World Wars; there were a variety of types, from professional groups to religious organizations. In addition, women's journals and books intended for female readers were published. Women had their own Parliamentary Society, there were women's funds and scholarships and women's clubs such as the Peasant Women's Clubs organized by the Farmer's Society. At the same time, in the Polish tradition, there was little separation of the sexes. This is illustrated by the absence of clubs from which women were excluded. It is something of a paradox that clubs refusing to admit women have only recently been imported to Poland through the influence of western clubs, even though such clubs are alien to the Polish tradition.

The situation changed radically after the Second World War. The 'grassroots' movements were replaced with institutions imposed from without. 'Equal rights for women' was one of the slogans of the new socio-political system, and its promotion was at times somewhat strange. Fair-haired female tractor drivers smiled down from posters as the symbol of the new equal rights of women who had won access to formerly male jobs. A single mass women's organization, the Women's League, was set up in 1945. Its aims included the promotion of women's professional work, the organization of assistance in everyday life and educational activities. But the League was an organization established by a superior authority as the only women's union and it came into being without the involvement of the women themselves. Like many other organizations set up in those days by the new authorities, it was treated as part of the imposed rule, failing to promote the interests of the group it was originally supposed to represent. Such an organization could hope for no social backing whatsoever.

Many activities at this time were really only window dressing, for example, one or two people with no party affiliation were co-opted to the administration to show that the Party was not the only ruler of Poland; the same was true of token women serving as evidence of women's equality. Such steps only served to discredit movements which used women's rights as their slogans. All activities carried out under that banner were seen as window-dressing, controlled from above and not genuine. The main effect was that women were burdened with much heavier duties. Women were exploited as a cheap labour force taking practically no part in decision-making and government (Limanowska 1989). There were persistent efforts to compromise women's culture, showing it as worse, less ambitious and less progressive than that of men; with time this led to the suppression of such culture. The discrediting of women's rights movements resulted in a lack of support and popularity for such movements. Women declared themselves in support of the struggle for the rights of all people, both men and women.

It is therefore not surprising that foreigners who at first consider Polish women enjoy a lot of freedom need only spend more time in Poland in order to change their opinion altogether, and to see the women as slaves who sacrifice themselves for their families. Women in Poland have jobs, look after the house and raise children and they have no access to organized help: there is a permanent shortage of places in day nurseries and kindergartens. Women's multiple duties have been particularly burdensome during Poland's present crisis. The effects on women were discussed at the UN expert consultation Women in Development in May 1989, in Warsaw. It is the women who pay for the crisis: stricken by poverty, the households have to give up various services and women must take over the tasks. They struggle to achieve the least possible reduction of their families' living standards, which, in practice, leads to proliferation of their chores such as queuing for hours, sewing and other additional duties. This extremely difficult situation is not accompanied by any move towards its transformation, but by a passive conviction that nothing can be done, and dignified efforts to cope with the growing burden.

Some achievements of the struggle for women's rights have had rather unexpected consequences. The superficial character and artificial nature of various activities supposedly undertaken in the interests of women has often deprived them of women's support. But in just one area, the post-war changes seem to accord with the demands of women. That area is the regulations, in force since 1956, concerning the admissibility of abortion. Today those regulations are accused of being too liberal, and a struggle is going on to change them.

THE ADMISSIBILITY OF ABORTION IN POLAND

In Poland, as in many other countries, debates about abortion and the conditions of its admissibility developed during the 1920s. New codes were then prepared to replace the legislation of the partitioning states, still in force in Poland during the first years of independence. At first there were plans to preserve the ban on abortion in the penal code, together with the penalties it provided. When the new draft penal code was submitted for discussion, those who supported the decriminalization of abortion were very active. Various arguments were used. Some concerned the inefficiency of punishment, the provision in question being 'dead' and seldom applied as most abortions remained secret forever. Others concerned its harmfulness, as abortions were being performed by amateurs which threatened the women's health, or even their lives. Furthermore, the price of abortion increased due to its illicit nature. Other arguments concerned the lack of effective care during pregnancy and assistance to mothers. It was argued that the birth of a child gives rise to its parents' duty to provide for it; but if they were to be unable to maintain the child, or if that child's birth would result in serious hardship for children already living, e.g. if the mother is employed and maintains the family but would have to quit her job to have another child, abortion should be admissible.

The Codification Commission included in the draft code a provision according to which an abortion performed by a physician to protect the mother's health, the family's welfare or an important matter of public interest, would remain unpunished.

The draft did not please everybody. Some found it too liberal, while others criticized what was, in their opinion, undue limitation of women's freedom. Eventually, the penal code passed in 1932 included a provision stating that an abortion should not be treated as an offence if it was performed by a physician to protect the woman's health or if the pregnancy occurred as a result of a criminal act such as rape, incest or underage sex (Bogunia 1980).

The discussion about conditions for abortion was resumed almost immediately after the Second World War. The voice of anti-abortionists prevailed. Their arguments were mainly demographic: the country had suffered great loss of population which now had to be made up. For that reason, some were demanding a total ban on abortion, including abortions performed for medical reasons. According to the chief ideologist of the anti-abortion camp, a physician A.B. Henke MD, the sense of duty to become mothers should be instilled in women even if they have to pay for it with their lives: 'a mother, a pregnant woman, finds herself in the forefront of the fighting line just like soldiers, policemen, doctors and nurses, and should be prepared to lay down her life for the child if necessary (Scientific Session of the Poznan Medical Society 1948). This natalist policy also led to a ban on advertisements which might hinder an increase in the population and even to the removal from bookshops and libraries of books dealing with birth control and abortions (Wolinska 1962).

On the other hand, the various arguments in favour of abortion indicate that they spring from broader ideologies and value systems. In the case of opposition to abortion, the ideology gave priority to social as opposed to individual interests. In a country exhausted by wars and occupation, the need to increase the population was considered the overriding interest to which the individuals – i.e. women – had to conform even if they were to die in doing so. A similar starting point can be found for the reasoning of other anti-abortionists, including those whose interests were the exact opposite of those of Poland: similar 'social interests' determined bans on abortion in Hitler's Germany and Stalin's Russia. We should stress that such arguments are not found in the present Polish discussions, during the present period of high birth rate levels.

The discussions which developed during the political 'thaw' which followed the death of Stalin in the mid-1950s were entirely different in tone from those of the 1940s. In 1956, a commission was created by the Ministry of Health to examine the implementation of the abortion provisions and to submit its own opinion on that issue. The commission favoured liberalization of the provisions and extension of the right to abortion. It was argued that preserving the old provisions simply helped to cover up the fact that many people could not afford a large family. It was therefore contrary to the public interest to force women of limited means to have their abortions performed by amateurs at great risk to their life and health. According to the commission, the provisions had proved ineffective and were commonly infringed (Zielinska 1986). The introduction of new regulations was proposed and the new act, passed in 1956, is still in force in Poland today.

The aim of this act is clearly stated in the preamble: i.e. to protect women's health against the effects of abortions performed in unsuitable conditions by persons who are not trained physicians.

The act provides a broad description of the conditions in which abortion is permitted. These are as follows: if there are medical reasons; if the pregnant woman lives in difficult conditions; or if there is a suspicion that the pregnancy results from an offence. The act does not, however, provide for the woman's right to make the decision. But in the current discussions, it is stressed that, in practice, the decision depends on the woman alone. This results from broad interpretation of the 'difficult living conditions' clause. Physicians base their decision on the woman's statement. After hearing it, they decide whether the conditions are sufficiently difficult or not. The enforcement of the act has, in effect, been handed over to the physician who chooses whether to perform an abortion. It should also be stressed that the implementation of the act was liberalized in the late 1950s. At first, physicians who decided that an abortion was admissible could not perform it themselves and abortions could not be performed in private surgeries. These restrictions were relaxed in 1959; the doctor who finds abortion admissible is now allowed to perform it and private surgeries can be used. As large numbers of abortions performed in private surgeries are not registered, this change has resulted in considerable difficulties in counting the number of abortions.

The act does not refer to time limits for the admissibility of abortion. The only indication of probable time limits is a general statement that abortion is prohibited in the case of medical contra-indications. The first document to deal specifically with this subject was a 1981 instruction which mentions a pregnancy of over twelve weeks as an example of a contra-indication.

The 1956 act was constantly and fiercely criticized in Catholic circles. It was argued that human life is sacrosanct and should be protected from the moment of conception. At the same time, fears were expressed about the wider impact on sexual morality. The act, it was argued, might lead to demoralization, lax morals, a cynical attitude to love and even to the physical and moral degradation of the nation.

In 1958, the PAX Catholic Association made an appeal to the Seym for the act to be annulled, and to the faithful, physicians and medical staff in particular, for its sabotage.

Discussions intensified again in the years 1980–1. Catholic groups made another appeal for the act to be abolished. Most active in this field were movements connected with the Catholic Church using characteristic names such as Care for Life, Gaudum Vitae or Pro Familia. They pronounced in favour of the protection of unborn children, explained the harmfulness of abortions and engaged in various activities to support women who were still hesitating over whether to have an abortion or not, such as providing telephone guidance and homes for unmarried mothers.

Criticism of the act at this time did have an effect. In September 1981, ministers' instructions were issued concerning the conditions for abortion. Physicians were required to provide a more detailed justification when allowing abortion on the grounds of difficult living conditions. The basic requirements, however, were not changed. The physician still makes the decision based on the woman's statement. However, the physician was instructed to try to persuade the woman not to have an abortion. The physician must now inform the patient about the harmfulness of abortions and the possibilities of receiving help if she were to decide to have the baby.

Those who criticize the act stress the fact that these instructions lack the force of a statute and only affect doctors employed in the public health service. Since most abortions are performed in private surgeries, their range is very limited.

In 1989, the anti-abortionists produced a draft for a new abortion act. The draft act gave rise to discussions in which highly emotional arguments were used. One of the arguments used against the present act is that it is a Stalinist regulation imposed from without and actually alien to Polish society. It is difficult to tell whether the act was really imposed from without, but its supposed Stalinist nature can easily be examined. We will therefore briefly discuss the Soviet abortion regulations.

Abortion was decriminalized in the USSR in 1920. This was motivated by the wish to protect the life and health of women and the need to protect them from 'greedy extortioners'. The performance of abortions free of charge, by physicians in hospitals, was permitted. Abortions performed by amateurs for profit were prohibited, leading eventually to a complete ban on abortions performed in private surgeries.

In 1936, during the rapid development of Stalinism, abortion was again banned. Only abortions performed for eugenic or health reasons were permitted. Penalties for abortion were included in the penal code.

It was not until after the death of Stalin that these provisions were changed. In 1955, the 1936 act that banned abortion was annulled. The new preamble justifying abortion mentioned the protection of women's health against the effects of illegal abortions and the failure of the struggle against abortion through offering social assistance and information. Furthermore, the act also emphasized the need to create conditions for the woman's independent decision about motherhood. Thus stress was put on protecting women's rights, including the right to make decisions about pregnancy (Zielinska 1986).

It is difficult to say whether other countries in Central and Eastern Europe were influenced by the Russian legislation when liberalizing their own regulations, or whether that liberalization was imposed on them. As we have seen in Poland and elsewhere, between the wars, the trend towards liberalization took place without Soviet influence. Most countries, namely Bulgaria, Czechoslovakia, Romania, Hungary and Poland, did liberalize their regulation of abortion in the years 1956–7. But the subsequent fate of those regulations varies greatly from one country to another. For example, in the German Democratic Republic, the woman's right to make the decision about abortion was held to be one of the conditions of their equality: the woman was to decide about the timing and number of births. Such decisions were treated as one of her chief rights alongside the right to education and professional training and the freedom to make decisions about marriage and the family (1972). In some other countries, such as Czechoslovakia, Hungary and Bulgaria, the admissibility of abortion was limited. The restrictions were justified on pro-natal grounds. The population increase was very low in those countries and the availability of abortions was limited in order to increase the birth rate.

The suggestion that the liberalized abortion act was an element of Stalinist legislation cannot therefore be confirmed. The question also remains unanswered as to what degree such processes were independent of or were influenced by Soviet liberalization in 1956. Today, however, this question has lost much of its importance.

After discussing the development of the legal regulations now in force in Poland and their rationales, some data concerning the practice will now be presented. Is abortion a frequent phenomenon? What are society's opinions about it? Why do women have abortions? Research findings can help to answer these questions.

ABORTION IN POLAND: RESEARCH FINDINGS

It is difficult to say how many abortions are performed in Poland each year as many of them are probably never disclosed and registered. It is thought that a number of abortions performed in private surgeries are kept secret by physicians in order to avoid taxes. Such abortions are legal but are not registered and the available statistics only refer to registered abortions.

In the 1980s, about 130,000–140,000 abortions a year were registered in Poland, that is 13.2 per 1,000 women aged 15–49, and 18.2 per 100 live births (still births excluded) (Zielinska 1986).

It is very difficult to estimate the number of abortions which are unregistered, and the data quoted by different sources vary greatly. Some estimate that there are between 55,000–85,000 per year (Klonowicz 1974). The pamphlets published by opponents of the new draft abortion act estimate the number of women who would be liable to punishment – that is, who have had an abortion – at 300,000 per year. Church groups quote the highest figure, estimating the number of abortions at 600,000 or even a million per year (Primate of Poland in Defence of Life 1982). As can be judged from the data on registered abortions, we are dealing with a steady trend: after the legalization of abortion, the number of cases registered went up rapidly but then became stable after 1970 and has plateaued year after year. Despite the high prices, the number of abortions performed in private and co-operative surgeries keeps increasing. According to the patients, such surgeries offer better treatment, greater secrecy and prompt admission. As reported by a Seym commission which examined the functioning of the abortion act in 1973, the most obvious impact was on the number of deaths and complications resulting from abortions. After the act was introduced, the number fell drastically, from 255 to 12 deaths per year.

What is the attitude of society towards the legalization of abortion? Studies carried out in the 1970s on various samples show that the number of those who opposed abortion never exceeded one-third of the sample. Those who support the ban are predominantly peasant women, lower educated persons and the elderly. Despite the fact that only a small proportion of women, 0.6 per cent, consider abortion to be morally right, over one-third, 37 per cent, said they would rather have an abortion than an unwanted child (Zielinska 1986). The reason for this is that those who declare themselves opposed to abortion do not think the ban should be unconditional. Their attitude depends on the motives for the abortion. When asking about abortion as a method of birth control, the proportion opposing abortion is high. But the disapproval decreases, or even disappears, if the reasons given for abortion are poverty, a threat to the mother's life, the mother's mental illness or a large family (Zielinska 1986).

The studies of abortion were small scale only. But there are certain common findings. A study of 200 women who had had a legal abortion showed the most frequent cause to be difficulties with finances and housing. One should bear in mind that the term 'difficult housing conditions' in Poland may mean that the family lives in a single room or with in-laws, having no hope whatsoever of getting a flat of their own.

The results of a study of 300 illegal abortions which resulted in court cases are more interesting still. The women had illegal abortions for the following reasons: ignorance of the possibility of a legal operation; instigation by another person, often the unborn child's father; and being afraid to consult a doctor. Women may also choose an illegal abortion if the doctor has refused to perform a legal one. These women may be refused for various reasons: the pregnancy may be too advanced; or they may be seriously ill; or they may have had many abortions before; or it may be only a short time since a previous abortion. If a legal abortion is unavailable, women will resort to illegal means. These findings confirm the suggestion of pro-abortionists who argue that women who are intent on having an abortion are sure to find an illegal operation, no matter how dangerous this might be to their life or health (Bogunia 1980).

Attitudes towards abortion have also been reported from a study of professional medical ethics. One of the questions concerned the respondent's attitude towards doctors who refuse to perform abortions because of their beliefs, despite the fact that they realize the danger of pregnancy to the woman's life and health. It should be mentioned here that there is no 'conscience clause' in Polish law enabling a doctor to refuse to operate for ethical or religious reasons. However, in a Catholic society where the church has repeatedly appealed to physicians to boycott the abortion act and the performance of abortion is generally perceived as a sin, one might expect the respondents to tolerate a doctor who refuses to perform an abortion for reasons of conscience. It appears, however, that this is not the case. A clear majority of respondents, over 70 per cent of a national random sample, considered such refusal to be wrong, improper or even inhuman. In the late 1960s, over 25 per cent of respondents accepted the doctor's refusal (Kurczewski 1972). Contrary to our expectations, these opinions were not related to the respondents' age, but rather to their level of education. The higher the levels of education, the greater the proportion of people condemning the doctor's decision. Similar findings were obtained when that same question was put again, in the 1980s, to a different sample of unmarried women aged 17–30 (Hordyniec and Grabowska 1982).

What is the general opinion about abortion? Does Polish society believe that the woman has the right to decide whether to have an abortion or not? The findings of many small surveys indicate that the view taken depends on the reasons why the woman is considering an abortion. In a 1988 study of a national random sample, the respondents were asked to express their opinion about a women who had an abortion because she did not want to become a mother (Kurczewski 1990). Most respondents thought the woman was wrong, 70 per cent, as opposed to 23 per cent who believed her to be right. Most of them thought that a woman has no right to make such a decision, 54 per cent, as opposed to 37 per cent who stated that she does have that right. Seventy-five per cent were aware of the fact that the law does not prohibit abortion in such cases; and 90 per cent believed that abortion is a sin.

An attempt has also been made recently by the Centre for Public Opinion Surveys, attached to the Committee for Radio and TV, to find out about society's backing for the new draft act which proposes a ban on abortion. Forty-six per cent of respondents supported the new regulation and 44 per cent were against it; 10 per cent stated that they had not formed an opinion. The findings are interpreted as further proof of society's almost equal division into advocates and opponents of the new draft. However, it must be remembered that it was very difficult to get information about the draft. First, there was a delay in publication; and then the only journal to publish it was *Polityka*, a weekly which is rather hard to obtain. The general public may be presumed to have heard about the basic assumptions of the draft, including the prospect of imprisonment for women who have an abortion. It seems doubtful, however, whether it is widely known that the draft provides for no exceptions whatsoever, that abortion is banned even when the woman's life and health are endangered or a grave injury of the foetus has been diagnosed. It may be supposed that, had the respondents been aware of this, they might have answered differently. This is possibly indicated by other findings of the study of a national random sample carried out by the Centre for Public Opinion Surveys; namely that a majority, 59 per cent, of respondents supported abortion in the case of an AIDS infected woman, while only 16 per cent thought that she should have the child. It may therefore be said that Polish society's opinions depend largely on the reasons for the abortion. The draft act, however, submitted to the Seym in recent months, fails to take this differentiation into account. Its main assumptions will now be discussed.

THE DRAFT

The new draft abortion act, submitted to the Seym by a group of deputies, is entitled 'the act for the protection of the unborn child'. Its advocates stress that penal provisions and bans are not its essential part, but only a consequence of its underlying assumptions. These assumptions include the inviolability of human life, and the distinct nature of the individual from the very moment of conception. Thus, the draft actually grants legal capacity to the foetus from the moment of conception. Once born, the child may demand compensation for injury it suffered as a foetus; but neither the possible kinds of such harm nor their potential perpetrators have been specified. It may also be judged that, with a regulation as broad as this, the child is also entitled to compensation from its mother for any behaviour or conduct that could have negative effects on the foetus. The draft act imposes on the child's parents the duty to care for it whether they enjoy parental authority or not. Parental authority concerns the period from the moment of conception to the child's majority. The duty to render certain services has also been imposed on the child's father if he is not married to the mother: this extends duties he has already under existing regulations. Despite the author's apparent aim of treating the child as an individual and autonomous human being from the moment of conception, there is not total consistency. Thus, the draft permits neither the establishment nor the denial of paternity before the child's actual birth. In those cases, the moment of birth still remains the date from which an action can be instituted.

The draft starts with a proclamation of the extensive assistance and care a pregnant woman is to receive. This takes the form of medical care, a pregnancy allowance, the institution of a family advisory service, and a place in a home for unmarried mothers if necessary. The Council of Ministers of the Polish People's Republic is to be charged with putting this into effect. As stressed, however, by opponents of the draft, these are only declarations, which will be impossible to implement in the present economic situation.

It is the provisions to be introduced into the penal code which have given rise to the greatest concern. They include the following provision, which is unconditional and provides for no exceptions whatsoever: 'Whoever causes the death of an unborn child shall be subject to the penalty of deprivation of liberty for up to three years.' The penalty may be aggravated if threats or deceit were used against the mother; or the court may renounce the infliction of punishment if this can be justified. The penalties for causing damage to the body or impairing the health of the unborn child, and for violating its genetic endowment are rather less severe.

The draft also proposes the introduction of a ban on all experiments and medical interventions in relation to an unborn child, other than those which serve the protection of its life and health.

IDEOLOGICAL AND PHILOSOPHICAL JUSTIFICATIONS

An individual's attitude towards the admissibility of abortion is usually part of his or her philosophy of life and moral attitude, which will concern a broad range of problems and cannot be discussed separately from a broader philosophy. We will therefore now present the justifications given by anti- and pro-abortionists, in the context of their underlying philosophies.

Opposition to legal abortion

In repeated discussions on the admissibility of abortion, the Catholic Church has taken up a position. That standpoint is particularly important in Poland due to the large proportion, over 90 per cent, of believers in the population; the large proportion of the population who attend church, listening to sermons and the Church's precepts, and the attendance of children and young persons at religious instruction. The Polish Catholic Church has joined the opposition to legal abortion; moreover, during the session of the Seym commissions that examined the discussed draft, the experts' Team of the Episcopate's Commission for Family Matters pronounced in favour of its introduction. We will therefore discuss the Church's attitude to abortion.

In recent years, the Catholic Church has constantly attacked the legality of abortion. This standpoint was justified in the 'Declaration on Abortion' of 1974, approved for publication by Pope Paul VI. The standpoint expressed in it is derived from natural law. It has been proclaimed in the Declaration that the right to life can be suspended neither by society nor by public authorities: such a right does not result from its recognition by any person or institution but precedes such recognition. Life should be protected and favoured. Admittedly, there are interests which may be more valuable than life: but life is the condition and basis for all the remaining values. The right to live cannot be subjected to any conditions which depend on the length of life.

The Declaration defines some grounds for abortion as 'not always wicked', quoting such grounds as a danger to the mother's life or health, the possibility of giving birth to an abnormal child or a loss of honour or a disgrace. It states, however: 'Never may any of these grounds result in a person's objective right to decide about another person's life, even if that other person has only just been conceived.' The law may renounce a punishment: but it ceases being law if it clashes with what is righteous and just. Man (*sic*) should never obey such law: he (*sic*) cannot even 'take part in a campaign propagating such law or vote for it' (Declaration on Abortion, Vatican 1974).

The guiding principles of the authors and advocates of the draft act on 'legal protection of the unborn child' are very much the same. As stated somewhat imperiously in the justification of the draft, it is a fact beyond dispute that: 'a human being is a separate individual from the very beginning of his (*sic*) development, and is autonomous, from the person of his (*sic*) mother in particular. Life is the supreme value and the carrier of human dignity, irrespective of the stage of development in which the human being finds himself (*sic*).' It is therefore proposed that 'any act that results in the death of the conceived child' should be treated as an offence. Life should be protected whether it develops in the mother's womb or *in vitro*. According to the authors, the entire contents of the draft follow from the recognition of the foetus as a separate human being from the moment of conception. As maintained, however, by opponents of the draft, the proposed regulation is inconsistent here. For practical reasons such as the inability to acquire proof, it does not permit the establishment or denial of paternity before the child's birth. Also the fact that separate penalties have been provided for abortion is criticized as inconsistent: if life were treated as one and the same value before and after birth, penal provisions that deal with murder should also deal with abortion. But in providing for different penalties, the authors are themselves admitting that they treat an individual differently according to whether or not he or she has been born.

The broader ideology underlining the Church's attitude towards abortion is quite apparent in the above mentioned 'Declaration on Abortion' among other documents, and in the encyclicals of Pope Paul VI. They deal not only with abortion but also with contraceptives and the freedom of sexual behaviour, as well as the aims of intercourse. As stated in the Declaration, sexual freedom 'is by no means human' if the person believes he or she may enjoy that freedom 'ignoring both the law and the essential orientation of sexual relation on giving birth to life' (p. 9 of the Polish translation). The Church accepts only a limited range of options for planning the size of one's family using natural methods of contraception only, and excluding not only abortion, but also contraceptives and all methods of artificial birth control. That standpoint can be found in, amongst other things, the encyclical Humanae Vitae proclaimed by Paul VI.

The natural methods of birth control only recently officially accepted by the Catholic Church are presented as effective and the only ones which are admissible. The Rev. J. Buxakowski who reported on the Church's standpoint during the Seym commission, stated that the natural methods of birth control 'are decidedly the safest and most reliable ones, and that artificial contraceptives cannot be compared with them in this respect' (Buxakowski 1989). No evidence has been quoted to substantiate that statement. The reliability of contraception is an essential issue in Poland. The authors of the abortion draft treat a large number of contraceptives as early-abortive and propose that they should be prohibited as such. Besides, the Church's view on this question is widely propagated, during religious instruction and at special courses preparing the young for life in the family. The propagation of belief in the exceptional reliability of natural methods of birth control may have far-reaching consequences.

The new draft is closely related to the Catholic philosophy of life and Catholic morals. According to that philosophy, sexual relations should take place between spouses only, and should be aimed at reproduction. Giving birth to children is 'the supreme mission of the woman' (Buxakowski 1989) and she should be prepared to risk her life or health to fulfil that mission. A very limited range of birth control is permitted based on natural methods only. From the viewpoint of Catholic philosophy, those methods have two virtues: first, they do not interfere with nature and, second, they lead to a periodical sexual temperance which is valued in this moral system as it encourages moderation and control over one's urges. The natural methods are thus presented as highly reliable, but no evidence is given to support this view.

Supporters of legalized abortion

During all discussions, the opponents of the draft act 'on legal protection of the conceived child' also pronounce against abortion. It might be supposed therefore that the pro- and anti-abortionists differ not in their respective attitudes towards abortion, but regarding the acceptable limits to be placed on availability. But a closer look at the two standpoints demonstrates the more fundamental nature of their differences.

First of all, the draft is blamed by opponents for lacking a positive programme. The mother is to receive support: but in the Polish socio-economic situation, this is not practicable. The draft provides for no educational programme; no activities for the propagation of contraception and no practical measures to help the woman. The only provisions capable of being implemented are the penal ones.

Another reason for opposition is the fact that the draft provides for no exceptions: even the performance of abortions to save the woman's life or health is prohibited. When asked about this question, the advocates of the draft failed to answer explicitly. But in the light of canon law, abortion is criminal, and 'the act's criminal nature remains unchanged, no matter how lofty the aim that leads to its perpetration . . . such as an effort to save the mother's life' (the Canon Code – a commentary, Lublin 1987). If, therefore, the draft reflects the Church's attitude towards this issue, abortions in such cases would be prohibited accordingly. Hence, the opponents of the draft argue that those introducing it are imposing the Catholic philosophy on the nation, irrespective of individual religious beliefs. The ban on abortion to save the mother's life is held to be contradictory to the authors' assumptions. They seek to defend life 'irrespective of the stage of development of the individual in question', as they put it elsewhere, but propose to sacrifice a more developed individual, the mother, in favour of a less developed one, the child, even if the latter might not even be viable.

A further argument concerns the effects of a ban on abortion. It is clear that a legal ban of this kind does not produce the intended effects, i.e. the end of abortions, but has other effects, both unintended and unwanted by the legislator, i.e. the deaths resulting from abortions performed in bad conditions, particularly for women without substantial financial resources.

Yet another argument points to the inadequacy of these legal measures. Even the advocates of the draft, when asked whether they really thought that women, including those who already have children, should be imprisoned on a large scale, stated that the sentences should not usually be carried out. According to the opponents of the draft, the attempted introduction of the ban reflects the Church's failure in this respect. Despite having widely propagated its view and informed the faithful that abortion is a mortal sin, the Church had failed to achieve its intended results and so now it tries to resort to legal measures which are, however, quite inapplicable to this issue.

Above all, the opponents of the draft demand the creation of a positive programme to prevent abortion. They demand straightforward sexual education for the young, and the accessibility of contraceptives. In Poland, where practically everything is in short supply today, there is also a shortage of contraceptives. According to some statements made during the recent discussions, abortion is practically the only method of birth control which is fully accessible to all Polish women. The women who decide to have abortions are victims of a situation where deficiencies in education and a shortage of contraceptives make abortion the only possible solution. These women, already victims of the system, would then suffer an extra punishment.

Finally, yet another argument appeared, though it has been used hesitantly: namely, that the woman has the right to make decisions about her own body and about the pregnancy developing in her womb. Some call the ban on abortion a compulsion to have children and a violation of civil liberties. The draft activated various women's groups which started coming out in defence of their own interests. Here the cause of defending women's rights forms a framework within which opponents of the draft operate. But before we consider the still tentative attempts to express that ideology and to create a movement to struggle for its implementation, a certain contradiction must be explained. We begin with a question: how is it that in a Catholic country where the faithful constitute over 90 per cent of the population, opinions and action concerning abortion clash so strongly with the Church's doctrine?

Our attempted explanation of this contradiction must begin with the answer to another question: what is the implication of the fact that over 90 per cent of Polish society are believers and define themselves that way? Are they acquainted with all the elements of the faith and doctrine of the Catholic Church, and do they accept the whole of that faith and doctrine? Obviously it is most difficult to find an answer to these questions; but we can try, using research findings. In the 1988 study of a national random sample (Kurczewski 1990), questions were asked concerning the respondents' belief in God, heaven, hell and the after-life, the last judgement, Satan and sin. Further questions concerned their attitude towards religion. As few as 3 per cent of the sample called themselves agnostics, and 1 per cent failed to give a decided answer. The remaining 96 per cent stated that they were believers; just 8 per cent were religious but never went to church. Thus, an overwhelming majority in society are practising believers who therefore also listen to sermons and have the opportunity to learn about the Church's attitude towards various issues. Does it mean, however, that these people necessarily accept all the separate elements of their religion? It appears that the greatest proportion believe in God, 93 per cent, and a large proportion also believe in the existence of sin, 86 per cent. Fewer believe in hell and Satan, 62 per cent and 63 per cent respectively. But 76 per cent believe in the last judgement, 71 per cent in heaven and 68 per cent in the after-life. It appears, therefore, that the fact that a person defines himself as religious is not actually enough to justify the conclusion that such a person believes in all the elements of the Catholic philosophy of life.

Answers to another question asked in the above survey seem more interesting still. The respondents were asked about the observance of religious dictates in the practice of everyday life. The most commonly expressed opinion was that the dictates which one finds wrong should not be observed at all (44 per cent). Some thought that one should ostensibly observe wrong dictates, but that, in practice, they should be circumvented (13 per cent). Thus, over half of the sample, 57 per cent, were of the opinion that the individual should not observe dictates that he thinks are wrong. Less than one-third maintained that such dictates should always be observed, even if one disagrees with them. Compared with the proportion of believers, the latter group is strikingly small.

Polish Catholicism should not be regarded simplistically. The fact that the vast majority of Polish society believe in God, consider themselves believing Christians and go to church, is by no means tantamount to a readiness to submit meekly to all dictates of religion and the Church. Nor is it tantamount to all the faithful having a universal and equally strong belief in all elements of their faith. If one's opinion clashes with a dictate of religion, most state that the dictate should not then be observed. The above findings may at least partly explain the contradiction between Polish Catholicism and the increase in abortion. This does not mean, however, that women who have abortions generally approve of them, or are unaware that they are a sin.

Sometimes these contradictions are explained at the individual level, and the woman's decision to terminate the pregnancy is treated as autonomous and free. In practice, according to the woman's statements, the choice they make is very seldom truly autonomous. Pressure is brought to bear on the woman by two conflicting sets of expectations. One is the Catholic system of values, which not only bans abortion but also prohibits contraceptives, demands a sexual temperance, and the fulfilment of 'the woman's mission', that is, maternity. The other set of expectations includes sexual values and needs, which the Catholic system either ignores or treats very specifically. Such values and needs matter not only to the woman herself, but also to her partners. Faced with an unwanted pregnancy, the woman's environment and partner may influence her decision to have an abortion. Even if he does not demand abortion in so many words, her partner may abandon responsibility, treating the pregnancy and the decision about abortion as the woman's problem only. In this situation, the woman submits to the pressures of life and not of faith. However, this may result in the woman feeling frustrated and being burdened with a bad conscience (Sokolowska 1983).

THE PREPARATION OF THE DRAFTS

The draft act 'on legal protection of the unborn child' was submitted to the Seym by deputies. It was signed by seventy-four deputies, of which only eight were women. It gave rise to much discussion and both proposers and opponents tried various ways of expressing their opinions. The draft was also discussed at a joint session of two parliamentary commissions: Social Policy and Health, and the Legislative Commission. The session took place in an atmosphere seldom found in Poland: a group of opponents of the draft picketed the Seym building, using the slogan 'Contraception – yes, imprisonment – no'. The session was interrupted to enable representatives of the Commissions to listen to the picket's arguments. The emotional tone of the debates spread to those participating in the session. Apart from members of the two Commissions, the participants included a group of representatives of the Episcopate of Poland. The 'Solidarity' daily *Gazeta Wyborcza* described the session as follows:

> The dramatic session could hardly be called a discussion. The twelve representatives of the Episcopate backed by several deputies, seemed to speak another language which the remaining speakers found it hard to understand. Even if the same words were used, their meaning differed.
>
> (Milewicz 1989)

The two parties used the same arguments to support entirely different standpoints. When the Church party argued that the present act violates women's dignity, opponents of the draft made an identical accusation contending that it is the draft which violates that dignity, treating the woman as nothing but a 'container for the conceived child'. Emotions prevailed over reasonable arguments. Finally, a motion to submit the draft for general consultation in society as a whole was passed. Afterwards, the chairman of the Episcopate's Experts Team, Jerzy Buxakowski, took the floor once again and stated that 'the laws of nature cannot be submitted to any plebiscites whatever. . . . Both abortion and contraception are against the laws of nature, that is of the human body.' Buxakowski expressed his opinion that the consultations should be carried out in selected circles only, scientific, ethical and the like, and found any other forms of consultation, such as a plebiscite or referendum, to be dangerous as they 'might set people at variance, disintegrate and antagonize society rather than unite it'.

Highly emotional discussions also took place on TV and radio, as well as in newspapers. Representatives of both camps came to the 'open studio' on TV to voice their opinion and the debates dragged on late into the night. The editors of newspapers received hundreds of letters from their readers: they now stress that those in favour of abortion prevailed. In various circles, signatures were gathered in protests against the draft. The writers of such letters were not only female students or intellectuals, but also various groups of workmen. In addition, the Seym, the Spokesman of Civic Rights, the Ministry of Health and other institutions received letters from the public. In letters of another kind, groups of female parishioners protested against young girls' statements on TV which called the draft a reversion to the Middle Ages and an attempted introduction of the Inquisition. Both parties to the discussions insulted each other, advocates of the draft calling its opponents murderers and Stalinists, and the opponents arguing that the advocates were trying to impose the Catholic Church's attitude upon the whole of society and that they were proposing a return to the Middle Ages and the Inquisition.

The timing of these discussions is important. The commissions examined the draft on 10 May, that is, about three weeks before the elections to the Seym and Senate. The elections were to be the first partly free elections in Poland since the Second World War, and the debates concerning the draft could be used in a variety of ways during the electoral campaign. Indeed, the draft both interested and divided society so much that it could not be left out of the campaign. At many pre-election meetings with the voters, candidates to the Seym and Senate were asked not only about their opinions of the draft, but also the way they would vote in the Seym and Senate if they were elected and the draft put to the vote. Those who asked such questions were not satisfied with evasive replies and insisted on explicit statements. Whatever the actual reply, it always met with a hostile reaction from a part of the audience.

The discussions on the fate of the draft were 'suspended', for the days of the elections, but afterwards the issue returned to the headlines.

The divisions caused by the draft can also be seen in Catholic circles. Such circles are admittedly consistent in their opposition to abortion; but some groups within them also oppose the draft. They believe it should be possible to appeal to the people's consciences, and to the Decalogue in the case of the faithful, but not to penal sanctions, when propagating the appropriate attitude to abortion (Standpoint of the Board of the Club of Catholic Intellectuals in Poznan Concerning the Legal Admissibility of Termination of Life Conceived 1989).

It must be admitted that not all opponents of abortion share the Catholic Church's opinions about other issues, and their opposition is not always based on the Church's arguments. Nevertheless, the strongest supporters of the draft are found in precisely such Church circles. In the Church, the faithful are taught that abortion is a murder and a sin, and are asked to sign the draft without being fully informed of its contents.

An attempt must be made to answer the question about the broader value system underlying the draft, and the moral approach it represents. Elements of that approach were expressed during the discussion and the introduction to the session of the parliamentary commission. It was held that no action which involves an intervention in the natural order of things can be acceptable. Any such intervention, like abortion or the use of contraceptives, is wrong and sinful. The woman is granted only limited influence over the number of her pregnancies. She may either abstain from intercourse and give up sexual relations, or use natural methods of birth control based on the menstrual cycle. From the moment of conception, the new human being is an autonomous individual and should not be destroyed, even if his further development is bound to result in the death of his mother in whose womb he is developing.

As a result of holding abortion and contraception to be equally wrong, the Church has lost the support of those who advocate a ban on abortion and believe the best way forward to be the development of contraception.

It is also noteworthy that opponents of the draft state during all public discussions that abortion is an evil that should be eliminated from our lives. But they propose entirely different methods for that elimination: i.e. sexual education and contraception. It should also be stressed that nowadays contraceptives are very difficult to obtain in Poland. Hence the opinion that if contraceptives were readily available, the need for abortions would disappear or at least be greatly reduced.

The most interesting effect of the submission of the draft to the Seym has been the activation of women's groups, the attempt to formulate women's needs and even the establishment of women's organizations. This trend is interesting because it is initiated 'from below' instead of being imposed upon the women. Many of the protests against the draft were spontaneous and poorly organized. These included street demonstrations, the signing of petitions and the sending of letters. Some of these actions gave rise to more permanent movements aiming to represent women's interests; for example, pamphlets distributed during a demonstration in Warsaw were signed by a 'Movement for Women's Self-Defence' from Bydgoszcz. Apart from information about the draft and the negative effects expected to follow a legal ban on abortion, the pamphlets contained an appeal for active steps to be taken, and a description of the situation of women in Poland: 'We are overcharged and overworked but we never rebel – and that is why we are not respected.' The pamphlets exhort women to take part in demonstrations and to protest by any means possible. The draft is defined as a violation of women's dignity and humanity, and a precedent which could lead the way for further violations of privacy in the future.

Another movement which has recently applied for registration is the Polish feminist association. For this group, the draft and events associated with it provided the impulse to become better organized.

Thus, there is evidence that the draft encouraged women to establish movements to provide education, to formulate their problems and to campaign for their rights. The opponents of the draft stress women's rights, particularly the right to make decisions about their bodies. Since a human foetus cannot grow entirely outside the woman's body, it cannot be considered an absolutely autonomous and independent being, in whose favour the woman should resign her right to make decisions about her own body and even endanger her life or health. Naturally, she may well decide to take the risk – but nobody should have the right to force such a decision upon her, and she herself should never be punished for deciding against it. According to this standpoint, abortion is either the woman's right, or at least a 'lesser evil', lesser than the woman's death, the birth of a disabled or sick child, one infected with AIDS for example, or the birth of a child whom nobody loves and nobody wants to raise from the moment of its birth.

The conflict between these two points of view still cannot be resolved. Admittedly we may agree with Mark Tushnet's opinion that a woman who decides to have an abortion today makes two different decisions: one concerning the removal of the foetus from her womb and the other concerning the destruction of that foetus. According to Tushnet, a separation of those two decisions will soon be technically possible: the woman's decision concerning her own body, a removal of the foetus, will not be tantamount to destroying that foetus and will not necessarily involve its death (Tushnet 1984). But for the time being, it is still impossible to separate those two rights: that of the woman to make decisions about her own body, and that of the new human being to live. Today if a woman wants to terminate a pregnancy, only one of those rights can be observed: there is no way of settling the conflict between them. Law has to choose one of the two options, compromise is impossible (Czynczyk 1989).

It is doubtful, however, whether the conflict we are now facing will be solved after the two rights in question are separated: the woman's right to make decisions about her body and the new being's right to live. Hopes to this effect seem rather illusory, as do the hopes that the accessibility of contraceptives might solve the problem of abortions in Poland; they have already proved false in the USA where contraceptives are easy to obtain. However, it may be supposed that the accessibility of contraceptives might at least reduce the number of abortions.

But can the problem of women's rights be separated from that of the child's rights at all, even if such a separation becomes imaginable in the biological sense? The answer seems to be: no, or at least such a separation will not be possible in Poland in the foreseeable future. Admittedly feminist movements have emerged and women's problems can at last be mentioned in public. However, the traditional model of a 'woman's role' in Polish society has changed very little. According to this model, women are expected to sacrifice themselves for their families, and this becomes particularly important in these days of economic crisis. This model still influences young people. Earlier this year, students of secondary schools aged 16–18 were asked about their conception of a modern man and a modern woman. Admittedly the sample was rather small, only thirty-three persons, but the findings are significant. It appears that a modern man is simply an ideal man. Instead a modern woman is an independent professional who develops her interests, is the man's equal and is smartly dressed and well groomed. But nearly all respondents – girls as well as boys – state that the ideal women should not be all that modern, at least in the current difficult conditions. The respondents stressed the multiplicity of the woman's duties, her specific role in the family and her dilemma resulting from the impossibility of reconciling work with family roles. Hence the belief that a modern woman should be single (Turczyn 1989). When asked about a conflict between the two groups of roles, all girls gave priority to the home and the family rather than to professional ambitions. It is rather striking that the young generation can think of no way of solving that conflict and perceive the woman's renouncement of her extra-familial aspirations as a necessity, and her role within the family as the paramount one. It seems that the feminist movement in Poland still has a great deal of work to do. The next generation of Polish women will probably still be hesitant about claiming their rights. Polish women still have a very long way to go before they reach equality, are assigned equal duties and are able to exercise rights fundamental to women.

REFERENCES

Bogunia, L. (1980) *Przerywanie Ciazy. Problemy prawnokarne i Kryminologiczne* (Abortion. Penal and criminological Problems) Wrockaw.

Buxakowski, J. (1989) 'Wprowadzenie do dyskusji nad projektem ustawy o prawnej ochronie dziecka poczetego' (Introduction to the discussion of the draft act of legal protection of the unborn child), Lad No. 26 of 25 June.

Czynczyk, A. (1989) 'Ethics and law on the first days of life', in A. Sajo (ed.) *Modern Technology and Law*, Budapest.

Declaration on Abortion, Vatican 1974, The Holy Congregation on Faith.

Hordyniec, W. and Grabowska, T. (1982) 'Spoleczna recepcja zjawiska przerywania ciazy i jej wplyw na system wartosci u kobiet poddajacych sie temu zabietogwi', (Reception of abortion in society and its impact on the system of values of women who terminate a pregnancy), unpublished master's thesis, library of the Institute of Social Prevention and Resocialization, Warsaw: Warsaw University.

Klonowicz, S. (1974) 'Legalizacja sztucznych poronien a dynamika rozrodczosci w Polsce', Legalization of Abortion and the Trends of Reproduction in Poland, Studia Demograficzne No. 36.

'Komentarz do kodeksu prawa kanonicznego' (1987) (Canon Code. A commentary) Lublin.

Kurczewski, J. (1972) 'Oceny i postulaty pod adresem lekarzy', (Opinions and postulates in relation to doctors', in J. Kurczewski and J. Solarz, *Zawod Lekarza w Opinii Publicznej*, (Doctor's profession in public opinion) Warsaw.

Kurczewski, J. (1990) 'Carnal sins and privatization of the body', *Zeitschrift für Rechtssoziologie* 1: 42.

Limanowska, B. (1989) 'Dlaczego ogorek nie spiewa?' (What prevents a cucumber from singing?) *Kobieta i Zycie* 11, March.

Milewicz, E. (1989) 'Ochrona dziecka poczetego' (Protection of the unborn child) *Gazeta Wyborcza* 5, May 12–14.

Prymas Polski w Obronie Zycia (1982) (The Primate of Poland in defence of life) Warsaw.

Rocznik Statystyczny (1988) (Statistical yearbook) Warsaw.

Sokolowska, M. (1983) 'Stanowisko kobiet wobec ustawy legalizujacej przerywanie ciazy' (Women's attitude towards the act of legalizing abortion) unpublished master's thesis, library of the Institute of Social Prevention and Resocialization, Warsaw: Warsaw University.

'Stanowisko Zarzadu Klubu Inteligencji Katolickiej w Poznaniu dotyczace prawnej dopuszczalnosci przerywania poc zetego zycia' (Standpoint of the Board of the Club of Catholic Intellectuals in Poznan concerning the legal admissibility of termination of life conceived) Lad No. 27 of 2 July 1989.

Turczyn, M. (1989) 'Potoczne rozumienie nowoczesnosci' (The popular interpretation of modernity) unpublished master's thesis, library of the Institute of Social Prevention and Resocialization, Warsaw: Warsaw University.

Tushnet, M. (1984) 'An essay on rights', *Texas Law Review* 8: 62.

Wolinska, H. (1962) *Przerywanie Ciazy w Swietle Prawa Karnego* (Abortion in the light of penal law) Warsaw.

'Zebrania Naukowe Poznanskiego Towarzystwa Lekarskiego' (1948) (Scientific Session of the Poznan Medical Society), Norwiny Lekarskie No. 2.

Zielinska, E. (1986) *Oceny prawnokarne przerywania ciazy. Studium porownawcze* (Penal law on abortion. A comparative study) Warsaw.

Name index

Subject index